P9-DIZ-836

SEX AND SOCIETY
IN NAZI GERMANY

HANS PETER BLEUEL

SEX AND SOCIETY IN NAZI GERMANY

Edited and with a preface
by HEINRICH FRAENKEL

Translated from the German
by J. MAXWELL BROWNJOHN

J. B. LIPPINCOTT COMPANY
Philadelphia and New York

English translation copyright © 1973 by Martin Secker & Warburg Limited
Printed in the United States of America

Published in German under the title *Das saubere Reich* and copyright © 1972 by Scherz Verlag Bern und München

This translation has been published in England under the title *Strength through Joy*.

U.S. Library of Congress Cataloging in Publication Data

Bleuel, Hans Peter.
  Sex and society in Nazi Germany.

  Translation of Das saubere Reich.
  Includes bibliographical references.
  1. Germany—Moral conditions. I. Title.
HN460.M6B5513   176'.0943   73-15517
ISBN-0-397-00980-1

Contents

v

List of Illustrations

Preface

By Heinrich Fraenkel

THIS is a remarkable book for a number of reasons. Above all it is indeed 'a previously unwritten chapter of German history' dealing with the 'theory and practice of mores in the Third Reich'.

True enough, even the more superficial student of that period of history is well aware of how the private lives of most Nazi potentates contravened the ideological demands of the régime; but I have never seen these contradictions more clearly revealed than in this book which presents a lucid (and thoroughly readable) account of 'Social Darwinism' and the 'racial' theories based on such claptrap. Moreover – and this is a very important point – most of the findings in this scholarly accumulation of facts with some 450 source-references are based on contemporary material which was freely available to any German at the time.

I found the final chapters particularly interesting in that they reveal the ineffectiveness of the régime's onslaught on the 'soul of the nation' as well as the degree of self-deception in its executives. When, in 1942, the authorities, more or less accidentally, stumbled on some cases of petty theft combined with rape and subsequent murder of (usually elderly) women it was assumed that since 'no German would be capable of such bestiality' the culprit must be sought among the foreign labour force. It turned out to be a German tramp who confessed to 84 (!) such crimes from 1928 to 1942 (which, incidentally, accounted for more than two-thirds of all sex-murders undetected in that period).

The final chapter provides some astonishing facts and figures on juvenile delinquency in the declining years of the war, significant not only for sexual aberrations with (preferably) Negroes and other 'exotic' types; what seems no less significant for the failure of 'Hitler-Youth' educational principles was the growing and almost passionate taste for what was then called American swing-music.

Ever since 1945 Germans have been mouthing that much abused

ix

cliché of their *unbewältigte Vergangenheit*, their undigested and 'un-
conquered' past. This book is candidly facing it, and this is what the
author has to say about it in his introduction: 'It only recounts what
any reasonably observant German could have perceived inside his own
country. It attempts to trace the moral guide-lines and mechanisms of
the Third Reich – phenomena whose existence was plain for all to see.
... Any attempt to demonize the erstwhile rulers of Germany amounts
to a disquieting essay in self-exculpation. However shocking and
atrocious the effects of their activities, they themselves were not evil
Titans. Theirs was government by unwholesome mediocrity, by
wholesome popular sentiment.'

Some of us who have been analysing that period of German history
for decades have been waiting for the first German generation that
would have the perspective and the courage candidly to face it. Hans
Peter Bleuel is among them; that is why this is an important book. It
is good to know that there are Germans now who are not afraid and,
indeed, are eager to face their *unbewältigte Vergangenheit*, thereby
proving that they have, in fact, 'digested' it and are about to 'conquer'
it for good and all.

Translator's Note

The Third Reich abounded in organizations and titles whose elaborate compound names permit of more than one rendering in English. Rather than litter the text with German designations, I have tried to use unstilted English equivalents (e.g. 'Reich Director of Health' as opposed to 'Reich Health Leader') and married them with their German originals in the Glossary (p. 246).

The end of 'good breeding'

'IN making Germany great, we are also entitled to think of ourselves. We have no need to cling to bourgeois notions of honour and reputation. Let these "well-bred" gentry be warned that we do with a clear conscience the things they do surreptitiously with a guilty one.'[1]

Thus spake the Führer. Not in public but to his private circle, and not at the zenith of his power but in early summer 1933, when his henchmen were just embarking on the task of 'making Germany great'. Middle-class aspirations, he assured his trusty comrades-in-arms, did not apply to them.

On his own submission, the Führer was a man of integrity. He waived his salary as Chancellor and made do with the royalties from *Mein Kampf*. The book was, *inter alia*, presented by government order to all couples marrying at registry offices and earned its author millions of marks. The 'saviour of the nation' also renounced marriage, as befitted his image: his bride was the German people. He devoted his entire private life to that cause and sacrificed himself in the service of the community.

In apparent contrast to their leader, his lieutenants were at liberty to indulge their personal whims. One such was Hermann Göring, originally No. 2 in the Nazi hierarchy and known, for his cultivated love of ostentation, as 'the last Renaissance Man'. Göring proved himself an exemplary husband, and not only by erecting a mawkish and self-gratifying monument to his Swedish first wife at Carinhall, the country seat named after her: he was equally fond and attentive to his second wife, Emmy Sonnemann, whom he wooed with all the boyish ardour of a sixth-former. His only daughter, Edda, derided by the scurrilous Julius Streicher as a product of artificial insemination, set the seal on his conjugal bliss. But this genial husband, this amiable Croesus, feathered his own nest with unparalleled effrontery, and became one of the most brutal and unbridled practitioners of Nazi despotism. Popular none the less, Göring fell short of his favourite Renaissance ideal in two vital respects: he possessed neither the intellectual superiority nor the aristocratic poise. And so, when burdens exceeded his ability to cope, he swallowed 100 tablets of paracodeine – a weak morphine derivative – every day, and revelled in his material possessions, entrusting the course of events to associates endowed with greater moral fibre.

Reinhard Heydrich, the scheming originator and ruthless director of the powerful Security Service (SD), had already demonstrated to a naval court of honour that his good breeding left much to be desired. Heydrich was an ambitious young man who aspired to a career in the naval arm of the Reichswehr. What ultimately drove him off course and attracted him to the militant possibilities of the Nazi Party was his insatiable sexual urge. In December 1930, by then a lieutenant, Heydrich became engaged to Lina Mathilde von der Osten, an attractive girl whom he had recently rescued after a boating accident. Another prospective bride – one of many – asserted her prior claims upon him. Unfortunately for Heydrich, her father happened to be a director of IG-Farben and acquainted with Admiral Erich Raeder. The case was referred to the naval authorities and came before a court of honour. Heydrich conducted his defence in such an arrogant and ignoble fashion that Raeder ruled in favour of summary dismissal for impropriety. Six weeks later, the cashiered and resentful ex-naval officer offered his services to Himmler, the Reichsführer-SS. As head of the Gestapo, Heydrich had ample opportunity to satisfy his horizontal needs without opposition. The only people to suffer were companions who incurred his wrath because ladies of easy virtue found them more attractive than their cold-eyed boss.

The 'earthy, humorous manners' of the Nazi Party's Director of Organization, Robert Ley, were a source of amusement even to his supreme lord and master. Hitler loved to hear stories of how Ley, a habitual drinker, used to turn up at the offices of Munich's urban planning department, elegant in summer suit, white gloves and straw hat, with his smartly attired wife in tow. 'I'll build the entire block. What'll it cost? A few hundred millions? Right, we'll do it. . . . We'll set all the fashions too – my wife will take care of that end. We'll need a whole building for the purpose. Let's do it! . . . And . . . and . . . and we'll need whores too! Masses of them – a whole houseful with all the latest décor. We'll handle the whole thing. A few hundred millions on construction? That's nothing!'[2] The Führer wept with laughter.

François-Poncet, the French ambassador, described Ley as a drunkard and a libertine. Himmler's masseur, Felix Kersten, tells of a visit to the Ley household during which his tipsy host treated him to a feast of feminine pulchritude by ripping his (second) wife's clothes from her body. The weeping woman called her husband a wild beast: 'He treats me outrageously . . . he'll end by killing me one day.' A year later she killed herself, and the grieving widower consoled himself with a cuddly young Estonian girl.

The vapid Joachim von Ribbentrop, Reich Foreign Minister, was the political handiwork of his wife Elise Henkell, daughter of the renowned wine firm which had employed him as a sales representative. She not only engaged all their servants, even his personal valet, but organized his social life and financed his political entrée at the opportune moment.

The Party veterans marched shoulder to shoulder in the same spirit, headed by the posthumously elevated Brownshirt bard, Horst Wessel. His mediocre rhyme *Die Fahne Hoch* (Raise the Flag) had quickened no pulses during his lifetime, but his status as a 'blood witness' or martyr of the Movement made him perfect material for Goebbels. The fact that the death of Wessel, a down-and-out ex-student, had no connection with his role as a minor Brownshirt leader was studiously ignored. He had just resigned from his unit, 'Schlägersturm 5', because of a recently kindled passion for a prostitute. Ali Höhler, who fired at him from among a squad of Red Front street-fighters, was in all probability an ex-pimp of Wessel's beloved and acted less from political motives than from a desire for personal revenge. With a vast outlay of propaganda, however, Goebbels managed to turn the obscure young Brownshirt into the idol of an idealistic movement and a shining example to the Hitler Youth.

Paragraph 4 of the Party Ordinance of 1926 stipulated: 'All are disqualified from membership who (a) commit dishonourable acts or of whom such acts become known subsequent to admission . . . (c) who by their moral conduct cause offence within the Party and thereby harm the same.' The body responsible for dealing with these lapses was the Investigation and Arbitration Committee (USCHLA). Its chairman, Walter Buch (Bormann's father-in-law), stated during the Nuremberg trials that he had himself been reprimanded because he rebuked Party members for drunkenness or extra-marital affairs.

In 1934, Party courts were issued with a new set of directives. To quote Paragraph 7: 'The jurisdiction of Party courts embraces: (*a*) all acts and omissions by Party members which violate the sense of honour and outlook of the NSDAP and thus jeopardize or injure the communal reputation of the Party, on application and indictment by the relevant Political Director.' Paragraph 13 again stressed that 'No proceedings may be instituted without application from the Political Director'. The SA was in any case excluded from the competence of the Party court. This meant, in effect, that only those who made themselves unpopular with their superiors could get into trouble. Senior ranks were almost automatically immune from disciplinary proceedings.

Hermann Rauschning, the early champion and first prominent apostate of National Socialism, diagnosed on the basis of personal experience that two different criteria prevailed. What was destined for the masses did not apply to the élite, who were bound by nothing – neither by programme nor by ideology nor by moral standards. This circle of initiates, the executive nucleus of the Movement and the National Socialist Government, were subject only to the Führer and the precepts of comradeship – precepts which, internal rivalries not-withstanding, are equally operative inside a mobsters' syndicate.

Goebbels once poked fun at the antediluvian moral concepts of the reactionaries and the tractarian spirit of their priggish bedfellows. Hitler seized the cue and whipped himself into one of his furious tirades: 'I abominate prudishness and moral prying. . . . What has it to do with our struggle? These are the outworn notions of reactionary old women like Hugenberg, who can only visualize national rejuvena-tion in terms of virtuous customs and austerity. "League of Virtue" and "Christian-German Table-Companions", "replacing the material losses of the nation with spiritual gains" – and all the rest of that tawdry patriotic mumbo-jumbo. Our uprising has nothing to do with bourgeois virtues. We are an uprising born of our nation's strength – the strength of its loins as well, if you like. I won't be a spoilsport to any of my men. If I demand the utmost of them, I must also permit them to let off steam as *they* please, not as it suits a lot of elderly church-hens. My lads are no angels, God knows, nor are they expected to be. I've no use for goody-goodies and League of Virtue-ites. I'm not interested in their private lives any more than I'll stand for any prying into my own private life. The Party has nothing to do with conventicles or vacuous speeches about moral rejuvenation based on the spirit and history of our nationhood.'[3]

Unfortunately, Pastor Adolf Sellman could not have heard this outburst, for Sellman, chronicler of the 'West German Morality League', saw the achievements of the Führer and his national uprising in quite another light. 'At a stroke, things changed in Germany. All filth and trash vanished from the public domain. The streets of our cities became clean once more. Prostitution, which had so brazenly ensconced itself in our cities and smaller towns, was banished. The government pursued a population policy in the best sense of the term.'[4]

On behalf of the Morality League, Sellmann welcomed the general directive issued on 22 February 1933 by the Prussian Ministry of the Interior, whose injunction to implement the Reich law for the control of venereal diseases 'is cleansing our streets of prostitution'. He welcomed the decrees of the following day, which ordained the closure of short-time hotels and places frequented by homosexuals. He welcomed the decree of 3 March 1933 for the control of nudism: beneficial to public health as sun, air and water might be, the naturist movement was a sexual aberration and should thus be stamped out by the police authorities. He welcomed the ordinance of 7 March 1933 against obscene writings, illustrations and performances, and he welcomed Göring's general directive to police authorities ordering them to oppose the installation of contraceptive vending-machines.

In the name of morality, the League rejoiced at the sterner penalties for homosexuality and assured the national government of its support in the campaign against injurious miscegenation and racial desecration, against Jews, Negroes and Mongols. The West German Morality League also approved the Aryan clauses, the law for the prevention of hereditarily diseased offspring (14 March 1933) and the law for the protection of the hereditary health of the German people (18 October 1935): 'Today, every law is an integrated whole created out of National Socialist ideology.'[5]

The West German Morality League was not an obscure bourgeois association. It was a rigidly Protestant body with half a century of tradition that went back to 1885, and had always been headed by worthy clerics and respectable schoolmasters. The League maintained homes for fallen women and girls in moral danger. Above all, it banged the drum of morality. It fulminated against prostitution and brothels, demanded heavy sentences for homosexuals and the prohibition of all activities which it considered vicious. The League's central figure had been Adolf Stoecker, the arch-conservative court chaplain who also emerged in 1887 as co-founder of an umbrella organization entitled

'Men's Association for the Control of Immorality'. The main concerns of the Morality League were national health, racial purity and sound genetics – three aims likewise championed by National Socialism.

An entry in the diaries of Count Harry Kessler summarizes this terrible consonance of aim, this naïve misconception, this haze of bigotry and moralizing: 'National Socialism is a delirium of the German lower middle class. The poison of its disease may, however, bring down ruin on Germany and Europe for decades ahead.'[6]

The new masters were also representatives of the lower middle class. If not petty bourgeois by birth, like the majority of their fellows, they were certainly so in outlook and in breadth of horizon. They never transcended the simple, mundane norm in their personal way of life and in their peccadilloes. There was nothing demonic or super-human about them, not even the dynamism of unbridled violence, neither in the leaders mentioned above nor in Himmler, Goebbels, Röhm, Esser and Bormann. Mediocrity predominated – respectable petty bourgeois mediocrity. Goebbels, who tried his utmost to slough off this quality, acknowledged its prevalence at the end of his life: 'Average human beings, at best. Not one has the makings of a mediocre politician, let alone the calibre of a statesman. They have all remained the Bürgerbräukeller bawlers they always were. As for the modicum of intelligence that once led them to join the Movement, many of them have drunk it away in twelve years of soft living.'[7]

In fact, this was just what commended the Party bosses to a nation whose idea of greatness was that of the worthy citizen to whom any-thing exceptional seems suspect; and this was just why the nation so readily allowed itself to be blinded to the exceptional criminality of a régime controlled by average citizens run wild. The same applied at the top of the ladder. What reigned there was the amorality of the worthy citizen who rejects the consequences of his narrow code and speaks of decency even when committing mass-murder on others – people from outside his own little patch. None of this was fortuitous, neither the parallels nor the perversities of these moral concepts. The modern historian Hans Buchheim speaks of the 'compost-heap of bourgeois thought' from which the SS mentality grew, and Hannah Arendt has defined the same state of affairs with her celebrated dictum about the banality of evil. The intellectual and mental disposition of wide sections of the middle class had long been profoundly corrupted by obsolete scientifico-philosophical dogmas in the Darwin-to-Nietzsche range, by an outmoded picture of society, by an inability to grasp the social implications of technological progress, and by an ingrained sense of national power and vocation. It had also been so stripped of moral substance that the old code of behaviour could be re-upholstered with new standards devoid of any ethical basis. The old code did not break down: the new one appeared to be identical – and probably was.

What became known under National Socialism as 'new morality' was simply the old morality under different auspices. The petty bourgeois rites of propriety remained intact and the new morality was the old upper-class morality, except that the ruling class now based its claim to superiority on certified racial purity or functional efficiency within the system instead of on noble descent or the accumulation of property.

The only new element was totalitarian intensification, though this too had its roots in authoritarianism of an earlier mould. Shortly after proclaiming the birth of the 'Germanic Reich of the German Nation', Hitler laid personal claim to supreme moral authority in an off-the-record speech made in 1937: 'Today *we* claim leadership of the people, that is to say, we alone are entitled to lead the people as such – the individual man and woman. *We* determine the conditions under which the sexes live! *We* fashion the child!'[8]

It only remained to reconcile this absolute claim with the mentality and expectations of the led, for harmony was dear to the soul, the 'folkish'* and national individuality of a people to whom nothing seemed more repellent and untoward than controversy and individual responsibility. The levelling process assumed two forms, and it succeeded effortlessly.

First, there was the appeal to solidarity: 'You are nothing, your nation is everything!' No maxim of this kind can fail to make an impact in societies afflicted by mental chaos and immature in self-analysis. It absolves individuals of the need to make decisions and beds them down snugly in the comforting lap of the community. A great deal of genuine yearning and true idealism was at work here after the Versailles treaty – the yearning of a torn and disunited, confused and bewildered nation for unity and stability. Given a people which could not cope with its economic problems and the demands of a democratic social system, this vague longing for harmony was able to focus itself on the figure of a leader, a charismatic redeemer. It was a role which Adolf Hitler, in this respect an authentic man of the people, knew how

* See Glossary, p. 246.

to assume and develop. He represented himself as the embodiment of the popular will.

The second route to harmony between the nation and its despotic rulers was a sort of feed-back process. Above and beyond all legal* ordinances, the Führer's will was equated with the natural will of the nation. As the régime's senior legal expert, Hans Frank, explained to the judge-members of the National Socialist Judicial Association (NSRB), whose leader he was: 'In any matter of consequence, think of the Führer. Ask yourselves: How would the Führer decide in my place? Act accordingly and you will find yourselves on a far higher plane. You will feel fortified by this thought and invested with an altogether new moral authority. Do not lapse into petty-mindedness or the service of hypocrisy or petty bourgeois disputes of any kind. Do not draw the inferences governing your decisions from any such mentality.'[9]

Here we encounter the magic touchstone known as 'wholesome popular sentiment', which transcends all legal codes and provides all totalitarian systems with a superlative pretext for their arbitrary acts. There are few sentiments more inhuman than the righteous indignation of the frustrated petty bourgeois who gives free rein to his outraged and virtuous sense of propriety. On this plane, the so-called decent average citizen can unhesitatingly identify himself with any government measure, however draconian and illegal.

The Nazi rulers followed this recipe when they decreed the following supplement to the civil penal code in 1935: 'Anyone shall be punished who commits an act which the law declares to be punishable or which merits punishment in accordance with the underlying idea of a penal law and with wholesome popular sentiment. Should no specific penal law be directly applicable to the act in question, it shall be punished according to the law whose intention most closely applies thereto.' This was only one of the manifold steps taken by the totalitarian régime to legalize its despotism, but it was one which could be sure of mass approval. The authorities could at last proceed against any offender uninhibited by minor legal considerations as to the demonstrability and definability of moral offences. Imprisonment, concentration camp or execution – any degree of punishment was feasible, even the most drastic. All that the respectable citizen deemed sexually improper, if not abnormal, all that conflicted with wholesome average notions of morality, could now at last be 'suitably' proceeded against and eliminated. Mediocrity triumphed and normality was satisfied.

This was not only a process to the taste of the dictatorship. It was also a law gratifying to the authoritarian personality, a law for the satisfaction of the little man who found in it pathetic confirmation of his status as an exponent of moral rectitude. 'Discipline and good order' was the slogan. It was to be implemented by 'deterrence'. No one would dare to behave 'abnormally' in the face of such dire penalties.

The authorities miscalculated, of course, and triply so in the case of this particular legal framework. Sex-criminals and the 'abnormally' inclined were neither deterred nor 'cured' by threats of retribution. For their part, the functionaries of the system tended to be reinforced in their miserable excesses and criminal instincts by these arbitrary provisions. And, finally, the younger generation entered a sort of vacuum, especially during the war years. Far from frightening young people, pseudo-judicial decisions merely confirmed that binding standards of behaviour had ceased to exist. The result was that they kicked over the traces – once again, especially in war-time – in a manner which cast doubt on all the maxims and claimed successes of the totalitarian system. Their recalcitrance was only random and took the form of juvenile delinquency, so-called, but it was manifest enough in the circumstances to spotlight the conflict between the moral assertions and moral credibility of their environment.

This book does not deal with what went on in concentration camps, in the occupied territories or at the front. It only recounts what any reasonably observant German could have perceived inside his own country. It attempts to trace the moral guide-lines and mechanisms of the Third Reich – phenomena whose existence was plain for all to see. The interpolated character sketches of Nazi potentates are intended merely to show how easily their aspirations could be gauged from their conduct and how closely their aims matched their personalities. Any attempt to see the Nazi rulers of Germany as ogres amounts to a disquieting essay in self-exculpation. However shocking and atrocious the effects of their activities, they themselves were not evil Titans. Theirs was government by unwholesome mediocrity, by wholesome popular sentiment.

1 Rich Man, Poor Man, Beggar-Man

THE ETHICS OF RESPECTABILITY

1898 was drawing to a close, and the editors of the *Berliner Illustrirte* had decided to draw up a 'centennial balance sheet': 'We who stand at the outgoing of the century and shall, in the natural course of events, witness the dawn of the new epoch, are entitled to recall the days marked by the major turning-point in time whose children we are, both materially and in spirit.'[10]

A go-ahead popular newspaper, the *Berliner Illustrirte* demonstrated that it was already a child of the new epoch by holding an opinion poll. Readers were invited to give their answers to twenty-seven questions, among them: *What name would you give this century? Who is its greatest thinker? Who is the century's leading woman? What was its outstanding cultural achievement? Which book has had the greatest influence? What do you hope for from the coming century?* It is easy enough to discern the purpose of this ingenious circulation-booster. The replies – and more than six thousand flooded in – were intended to show how far the nineteenth century had wrought a change in customs and conventions, attitudes and ideas. But how did the readers' balance sheet turn out in practice? It was only to be expected that Bismarck, Napoleon, Goethe and Wagner should figure among the outstanding personalities of the period. An emphasis on patriotic and national events – the defeats at Jena and Auerstädt, the Battle of Leipzig, the war of 1870–71, the unification of the Reich – was likewise to be expected in a youthful German Empire whose citizens held Kaiser Wilhelm I to be the hero of the century and its last three decades a golden age. But how exactly did this age see itself, what ideas did it entertain on the eve of the 'new epoch' and what had it learnt from the upheavals of the nineteenth century if the representatives of that century nominated Field Marshal Helmuth von Moltke its greatest thinker?

Shining examples: Queen Louise and Moltke

The change in attitudes and ideas was confined to the world of outward appearance. Deeper consequences went unheeded. Enthusiastic participants in the poll glorified the century as an age of invention, of steam and electricity; they named Thomas Edison its greatest inventor and the railway its most beneficial achievement.

What splendid progress we've made! – such was the confident tenor of the replies. No reference was made by these self-assured middle-class voices to the immense economic and social problems which the rapid growth of industrialization had created and was steadily aggravating. Yet the whole structure of society was already in the throes of radical change. Old social categories and divisions were beginning to dissolve. Novel views were gaining ground and affecting customs and conventions, social conflict was throwing up new concepts and ideas. Despite this, the imagination of the Wilhelmine bourgeois barely scratched the surface of events. He refused to recognize the underlying and, to him, profoundly disquieting trend.

The middle-class readers of the *Berliner Illustrirte* pronounced Queen Louise of Prussia (1776–1810) to be the century's outstanding woman, but not because of her courageous stand during the years of Napoleonic tyranny, which made her far more politically effective than her irresolute husband Frederick William III. Her enduring popularity stemmed rather from sympathy for her fate as an exile and admiration for her womanly simplicity of character. She was, so to speak, a patriotic 'women's mag' personality, whose vastly exaggerated virtues had been rammed down the throats of generations of German schoolchildren. Second to Louise came Britain's Queen Victoria, a truly epochal figure, though one who had given her name to an era of smug middle-class decorum and prudery.

This example is enough in itself to show how immutably the old ideals had survived the new upheavals. The royal order of precedence – Louise and Victoria – still characterized the middle-class image of woman at the turn of the century. There was scant connection with reality or with what was expected of women, still less with what women outside the cosy confines of the middle class were compelled to do. The latter were a majority, but they did not count.

The Wilhelmine era was the heyday of the educated middle class. Knowledge meant power, and the spirit of the Enlightenment had been consigned to a bourgeois limbo in 1848, along with other liberal ideals which hampered the growth of State-sanctioned affluence. People lived on surrogates, on moral substitutes, and busily strove to conform as best they could to the customs and conventions of the ruling class. Life behind the façade of Wilhelmine propriety and pseudo-feudal etiquette was cramped but comfortable.

No one could have expected a readers' poll of this kind to supply detailed information. The replies naturally concentrated on spectacular phenomena, but their very nature permits inferences to be drawn about the mentality and social concepts of those who sent them in. The *Berliner Illustrirte* was read mainly in the middle-class circles which set the tone in morals and behaviour. What did they consider spectacular?

The abolition of slavery and – what a contradiction! – the colonization of Africa and Asia: were these really the major cultural achievements of the century? Were its greatest economic developments the introduction of railways and the building of the Suez Canal? Had the war of 1870–71 really been the most important event in the history of Germany? Had not the domestic political scene been dominated, notably in the closing decades of this complacent century, by slogans and catchwords of a quite different and highly explosive nature: industrialization, proletariat, anti-socialist legislation, the emancipation of women?

It was this last category which encompassed the events and problems that were to govern future development in the 'dawn of the new epoch', with its social and moral transformations.

The good old days

The population explosion and its far-reaching effects were already bearing down on Germany during the nineteenth century. The population grew from 24 million in 1816 to approximately 65 million in 1913. Over 6 million Germans emigrated and the birth-rate declined by about 25 per cent during this period, it is true, but advances in medicine and hygiene – elimination of puerperal fever, antiseptics, vaccination, purification of drinking-water – more than offset such losses: the death-rate declined by over 40 per cent.

At the same time, social stratification underwent an immense change. In 1840, between 60 and 70 per cent of the population were employed in agriculture and forestry. The figure had dropped to 50 per cent by

1870 and 30 per cent by the turn of the century, and the decline persisted. Meanwhile, the proportion of those employed in industry and manual trades rose during the four decades between 1870 and 1913 from 30 to 40 per cent. Commerce and communications became major spheres of activity and by 1907 supported 15 per cent of all employed persons. Child labour declined – over 6 per cent of factory workers in mid-nineteenth-century Prussia had been children – but the proportion of female labour doubled: by 1907, 30 per cent of all wage-earners were women. The agrarian state had turned into an industrial state.

Distribution of population, too, changed entirely. As late as 1871, only 36 per cent of Germans lived in towns with more than 2,000 inhabitants. By 1910 the figure was 60 per cent. The population of medium-sized towns grew rapidly. Only two cities – Berlin and Hamburg – boasted more than 100,000 inhabitants in 1800. Munich and Breslau joined them in 1850, but twenty years later there were eight large cities, in 1900 thirty-three and by 1913 no less than forty-seven.

Provincial towns turned into spreading industrial centres. Conurbations took shape on the Rhine and Ruhr, in Westphalia and round Berlin. In the capital itself, population density per square kilometre shot up from 6,679 (1830) to 13,951 (1871) to 29,793 in the year 1900. Trade and industry became concentrated in the towns and people flocked there in quest of work and wages. Their hopes far exceeded the employment available. Not enough vacancies awaited the converging masses of migrants from the land, the impoverished craftsmen and unskilled labourers, the massive influx from the agricultural areas of the East, and because labour was abundant wages tended to be wretchedly low.

Slums proliferated in the major cities. Working-class families rented sleeping-places in their one-roomed homes to paying lodgers. Tenements, basements and attics overflowed with people who lived below the subsistence level. Women and children did outwork for starvation wages while their unemployed husbands and fathers queued outside factory gates. Riots and strikes flared up. An industrial proletariat came into being, the class struggle erupted, the labour movement began to stir. The middle-class world evolved a genteel name for such phenomena: the social problem.

This radical change in social structure, coupled with the appalling conditions under which a large part of the population lived, could not fail to have an effect on the mores of the society in question. The old patriarchal order that had prevailed in agrarian society began to break up. The traditional family group, whose ramified ties of kinship had constituted a system of mutual economic support and assistance, gradually disintegrated. The husband and father – often out of work or poorly paid and with no form of social security to fall back on – was engrossed in a naked fight for survival and had ceased to be the undisputed head of the family or even its sole breadwinner. The wife was sucked into the economic vortex and in many cases obliged to contribute to the family budget. Her tasks were no longer confined to home and hearth. She sallied forth as a worker in her own right, and this affected her status inside the family. The ineluctable loosening of family ties also conferred earlier independence on children and adolescents. Schools hastened this process by removing children from the parental home, and among the lower classes the employment of both parents or the exigencies of family life contributed to a decline in parental guidance and authority. It was inevitable, under these circumstances, that traditional principles of upbringing should change and relations between the sexes relax. In the wretched conditions that prevailed inside the metropolitan slums, good manners and traditional moral concepts suffered a total slump. They had become unserviceable.

Small wonder, therefore, that this urban industrial proletariat should have come to be regarded as the source of all evil, as a breeding-ground for immorality and moral decay. The machine age and its pressures were held responsible for the destruction of family life. Urban rootlessness and lack of cultural refinement were unfavourably contrasted with the natural way of life and wholesome outlook cherished by sons of the soil.

Obvious though this interpretation seemed, it missed the point. The new trend necessarily exerted its first and crudest impact on the mobile sections of the community, the urban settlers, those who had migrated to the industrial centres of Western Germany in search of employment, destitute craftsmen and members of the old middle class who had lost their inherited ties and native environment and now formed the broad new substratum. But the trend was not confined to the lower orders of society alone. Industrialization and its consequences extended to the middle class, creating unrest and novel conditions there too.

The new Eve

Born at the turn of the eighteenth and nineteenth centuries, the feminist movement arose from a spirit of emancipation, not for social reasons. The ideas of the Enlightenment and human rights had kindled a desire for education among women belonging to liberal-minded sections of the upper middle class. Names like Karoline Schelling, Dorothea von Schlegel, Henriette Herz, Rahal Varnhagen von Ense, Bettina von Arnim and Madame de Staël testify to the stimulating and enduring influence of these intellectually gifted women upon their age. Their salons were cultural meeting-places and their admirers included the most eminent minds of the day. Although members of a small and exclusive circle, they were enough to pour scorn on the dogged reactionary assertion that women were incapable of superior intellectual attainment and personal independence.

As in France and the English-speaking countries, though somewhat later, the feminist movement attracted strong support in Germany and called for the participation of women in public life. The middle-class feminist movement was primarily concerned, however, with securing equal rights for man and woman. This meant not only political enfranchisement but, first and foremost, educational opportunities which would usher women into independent economic and intellectual activity and prepare them for professional careers. The Universal German Women's Association, founded in 1865, campaigned for the establishment of girls' grammar schools and the right of young women to matriculate and graduate. Helene Lange founded one such school at Berlin in 1889. In 1896 girls were permitted to matriculate, and general admission to university studies was finally granted in 1908.

Nevertheless, the popular idea that women elbowed their way into professional life forcibly and solely of their own volition is more than deceptive – it is a fallacy. Eight-and-a-half million women were employed in the year 1907, and there is little doubt that only a dwindling minority still equated work with a vocation or would have worked in the absence of economic pressure.

Industrialization and the complete metamorphosis of production relations were far more responsible for harnessing such a multitude of women to the juggernaut of industrial expansion. The modern factory system, with its work-sharing methods of manufacture and discrete series of simple and limited manual operations, absorbed women as cheap labour. A lot of men, notably craftsmen, had been robbed of a livelihood by the mechanization of production, while others did ill-paid and unskilled jobs. Thus, many women were forced to play their own part in maintaining the family. They could not choose their jobs and were exploited by every means consistent with the capitalist profit motive. In 1905, when so-called protective laws covering female labour were already in force, the average working woman earned 9 marks per week for a thirteen-hour day.

This was the aspect on which the socialist women's movement concentrated its endeavours. It was not concerned with the right to pursue a profession. The women whose interests it represented had not wanted to work, yet they were forced to do so under conditions which made absolutely no allowance for their 'feminine disposition'. Driven to extremes of physical and mental fatigue, they performed men's work simply because they could be hired more cheaply and tended to be less rebellious than their husbands, who were starting to form workers' associations and trade unions.

It was against this ruthless overtaxing of female labour that this second, socialist-oriented, wing of the feminist movement took up arms. It advocated better and more suitable working conditions for women, not the right of women to work. Political demands were also raised, of course, and the middle-class feminist associations took a similarly keen interest in social problems and the lot of the working woman.

It was a tough and protracted struggle punctuated by meagre and infrequent successes. Not unnaturally, factory-owners were disinclined to prejudice their own position and cut profits by introducing better conditions and wages. Such was the success of the liberalistic economic system that for a long time the government hesitated to intervene. Its modest socio-political protective measures were easy to circumvent in practice, and, even when the pressure of events compelled it to introduce some rudimentary social welfare legislation towards the end of the century, this too consisted of half-measures. The labour protection law of 1891 imposed a general ban on Sunday working and the factory employment of children under thirteen – though outwork was not prohibited until eleven years later. Adolescents under sixteen were forbidden to work more than ten and women more than eleven hours a day.

Decades of agitation and public appeals had failed to secure equal regard for the labour output and professional status of women and men, but it came about quite spontaneously during the First World War. Women on the 'home front' stepped into the vacancies left by men who had been called up. They worked as tram conductresses and in government offices, behind counters and in heavy industry. Three million women were employed in munitions factories alone.

The country was now dependent on the employment of women. All at once, in a false glow of chauvinistic fervour, Germany hailed as patriotic what it had previously spurned as an offence against the nature and function of womanhood. Professional activity on the part of women was not only acknowledged – it was taken for granted.

The old Adam

The traditional conception of the role and function of women was quite unaffected by this fundamental change in their actual circumstances. The patterns and social criteria to which a woman had to conform and by which she was assessed took no account of changed conditions. The true woman, it was thought, remained true to her feminine state and confined her activities to the household and the rearing of children. She had also, when required, to demonstrate matrimonial harmony in public, preferably mute and always at her husband's side. Ambitions in the field of arts and crafts were allowed, musical ambitions permissible only in the higher reaches of society. A woman's topics of conversation were limited to the modest pleasures of a housebound existence. While sometimes capable of a profound grasp of spiritual problems by virtue of her feminine instinct – for that much *was* conceded – she was 'by nature' incapable of strictly logical discussion. A woman did not belong in public. Politics were anathema to her: politics were a man's business.

All these precepts were epitomized in one cardinal rule: women are inferior to men. The middle-class code duly exploited the 'natural destiny' according to which Providence had assigned woman a subordinate role and made it her lot and aptitude to tend and nurture, to care for and cherish – in short, to serve.

The incompatibility of such guiding principles with social reality is quite obvious. Three factors should be borne in mind here. In the first place, one cannot evade the concept of a ruling class. During the Wilhelmine era, the tip of the social pyramid consisted of the aristocracy and officer caste. Bourgeoisie and officialdom formed the 'politically supportive' basis of this upper social category. A far from homogeneous foundation, it ranged from the reactionary entrepreneur, via the rank-conscious tax inspector, to the humble office clerk – the 'wing-collar proletarian' – who timidly sought to dissociate himself from the socialistic sentiments of troublemaking factory workers. It also included certain craftsmen who combined their ingrained abhorrence of mass production with chauvinistic fervour and loyalty to the Emperor. For all their class differences and social disparities, these groups were cemented by a common factor: the imitation of moral concepts and manners which they regarded as a prerogative of the admired feudal class. Distortions were inevitable. There was the *laissez-faire* of the dual morality which permitted men what was strictly forbidden to women, which winked at conduct in a superior to which a subordinate would never presume. There was also the hidebound narrow-mindedness of the master-in-my-own-house attitude. Yet the system worked. A middle-class code of propriety – elastic within certain limits, *entre nous* – was established and proclaimed to be binding on society as a whole.

Secondly, the middle-class exponents of this code were little affected – at first – by the dissolution of the traditional family structure. Unemployment struck at the working class, at middle-class rejects and fugitives from the land – the Lumpenproletariat. There, the authority of the breadwinner was eroded by poverty. There, millions of women were compelled to step in and earn a pittance. There, children worked twelve or fourteen hours a day for the privilege of bringing home a few coppers. The middle class, whose meagre liberal heritage had left it with some very private and individualistic conceptions of personal happiness, experienced little destitution, much material prosperity and no social change whatsoever. Here, as in the country, family relationships remained intact and moral standards unimpaired. There was no incentive to overhaul prevailing ideas, let alone revise them.

In the third place, although the feminist movement sprang from the middle class it did not aim to dispute the social assessment of women. Its pioneers sought to abolish the minor status of women in an idealistic sense, intending that they should have parity with men in terms of civil rights. The feminists did not aspire to upset the relationship of the sexes or establish a dominion of their own. On close inspection, their plans did not threaten the patriarchal claims of the man inside his family circle. Their efforts were directed towards securing respect for women once they had left this limited environment and debouched into the life of the community. Inside the house they were quite ready

to accept the traditional rules of feminine subordination and pay
tribute to the hereditary right of supremacy claimed by the spouse and
paterfamilias.

The feminine image corresponded with the neatly graduated and
attuned conditions of private and economic life that had reigned in the
class society of yore. That it could still serve as a model in the wholly
transmuted social system of the nineteenth century and force women
into a tight moral corset is attributable to the following circumstances:
it was espoused by a broad-based middle class which, differences
in status notwithstanding, regarded itself as the backbone of the nation
and was able to dictate social standards by its conformity with conservative ruling circles. Not only was it minimally affected by social
regroupings, but – on the contrary – it enjoyed a brief spell of unwonted
consolidation and economic prosperity.

Menaced by social degradation, the lower strata of this middle class
fought all the more fiercely for their petty bourgeois moral code – in a
sense, for the badge which symbolized their membership of better-
class society. What aggravated this conflict was that, after the failure
of liberal endeavours in 1848, the middle class had withdrawn from
political activity and sought its own private salvation in the abandon-
ment of all progressive trends. Hence the steadily and inevitably
widening gulf between social reality and middle-class moral concepts
and notions of propriety.

A semblance of freedom

The Weimar Republic granted women what they had vainly demanded
even in the closing years of the Empire: political enfranchisement.
What they did with the vote demonstrated a striking correspondence
between the prevailing image of woman and her political behaviour.
The more conservative and religious a party's pretensions during the
1920s and 1930s, the more heavily it could rely on feminine support.
The German National People's Party and the Catholic Centre attracted
more women's votes than any other party, whereas the liberal and
socialist parties enjoyed a vast preponderance of male support. This
seems to confirm that even the socially retrogressive aims of the former
parties were better attuned to the female temperament. At the same
time, attention must again be drawn to the conflict between the
accepted image of women and their actual way of life.

Men returning home after the war reoccupied many of the posts that had provisionally been filled by women. Much professional terrain was taken away and again declared a male preserve. From a long-term point of view, however, female employment continued to show a substantial rise. By 1925 the female share in Germany's 32-million labour force was 11.5 million, or over one-third.

It appeared during the Republican years that professional emancipation was being succeeded by an emancipation of morals and conventions. With a self-assurance born of their war-time activities, women moved naturally in every sphere of public life. The new lack of constraint was most noticeably reflected in their outward appearance – in fashion. Tight little cloches replaced the huge milliner's confections which had once reduced the head to insignificance. The ankle-length skirts which had obliged their wearers to walk with measured tread now shot up to knee-height and emphasized those parts of the anatomy which had earlier been modestly shrouded, even in the conjugal bedchamber. The tight-laced bosom, at once a symbol of motherhood and a coyly concealed eye-catcher, not only reassumed its natural shape but became a positive encumbrance to devotees of the tomboy style. The elaborately unsophisticated draped hair-style fell prey to the scissors and the casual Eton crop came into vogue.

This drastic infringement of long-standing conventions did not by any means entail a loss of femininity, which was simply brought to bear in a different way, more deliberately and with fewer inhibitions. Proximity at work and a growing awareness of woman's independent role had an effect on relations between the sexes. On the one hand, they became more businesslike and encouraged the growth of new forms of comradeship between man and woman. On the other, there was a more liberal recourse to sexual stimuli: charm, coquetry, youthfulness, lack of constraint – a whiff of eroticism. The same went for social relaxation: women no longer shrank from smoking a cigarette or drinking a glass of wine in public. Was this the new reality? It was a part of it, a trend – seen against the background of previous conventions, a very striking trend.

The new tendency encountered resistance among many eminent women who had devoted a lifetime to the emancipation of their own sex. They feared that lack of constraint was breeding superficiality and hedonistic attitudes which would swamp the feminine values they had campaigned for.

Ideas of this kind were stylized by conservative cultural critics into doom-laden portents of disaster for the German nation, if not for

Western civilization as a whole. The masculinization and alienation of woman, moral depravity in the quagmire of urban existence, the degradation of women by morally subversive novels about city life, neglect of the true function of motherhood, juvenile demoralization – such was the reactionary line.

The steady emancipation of mores and relaxation of antiquated moral precepts was illusory, however. For all the legal reforms and changes in fashion, only a very small section of society had the determination and could muster the strength to renounce the traditional moral code. The pert and risqué offerings served up by cheap newspapers and illustrated magazines were in no way representative. Traditions do not die so easily, still less key principles which govern the personal conduct and coexistence of man and woman, the social rules of propriety and etiquette. These are handed down even after revolutions, and especially after so half-hearted a revolution as the German upheaval of 1918, which left the politically supportive class unchanged. The bourgeois middle class – civil servants, white-collar workers, small businessmen, the self-employed – continued to dictate the bounds and norms of social convention. In concert with self-styled authorities on such matters, it dictated the prevailing moral code as well.

Target: four children

'Sexual intercourse takes place within wedlock. Woman must remain chaste until marriage and man must strive to be continent. In his own interests, for intercourse with venereally diseased prostitutes exposes him to grave health hazards, and all prophylactics – of which the most effective is still the condom – are inadequate. Active sexual relations are beneficial to conjugal life and promotive of physical well-being, though the female partner in the sex act should preferably adopt the conventional supine position, this being the most natural. Undue frequency is inadvisable, but married couples may safely indulge in intercourse two or three times a week. The purpose of marriage is the procreation of children and their upbringing. National growth requires each marriage to produce at least four offspring. No woman should be expected to undergo more than seven or eight confinements. More will exhaust her womanly energies and be additionally reflected in the frail constitution of subsequent children.'

These precepts were imparted by Professor Max von Gruber of

Munich University in his best-selling book *Hygiene des Geschlechtslebens* (Sexual Hygiene). This popular treatise by a reputable hygienist – an edition of 325,000 copies appeared in 1927, the year of his death – was representative of the more liberal branch of contemporary literature on sex education. It contrasted strongly with the spate of well-meaning tracts which preached that morality was the young girl's sole and finest preparation for marriage while clouding the real issue with mysterious allusions. The new sex primers described, boldly and in detail, the physiological requisites and processes of reproduction and birth, and they described them in such a way that mature students could read them with profit and simple minds comprehend them with ease.

More clearly than any turgid treatise, these down-to-earth texts demonstrated the moral standards of the time and the limits which they imposed.

Of course, even the scientists and scholars of those years were still far removed from the liberal views on sex education which have grown out of modern psychology and sexual research. Max von Gruber was convinced, for example, that masturbation inflicts serious mental damage on adolescent boys, a view which still persists in isolated quarters, and the professor recommended precautionary measures: 'Children should wear buttonless trousers so that they cannot easily manipulate their genitals; on the other hand, trousers should be roomy enough to preclude pressure and tension. Put your children to bed tired so that they fall asleep at once, and get them up as soon as they wake. Don't allow them to slide their hands beneath the bedclothes; equally, don't let boys walk around or sit down with their hands in their trouser-pockets. Check frequently to see that the seams of their pockets aren't torn, thus opening up a concealed route to their sexual organs.'[11]

These solicitous remarks were based on the characteristic assumption that masturbation is indecent, but that the problem can be solved by minimizing the possibility of such moral offences and making them punishable. In other words, the line of demarcation between natural and unnatural behaviour is drawn by decorum and propriety. Max von Gruber's approach to homosexuality was in perfect accord with the same principle: it should be banned by the State, otherwise there would be an astronomical increase in the numbers of those who were, if not homosexual, bisexual. Paragraph 175 of the penal code prevented and achieved nothing, however, as one can infer from the findings of Magnus Hirschfeld, founder of Berlin's Sexual Research Institute.

Hirschfeld put the number of homosexually inclined people in the German capital at 56,000 and in the whole of Germany at approximately 1.2 million.

None of this literature on sex education betrays the least sign of a change in the relations between the sexes. Terms such as eroticism and sexuality were used only as verbal bogeys. Professor von Gruber, the voice of authority, declared that 'The sexual urge expresses itself in various ways: as a desire for sexual union and as a desire for offspring. In untouched women of good character the latter desire tends to be far stronger than the former'.[12]

This categorical assertion was quite as unscientific and open to doubt as the argument with which he assailed the idea of female employment. 'The most pernicious feature of so-called feminine emancipation and the employment of married women is that in the conflict between motherhood and professional duties the former generally gets the worst of it. If there are any children at all, they tend to be sickly.'[13]

To Max von Gruber, this new social trend – the extramural employment of women – spelt ruin for civilized peoples. Mothers were the target of Gruber's condescension. His idea of chastity embodied the most primitive motive underlying any patriarchal code of morality, though in a new guise: 'We must esteem and cherish feminine chastity as the supreme national asset, for in the chastity of women lies our one sure guarantee that we shall truly be the fathers of our children, that we toil and labour for our own blood.'[14]

In other words, a woman must be chaste so that her spouse can feel assured of his fatherhood. The principle here was to protect the supreme national asset, healthy stock and good blood. Choice of spouse was primarily to be determined by the same factor. Avuncular inspection, or the examination of a chosen mate in the nude by a reliable relative, was rejected by Gruber as wholly inadequate. 'It is, therefore, absolutely essential to take account of the ancestry of the individual to be married, not only of his or her physical attributes. On the whole, good breeding is the best guarantee of good offspring.'[15]

The form of sex education to which the learned hygienist really aspired had little bearing on the nature and practice of intersexual relations. He called a spade a spade, true, but he never went beyond platitudes and prejudices nor ever intended to. Gruber aimed to harness the traditional moral code to an overriding 'folkish' or nationalistic ideal. On this basis, the family ceased to be more than the 'germ cell' of the nation in a purely biological sense; its process of development was prescribed by the national requirements which governed its germination. Growth was to be determined by the organism, not the cell.

When Gruber spoke of sexual hygiene, the allusion to medically healthy relations between man and woman was secondary. These were important only as a prerequisite of 'hereditary national health', which entailed systematic selection. The guardian of Germany's racial heritage rhapsodized over the splendid successes achieved by selective breeders of domestic animals: 'There can be no doubt that, if we practised selective breeding in the same painstaking manner, we could within a few generations breed human strains which would far surpass all their predecessors in beauty, strength and efficiency. *The human condition suffers from nothing so much as from the fact that far too many inferior, stupid, weak, idle, antisocial and unscrupulous persons are begotten and far too few superior, intelligent, strong, industrious, public-spirited and conscientious ones.*'[16] Here, modish conservative cultural pessimism joined hands with a medically camouflaged brand of Social Darwinism. Among younger advocates of racial hygiene and eugenics, the latter assumed a still more drastic form.

Selective breeding, Germanic version

Even more widespread was the culturally pessimistic view that the decline in good old standards was sending the whole of society to Babylonian perdition. In February 1930 the gynaecologist August Mayer was invited to give a lecture by the Red Cross organization. Born in 1876, Mayer directed the women's clinic at Tübingen University from 1917 to 1950 and was regarded as an oracle in his own field. His life's work, to quote the encyclopedias, was the study of physical, hereditary, mental and social factors in relation to gynaecology.

Mayer's lecture was entitled 'Reflections on Modern Sexual Morality'. His interpretation of 'social factors' is noteworthy because it amounted to a concentrated attack on liberal trends in modern child education and the new role of woman.

Years earlier, Max von Gruber, whose intentions were admittedly somewhat different, had given his blessing to sex education for young people while recommending that it be reserved for more senior age-groups. August Mayer rejected this outright. In his view, newfangled sex education of the young went altogether too far. He found the postulated harmfulness of sexual self-control quite as absurd as the 'gospel of the flesh'. The result: in place of man's ennoblement, his destruction. Mayer declared that those who championed 'the right of the young to self-education' were merely encouraging young people to reject the prevailing social order and its standards of conduct, stimulating lack of moral restraint and promoting the spread of venereal diseases.

Mayer condemned the aims and effects of the feminist movement no less harshly. Indignation at the 'double moral standards' of the middle class had prompted women to call for equal rights. They were now proclaiming the 'right to free love' and thus declaring war on marriage.

Mayer crudely oversimplified the social factors involved, so his account was crudely erroneous. Like many others, he attacked the compound evil labelled 'feminist movement and sex education'. He really meant something else. The whole trend – the new sexual morality, so-called – was repugnant to him.

The feelings of every true woman, Mayer declared, culminated in motherhood; her only additional desire was to be a 'comrade and fellow-wayfarer', or concomitant, of her husband. Natural law entailed a respect for all that was genuine. Contraception, claimed the eminent gynaecologist, was a rape on nature and a betrayal of the soul of every natural woman. 'What we need are women *of high quality* as vehicles and guardians of moral conduct . . . The maternal function must again become a cardinal function. Maternal dignity and maternal worth must rise in value because they are the source of perpetuation, both for the family and for the world'.[17] Clumsily put, but a straightforward avowal of faith in the old order and a flat rejection of the new.

The modern degeneracy of the modern age

The modern age . . . This was the watershed between two schools of thought. Some regarded it hopefully as a new beginning untrammelled by the strait-jacket of the old social order, readily forgetting that a new political system and liberal legislation may create a different framework but cannot shield it from the potent effects of traditional ideas and usages. Their opponents on the conservative side suffered from a similar blind spot. They refused to acknowledge that the new situation was a product of manifold political, economic and social changes which had been in progress for a considerable period. To them, the modern age was at once a sad decline and the root of all evil.

The Weimar Republic, the majority of critics argued, had ordained that woman be granted an equality of status which conflicted with her natural lot and estranged her from her function as a mother and guardian of the home. In their eyes, the adherents of the democratic system held views which militated against every tradition and well-ordered social structure: they spoke of liberty and meant disintegration. The result could be seen in the cities, where children lost all respect for their parents and left home far too young. The sense of family solidarity was evaporating. Young women abandoned their proper reserve and brazenly consorted with young men, unmarried girls went hunting for husbands. Small wonder, said the critics, that vice ran riot in the streets or that prostitution was assuming the dimensions of an industry (though Hirschfeld estimated that there were 20,000 prostitutes in Berlin even before the First World War). Venereal diseases were allegedly contaminating the population and homosexuality was rife in public lavatories, men's clubs and youth organizations.

This alarming picture of demoralization was an indictment of the unloved Republic: all blame rested with the so-called System State. Berlin was branded the sinful Gomorrah of a degenerate civilization. The self-styled upper crust exploited the system, throwing wild parties and extravagant banquets which violated every rule of propriety. Culture was dying fast. The theatre had become a temple to unbridled sensuality, the music-hall pandered shamelessly to the lust for amusement. Cinemas contributed to the general superficiality with jejune entertainment and frivolous spectaculars. What the modern age called art was rootless urban culture. Literature was dominated by decadence, obscenity and pseudo-sophistication. The fine arts had degenerated into a repulsive display of all that was hideous and abnormal. Barbaric primitivity and loathsome cacophony were the distinguishing features of modern music. All that was good, beautiful and true – the classical German heritage – was rejected, scorned and subverted.

This gloomy genre-picture of the 'Golden Twenties' was painted by genuinely alarmed conservative moralists and ambitious reactionary politicians alike. The motive that prompted such critics was immaterial, nor did it matter whether their assertions really matched the facts. What mattered was that this horrendous panorama of moral decadence and cultural decline accorded with the resentment harboured by a broad section of the public which still dwelt in the nineteenth-century world of ideas. To the bourgeois middle class, the Wilhelmine era from whose smug, snug security it felt so brusquely wrenched now seemed the acme of justice and morality, peace and good order. As for the lower middle class – the people who had been overtaken by events and socially uprooted, the mass of discontented petty bourgeois – they now compounded their social envy with middle-class bitterness towards the prevailing system. Resentment of the Republic went hand in hand with disquiet at the new customs and conventions. It was obvious that this mood could be turned to advantage in the field of political controversy. Solemn lamentations over the universal disappearance of decorum and decency assured the right-wing parties of broad support, just as a rancorous campaign against alleged corruption under the parliamentary system won guaranteed backing for radical splinter-groups.

The recipe for success was simple in the extreme and intelligible to all: the Weimar system of government was to blame for everything. Democracy signified cultural disintegration and moral decay.

Party veterans versus new ways

In the lower reaches of this resentful middle class a locksmith named Anton Drexler won a few hundred supporters for his 'German Labour Party'. The name was both high-flown and misleading. The members were Drexler's workmates from the Munich railway yards, craftsmen, small shopkeepers, a few academics, and demobilized soldiers who were finding it hard to re-establish themselves in civilian life. Drexler's political aims were modest. For reasons still obscure, he cherished a profound hatred of socialist workers in general, also for the Jewish-masonic conspiracy which, he was firmly convinced, had sent Germany plummeting to disaster. The petty bourgeois politician was no stranger to class differences, but his concept of class was somewhat surprising: officers and civil servants were not bourgeois, but the worker, by contrast, was. It should be added that Drexler supported 'healthy' capitalism and had left the middle-class 'Patriotic Front' partly because its development was insufficiently nationalistic for his taste and partly because he sought access to the masses. He was not so wide of the mark in adopting this limited approach. It appealed to the steadily growing number of petty bourgeois malcontents who felt enviously inferior to the better-class sections of the German national bourgeoisie on the one hand, and, on the other, looked down contemptuously on the largely Marxist and 'unpatriotic' mass of industrial workers. The muddled chauvinistic ideas of the German Labour Party gave this essentially unpolitical class a chance to transmute its social sentiments into political self-awareness.

After all, everyone was at liberty to feel himself a German worker according to Drexler's almost comic definition: 'If someone labours for the common good of his Fatherland, whether physically or mentally, he is a worker and on that account belongs to the "German Labour Party". So stop taking exception to the name.'[18] At the beginning of 1920 this 'party of all working people' was made up as follows: craftsmen and skilled workers, 33 per cent; academics and students, 20 per cent; officers and other ranks, 13 per cent; civil servants and white-collar workers, 14 per cent; commercial employees, 12 per cent. The balance consisted of a few small businessmen and unskilled workers.

The whole thing was a manifestation of vague lower-middle-class disquiet. Woolly slogans like 'Jewish conspiracy', 'smashing the dominance of invested capital', 'healthy capitalism' and 'German socialism' reflected this. Emotion took the place of analysis, rhetorical claptrap deputized for political objectives.

Although the founding of the Munich party was correctly aimed at a gap in the political market, it won little initial success and barely achieved local importance. This state of affairs changed abruptly when, in September 1919, there appeared on the scene a man who knew how to convert general disquiet into organized protest. Within a few years, Adolf Hitler transformed the petty bourgeois political association known as the German Labour Party (DAP), whose dim existence had been confined to the back rooms of Munich beer-halls, into the National Socialist German Labour Party (NSDAP), a nationalist mass movement which proceeded to attack the democratic system of government.

Hitler's first encounter with the DAP was largely fortuitous, but his decision to join it can hardly have been as agonized as he alleges. He had, after all, discovered a ready-made political group which accorded perfectly – in embryo – with his own idea of the small movement which could pave the way for 'national resurgence'.

The man who, in face of Germany's national impoverishment and his own rather aimless personal position, determined to become a politician, had already contemplated founding a party of his own in opposition to the 'parties of the November Crime' (of 1918) as well as to 'the so-called "bourgeois-national" structure'. He had a name all ready for it: the Social Revolutionary Party. His was no programme, more of a mousetrap: 'The name of the movement to be newly founded had from the very outset to offer a prospect of approaching the broad masses; in default of this quality, the whole task seemed pointless and unnecessary.'[19]

As a civilian agitator in the service of the Reichswehr, Hitler had already gained enough experience to know what classes could best be mobilized for his purposes. He unwittingly portrayed this target-group in *Mein Kampf*: 'What prerequisites did I myself bring to this task [of leadership]? That I was poor and without resources seemed to me the most tolerable aspect, but it was harder that I should be numbered among the anonymous, that I was one of the millions whom chance suffers to exist or recalls from existence without even their closest neighbours deigning to notice the fact. In addition, there was the difficulty which inevitably arose from my lack of schooling.'[20] There could be no more vivid description of the mentality of someone who, in his own estimation, has had a raw deal, of the misjudged and disdained, of the sufferer from social and personal frustration.

With the groping instinct of the nascent demagogue, Hitler realized how much power would accrue to anyone who provided this suppressed craving for recognition with an outlet. It was futile to come forward, like so many splinter-groups, with a cut-and-dried party programme or detailed statements of policy. In order to activate these millions of nameless people he must offer them a grand design, a framework in which the individual could seek his own place, an ideal nebulous enough to fulfil all expectations. As he himself put it: 'The theoretician of a movement must lay down its goal, the politician strive for its fulfilment. The thinking of the one, therefore, will be determined by eternal truth, the actions of the other more by the practical reality of the moment. The greatness of the one lies in the absolute abstract soundness of his idea, that of the other in his correct attitude towards given facts and their advantageous application; and in this the theoretician's aim must serve as his guiding star.'[21]

Hitler, who combined the politician and the theoretician in a single person, certainly had the 'correct attitude'. He possessed during his years of ascendancy and triumph a positively uncanny ability to sense inclinations and an almost incredible knack of exploiting them for his own ends. At the same time, his demagogic brilliance invested even the most deplorable exaggerations with a semblance of credibility.

As a popular orator and party leader, Adolf Hitler was, if anything, even less inclined to commit himself on matters of ethics and morality than in the politico-social sphere. Few firm guide-lines can be detected apart from the inferences to be drawn from his pronouncements on racial theory. He laid down no eternally valid code such as would have done justice to the pretensions of a Thousand-Year Reich, no immutable moral laws appropriate to the Messianic spirit of the Führer-State.

This does not, of course, mean that Hitler left this area blank and adopted an attitude of *laissez-faire*. It is a tribute to his powers of insight that he made use of only two factors. The first was that huge popular success can be gained by delivering morally embellished condemnations of an unwelcome political opponent or social trend if the opponent's way of life incurs the patent disfavour of the 'masses' or if the steady development of the trend encounters their habitual lack of comprehension. Both can duly be pronounced offensive to wholesome popular sentiment.

The second factor was that it is beneficial to the imposition of a totalitarian social order, in particular, if it initially adopts – with slight modifications – the moral concepts already prevailing among wide sections of the public and leaves the private sector a personal preserve of the individual. Apparent tolerance towards the individual enhances his readiness to comply with the apparent dictates of the mass, of wholesome popular sentiment.

During his struggle with the Weimar Republic, Hitler took up arms against the 'ethical and moral contamination of the body politic' with all the righteous indignation of a respectable man and folkish prophet.

By 'contamination of health' he meant syphilis, which on his submission was infecting whole cities. It had to be stamped out, not by a 'remedy of questionable character' – viz. Salvarsan, discovered in 1909 by the Jewish biochemist Paul Ehrlich – but solely by fighting its causes: the prostitution of love, the Jewification of spiritual life and 'mammonization' of the mating instinct, the *mariage d'argent*. The rising generation was being ruined, 'for the robust children of a natural emotion will be replaced by the miserable creatures of financial expediency'.[22] These children were 'the sad product of the irresistibly spreading contamination of our sexual life'.[23]

All this hazy but effective stuff came from the same source, the well from which any successful orator could at any time draw thunderous applause: the anti-Semitism of the man in the street.

In Hitler's monomaniac vocabulary, syphilis became a typical Jewish attribute, a quasi-asset – or liability – of Jewry in general. The 'French disease' of the age of chivalry was replaced by the 'Jewish disease' of the folkish epoch. The Jews were the infamous foes who had aspired to debilitate the German people, *ergo* miscegenation with those of Jewish blood was the world's 'original sin'. This was the very sin so persistently committed by the 'contemporary bourgeoisie', whose most fervent ambition – according to Hitler – was to wed the daughters of wealthy Jews. This accounts for his 'mammonization of our mating instinct' and his 'miserable creatures of financial expediency'.

It would seem at first sight that Hitler had declared war on the prosperous middle class as a whole, and this impression is reinforced by the catalogue of omissions with which he charged the Wilhelmine bourgeoisie, by his tirades against traditional usages and the '[hypocritical] saint's cloak of prudishness'[24] assumed by certain sections of society. But this impression blinds one to Hitler's adroit tactics. He only inveighed against 'certain circles' – in concrete terms, those whom he attacked as supporters of the democratic system. Just as his concept of 'workers with head and hand' made the German Labour Party accessible to anyone who was not a Jew, Marxist or democrat, so nothing could have been further from his mind than to scare away the upper echelon of the middle class *en bloc*. It, too, was subject to the above disqualifications and no more, though mingled with an anti-intellectual bias. The Führer of the German Reich was still pursuing the same strategy years later: 'I wish to draw a distinction between the people, in other words, the wholesome, full-blooded and patriotic mass of Germans, and a decadent "high society" which is untrustworthy because of its limited ties of blood. Sometimes termed the "upper class", it is really only the excremental product of a social misbreeding whose cosmopolitan infection of blood and intellect has rendered it unstable.'[25] Fiercely attacked as it seemed to be, therefore, the middle class enjoyed the same privilege as any other: those who wanted to join were at liberty to do so. Hitler was adept in trimming his sails to suit an audience. His vituperative outpourings in Munich's Sterneckerbräu beer-cellar differed considerably from the criticisms he voiced at Dusseldorf's Industrieklub.

The main effect of his slanders on the upper middle class was to provide the social envy of the lower middle class with a moral pretext and so render it productive from his own point of view. Bitterly as he attacked bourgeois morality, his own 'socio-revolutionary' concept was merely a variant intended not to stifle the better instincts of the 'wholesome' bourgeois. As a Party orator, Hitler sought to combat prostitution by promoting early marriage, 'particularly for the man, the woman being in any case only the passive party'.[26] This entailed the somewhat erroneous but flattering assumption that prostitution was not sustained chiefly by married men. He railed against the upper-class mother who wanted her children sired by a husband who had already sown his wild oats. He also bewailed 'limited propagation' in so-called 'sensible' families and demanded instead that the State should encourage prolific families and practise racial hygiene, inter alia by using medical treatment to remove any obstacles to reproduction in families of sound stock. 'Marriage, too, cannot be an end in itself, but must serve the one great goal: the multiplication and preservation of the species and the race. This alone is its meaning and function.'[27] The bourgeois Professor Max von Gruber would have put it in much the same way. Hitler was following the eugenic line when, in 1925, he demanded that a folkish State should prevent the sick or hereditarily disabled from reproducing by means of sterilization or 'ruthless' segregation: 'The right of personal freedom recedes before the duty to preserve the race.'[28]

Hitler's educational theories were calculated to win the respect of the most unsophisticated citizen and the most hidebound martinet of a schoolmaster. The Führer-to-be extolled the army – the old finishing school of the nation – because, 'in the morass of universally spreading enervation and effeminization',[29] it had annually produced 350,000 vigorous young man whose term of service had taught them to obey orders. The task of schools, Hitler said, was to eliminate the harm caused by excessive intellectual instruction, this being unsuited to a period in which issues were decided by physical might. He did not omit to add some tips on sex education: 'Undue emphasis on purely intellectual instruction and the neglect of physical training also encourage the emergence of sexual ideas at a much too early age. The youth who achieves the hardness of iron by sports and gymnastics succumbs to the need for sexual satisfaction less than the stay-at-home fed exclusively on intellectual fare. And a sensible system of education must take this into account. Furthermore, it must not lose sight of the fact that the healthy young man will expect different things from a woman than the prematurely corrupted stay-at-home.'[30]

The picture would have been incomplete without an indictment of the sensually oppressive atmosphere that brooded over the whole of public life, that 'hothouse of sexual ideas and stimuli'.[31] Cinema, vaudeville, theatre and advertising were plunging young people into a sink of iniquity, aided by foppish fashions in dress. The filth of urban 'culture' must be swept away. 'Theatre, art, literature, cinema, press, posters and window displays must be cleansed of the manifestations of our rotting world and placed in the service of a moral political and cultural idea. Public life must be freed from the suffocating perfume of our modern eroticism, as from all prudish hypocrisy.'[32]

The average man in close-up

But where were the outlines of this better and more genuine morality which Hitler contrasted with his vision of a decaying world? Spartan upbringing, early marriage, reproduction by the racially pure, genetically sound offspring, a public life cleansed of sexuality – did these demands really oppose new values and standards to the alleged moral corruption and erotic depravity of the hated democratic system? Were not even these meagre promises rendered implausible by the brutal conduct of brown-shirted strong-arm squads and the life-style of many notorious Party bigwigs such as Christian Weber, Hermann Esser, Julius Streicher, Ernst Röhm, Edmund Heines and Robert Ley?

The Nazis had no new morality to offer. They contented themselves with furious attacks on the spectre of prevailing immorality which Party orators paraded at every meeting to guaranteed acclamation from their embittered audiences. Their own scanty ideas, which they prescribed as a radical cure-all for the body politic, were based on nationalist-racialist misconceptions and the moral concepts of a pre-industrial agrarian society. This is nowhere more apparent than in the role which National Socialism assigned to women – one of the few points on which Hitler committed himself from the outset. Female education had to be firmly directed at the 'mother-to-be'. This was the sole context in which women rated a mention in the '25 Points' comprising the 'Programme of the NSDAP', drafted by Gottfried Feder. Point 21 in the socio-political section declared that 'The State must provide for the improvement of national health by protecting the mother and child . . .'.[33]

Women had to be protected above all from the world of labour, meaning employment outside the home. That, so the argument ran, was a violation of the feminine disposition, jeopardized a woman's chances of bearing children and prejudiced the rearing of healthy offspring. Existing circumstances – one-third of the working population was female – did, however, impose some concessions on the vote-hungry National Socialists. Women were granted the right to earn a livelihood in special 'feminine' occupations. By a fortunate coincidence, these happened to be just the occupations in which the wives and daughters of the lower middle class were obliged to earn their keep or lend indispensable assistance to their menfolk: domestic service, the retail trade, farming, nursing, social welfare and the education of the young. 'The working woman,' Gregor Strasser magnanimously declared in election year 1932, 'enjoys equality in the National Socialist State and has the same right to State protection of her livelihood as the married woman and mother.' Pursuing this tactical line, he simultaneously gave notice of future restrictions: 'Within this necessary and forthcoming transition to suitable female employment, the dismantling of the present structure can only proceed as opportunities present themselves, under the guarantee of economic security.'[34]

National Socialist political theory provided for the civic equality of women in certain circumstances only. Women were barred from membership of the Party executive as early as 1921. As Party members of junior rank, they confined their duties to plying the exhausted or injured heroes of assembly-room scuffles with refreshing drinks and soothing bandages. They were good at spreading joyful enthusiasm but had to steer clear of political controversy, which was man's work. Hermann Esser, one of the Führer's oldest cronies and notorious for his many love affairs, was moved by national solidarity to declare that 'Women belong at home in the kitchen and bedroom; they belong at home and ought to bring up their children'.[35] Gregor Strasser, representing the Party's anti-capitalist wing, exemplified the same basic moral pattern – one which documented the claim to superiority of a masculine and misogynistic movement. It formed the central tenet of the bourgeois code which he embodied in NS-Briefe (National Socialist Letters), though in a more refined guise: man owes woman purity of soul; woman owes man purity of body.[36] The value of woman reposed solely in motherhood, preferably of frequent recurrence. In a theoretical treatise written in 1932, the Nazi Amazon Amalie Lauer flatly informed her fellow-women that the National Socialist scheme of things allotted them biological importance only – provided always that they could guarantee to produce racially pure offspring.

Gregor Strasser had already (in 1926) broached the possibility of rewarding motherhood with political privileges – a multiple vote, for example – and of equating it with military service for men. Hitler thought this an excessive recompense for a natural duty. In his projected State, a woman would not gain full recognition until she became a mother, and a single woman would not be a full member of the

national community: 'The German girl is a subject and becomes a
citizen only when she marries. But the right of citizenship can also be
granted to female German subjects active in economic life.'[37] It goes
without saying that this was merely a sop to the mass of employed
female voters and did not stem from any genuine regard for female
attainments.

For the middle class, who abhorred intellectual feminists as much as
they did the Republic which had yielded to their demands, and for the
lower middle class, to whom the whole newfangled fuss about women
was repugnant – for these classes, views and attitudes of this kind held
a considerable attraction. This is evident from the social background
of Party members and the stratification of National Socialist voters.

Almost half the registered National Socialists of 1930 were employees
– office and domestic staff – or self-employed persons, shopkeepers,
craftsmen and professional people. The farming community and petty
officialdom, including teachers, were strongly represented. Most conspicuously under-represented were industrial workers, who made up
almost 50 per cent of the population but supplied less than 30 per cent
of the Party membership.

The composition of NSDAP voting strength renders this picture even
clearer. The Party drew support from the agricultural and provincial
urban middle classes, who bitterly opposed the modern trend towards
bureaucratization and centralism. It was also backed by small independent farmers and businessmen. Most of its votes came from the
lesser townships and rural areas where hostility to the growing influence
of urban authority and culture was strongest. In towns with over 25,000
inhabitants, the National Socialists always polled fewer votes than the
other big parties – SPD, Centre, German National or Communist.

'In 1932, the National Socialist Party's typical ideal voter was a self-
employed Protestant member of the middle class who lived either on
an estate or in a small township and had formerly voted for a party of
the political centre or for a regional party opposed to the power and
influence of big industry and the trade unions.'[38] This 'labour' party was
nourished, not by urban rootlessness and destitution, but by provincial
backwardness and atrophy, and it was an essential article of faith in
this social group that woman should limit her activities to hearth and
home, kitchen and nursery.

There is no doubt that, all secondary objectives apart, this principle
corresponded with the sincere beliefs of the Nazi vote-catchers, whose
mentality bore a fundamental resemblance to that of their supporters.

On the other hand, principles of this type run the risk of complete distortion as soon as they enter the political calculations of a radical movement. The successful use of a simple cliché encourages people to simplify it still further and, ultimately, carry it to extremes. The brilliant demagogue finds this the obvious course to adopt, and there is method in it.

'Like woman,' philosophized Hitler, 'whose mental state is governed less by considerations of abstract reason than by an indefinable emotional craving for complementary strength, and who, in consequence, would rather yield to a strong man than dominate a weak one, so the masses love a dominator better than a suppliant and feel inwardly more satisfied by a doctrine which tolerates no other beside itself than by the granting of liberal freedom. They have no idea what to do with it, as a rule, and even tend to feel that they have been abandoned.'[39] At the end of this road lay contempt for humanity. 'The ordinary man in the street respects nothing but brutal strength and ruthlessness,' Hitler told Rauschning in autumn 1933, '– women too, for that matter, women and children. The people need wholesome fear. They *want* to fear something. They want someone to frighten them and make them shudderingly submissive.'[40] Hitler could produce an ostensibly cogent argument to support his assertion: success. In the Reichstag elections of September 1930, which brought the Party its first real break-through, the 6.5 million NSDAP voters included 3 million women. Undoubtedly, what clinched matters was feminine instinct rather than feminine intelligence. For National Socialists, it was reason enough to pay the fair sex a special tribute: they marvelled at the 'unerring instinct' which had prompted women to throw in their lot with Adolf Hitler. Millions of women voted Hitler to power, and millions more idolized him as their Führer.

Adolf Hitler: Not made for woman

'Face and head ill-bred, hybrid. Low, receding brow, unlovely nose, broad cheek-bones, small eyes, dark hair. Facial expression that of an insanely excited man, not of one in full command of himself. Finally, an air of delighted self-esteem.'[41] So much for a personal impression of Adolf Hitler's appearance by the racial hygienist Max von Gruber. His objective verdict concluded with the statement that, racially, Hitler was of typically un-Nordic, Alpine Slav stock.

A few years later Gruber's fellow-experts arrived at quite another conclusion. In 1933, 'With official Party and police authorization' – thus the imprint on the volume – Alfred Richter published *Our Führer in the Light of the Racial Question*. Richter, who described himself as 'Director of the Private Institute of Practical Characterology and Ethnology' at Bärenstein in the Erzgebirge, unveiled for his 'Germanic brothers and sisters' an entirely new Adolf Hitler, radiantly illumined by the most limpid of northern lights: 'Brilliant, creative, spiritual leader-nature, vigorous, tough, endowed with great love, infinite suffering and self-sacrifice.' The findings of practical characterology were neatly corroborated by those of scientific ethnology. Studying the photographs on which he based his assessment, the characterologist was struck by more than the Führer's Nordic brow: 'Hitler, who is blond and has rosy skin and blue eyes, is thus of a purely (Aryan-)Germanic nature.'[42]

However generally indifferent we may be to a person's Germanic nature and racial type, they merit our attention in Hitler's case. His manic racialism had results more than terrible enough to warrant an inquiry into his own parentage and descent. The facts that emerge are such as to shed light on the enduringly horrifying character of his racial ideology and its devotees.

Hitler's forebears lived in the rural Waldviertel of Lower Austria, a stony tract of land between the Danube and the Bohemian–Moravian border. In Third Reich parlance, this meant that his veins pulsed with the healthy German blood of peasant forefathers who were sons of the soil.

The Führer of a subsequent Greater Germanic Reich could not have been over-eager to have his family history investigated too carefully. It was clear to him, if to no one else, that his entitlement to the 'minor certificate of Aryan stock' required of every official under the law of 8 April 1933, which reconstituted the civil service, was debatable for the simple reason that his grandfather's name was unknown.

In 1837, in the Lower Austrian village of Strones, the spinster Anna Maria Schicklgruber gave birth to a male child who was christened Alois Schicklgruber. Five years later she married the itinerant miller Johann Georg Hiedler, brother of the man at whose farm she lived with her child. It is nevertheless improbable that Hiedler was the child's father. In 1930, when Adolf Hitler received some vague disclosures about his ancestry from a distant relative, he commissioned the Party jurist Hans Frank to follow them up. The trail led to Graz in Styria. Before her confinement, Anna Maria Schicklgruber had been employed there as cook to a couple named Frankenberger, who had a nineteen-year-old son. What argues in favour of the latter's paternity is that the Frankenbergers paid Anna Maria an allowance and continued to do so for fourteen years; what militates against Johann Hiedler's is that he took no steps to legitimize his wife's child. Alois remained Alois Schicklgruber until he was nearly forty, and his parents had been dead for decades when he finally took the name Hitler. In 1876 his step-uncle Johann Nepomuk Hiedler persuaded the parish priest at Döllersheim to make an improper alteration in the baptismal register by swearing a dubious affidavit confirming his late brother's paternity. The word 'illegitimate' was scratched out and Alois acknowledged to be the son of Johann Georg Hiedler – more fluidly, Hitler.

All attempts to elucidate the matter have so far failed. It is, for instance, uncertain whether Hans Frank was correct in stating that the Frankenbergers – and, thus, Adolf Hitler's putative grandfather – were Jewish. Hitler, who must have been extremely annoyed by these revelations, did his best to plug their turbid source for good. In May 1938, a few weeks after Germany's union with Austria, Döllersheim and its vicinity were declared a Wehrmacht training area. The birth-place of Hitler's father and his grandmother's grave were flattened by manoeuvring tanks – a circumstance which, in view of the Third Reich's Führer-worship and careful preservation of national monuments, appears highly significant.

Adolf Hitler's family background was neither as humble nor as worthy as his own accounts and those of his admirers make out. His keen and ambitious father, Alois, attained senior rank in the Imperial and Royal Customs Service, a position which carried a fair salary – ultimately

2,600 Kronen a year – and brought him local prestige in the various Upper Austrian townships where he served. His private life was not, however, quite as blameless as one might have expected in an honest servant of the Crown.

Alois Schicklgruber's first marriage to Anna Glasl, the daughter of a fellow-official, did not prosper. His first wife was in failing health and remained childless. Alois turned to other women. A month after Anna's death in 1883 he got married again – now styling himself Alois Hitler – to a hotel cook named Franziska Matzelsberger, who had earlier presented him with a son, Alois, and three months later gave birth to a daughter, Angela. The marriage was of short duration. Franziska, who suffered from tuberculosis, died in 1884. The widower was obliged to wait six months before he could marry yet again. As a girl of nineteen, Klara Pölzl had lived for a while at his home in Braunau, both during his first ill-starred marriage and after the start of his affair with Franziska Matzelsberger. She was the granddaughter of his legal uncle Johann Nepomuk Hiedler, so their marriage required a certificate of dispensation from the Church. It finally took place in January 1885, and in May Klara give birth to a son.

The third child of this marriage was Adolf Hitler, born on 20 April 1889 at Braunau am Inn. His mother was twenty-nine years old. His father, who was over fifty, retired at the age of fifty-eight and died at Leonding in 1903. A stern and irascible man, Alois was as incapable of paternal affection as he had been of marital fidelity. Besides, son Adolf gave little cause for parental pride. While conceding that he showed adequate ability, his teachers charged him with lack of perseverance. The good primary-school pupil twice missed promotion to a higher form when he reached secondary school and was eventually failed in mathematics, natural history, French and German. When he dropped out of school in 1905, his vaunted interest in history earned him a mere pass. His only 'Excellent' was for gymnastics.

It is difficult not to relate these performances at school with the Führer's views on education, which condemned undue intellectual instruction and stressed the value of physical training. Hitler's youthful attempts to win academic laurels were a dismal failure. In 1907, after loafing round the provincial city of Linz for two years at his mother's expense, he headed for Vienna with the aim of becoming a painter. The young man's test drawings were adjudged unsatisfactory, however, and he was not accepted as a candidate for examination by the Academy of Fine Arts. The alternative solution, architecture, was also ruled out because applicants were required to have completed their time at school. True to the National Socialist ideal of boyhood and his Führer's image, Adolf Hitler liked to portray himself in retrospect as a dashing schoolboy gang-leader and youthful daredevil. In his private circle of favoured listeners – secretaries, aides and a few unsophisticated cronies – he courted applause with lively stories of his boyhood days.

He claimed, for instance, that he cheekily accosted any young girl who took his fancy, or, if she was accompanied by her mother, boldly asked to carry the latter's parcels as a pretext for escorting the girl to her door. He also used to play all kinds of pranks in church, pulling faces or brushing his non-existent beard with his father's moustache-brush to attract the girls' attention and make them giggle. These anecdotes are no more credible than the legend of his aunt's dairy-maid, who made eyes at him while milking. It was a close shave, apparently, but at the last moment he regained control of himself and left the poor girl flushed with shame and embarrassment.

In fact, young Adolf was neither a gang-leader nor a daredevil. He was far too domineering and arrogant on the one hand and far too solitary and unsociable on the other. His contacts with the opposite sex were, by all accounts, meagre in the extreme. Tradition relates only one story which merits some degree of belief. It demonstrates the narrowness of this presumptuous but inhibited young man's social horizons.

The girl's name was Stefanie. In 1904, while Hitler was still agonizing at school, she matriculated at Linz. She spent the following two years at college in Munich and Geneva. By the time she rejoined her widowed mother – her father had been a senior government official – she was a budding beauty with bright, expressive eyes and pure blonde hair which she wore in a chignon. Hitler must have encountered her in 1907, his last year at Linz. Strolling idly through the city, forging plans, he sometimes caught sight of his beloved walking arm in arm with her mother. He never accosted her – according to the fancifully embroidered account given by August Kubizek, his only friend of the period, he didn't dare. He planned to wait until he could dazzle the girl with an imposing professional title – 'academic painter' – and then marry her. In the meantime, he adored her from a safe distance. There was never any real question of a match between them. For one thing, the carefully nurtured girl belonged to a circle in which he would have been unacceptable, even as an academic painter. For another, she was already at her most marriageable age (she became engaged to an officer in 1908) and would have regarded eighteen-year-old Adolf as a mere boy.

Is this to exaggerate the importance of a youthful passion? Franz Jetzinger, the biographer of Hitler's early life, ran Stefanie to earth and interviewed her. She could not recall her diffident admirer but she did remember a strange letter she had received as a girl 'in which the writer said he was now going to attend the Academy of Fine Arts, but I was to wait for him – he would return and marry me'.[43]

This typifies the delusions to which Hitler was obviously becoming ever more prone. He composed a callow love-poem entitled 'Hymn to the Beloved', whose theme Kubizek describes as follows: 'Stefanie, a noble damsel clad in a flowing gown of dark-blue velvet, rode across flowering meadows on a white steed. Her unbound hair cascaded from her shoulders like a flood of gold. Above, a bright spring sky. All was pure, radiant happiness.'[44] Stefanie became stylized into an ideal figure with whom Hitler aligned his every expectation and interest. 'He always said it would be quite sufficient if he confronted Stefanie one day. Everything would fall into place without the need for a single word to pass between them. To people as exceptional as Stefanie and himself, customary forms of verbal communication were unnecessary. Exceptional people understood each other with the aid of intuition, he told me.'[45]

Here we see Hitler displaying a precocious knack of bending reality to his wishes. In his mind's eye, a relationship which could not in reality have been more one-sided assumed forms which already constituted a firm component of his presumptuous plans for the future. The nature and timing of his sole sign of life to Stefanie – the letter giving notice of their future marriage – show that he was incapable of overcoming his timidity or constraint until he had penetrated far enough into the dream-world of his tangled pretensions and unfulfilled desires to believe in it himself.

Hitler's relations with the opposite sex do not seem to have become any more active during his subsequent years in Vienna. The young man's outward appearance grew less and less prepossessing. His threadbare frock-coat had been given him by a Hungarian Jew, shaggy hair hung luxuriantly to his collar beneath a greasy bowler, and his chin sprouted black stubble.

This was the period during which Hitler cobbled together his philosophy of life in doss-houses, soup-kitchens, coffee-houses and places of casual employment. Filled with hatred of the masses and abhorrence of the socialist labour movement, he whittled rancour, prejudice and contempt into a crude Social Darwinism which equated right with might and transfigured the brutal fight for survival into life's dominant idea.

The social background for such views was provided not only by doss-houses but also by Vienna's petty bourgeois society, where, in addition to anti-socialism, nationalism and Pan-Germanism, anti-Semitism had come into vogue.

Hitler showed himself highly susceptible to this world of ideas. All at once, in everything that was filthy, obscene and malignant, he discovered 'like a maggot in a rotting body . . . a Yid!'[46] It must have been a happy release. At last he had an identifiable target for his social hatred, a personal foe on whom he could vent his dull but insistent feelings of rage. He developed his anti-Semitism into a racial category, 'enlightening' himself with the aid of trashy pamphlets.

Racialism of this type always contains a primitive admixture of sex. The blond and blue-eyed creature of light acquires sublimity, distinction and exclusiveness only when contrasted with its slimy, repulsive, malignant counterpart. Racial theories based on such sentiments employ the obscene emotive power of language and cadence as a weapon aimed consistently below the belt.

It is hardly necessary, therefore, to ascribe the sexual undertone in Hitler's anti-Semitism to a hypothetical encounter with a Jewish girl or prostitute who left him with syphilis – a theory which has never been verified. The simpler explanation is that Hitler, with his singular lack of sexual experience, unloaded all his sexual envy, abnormal attitudes and resentments on to the Jewish 'counterpart' and made it the target of his unbridled fury. 'For hours on end, with satanic joy in his face, the black-haired Jewish youth lies in wait for the unwitting girl whom he defiles with his blood, thus stealing her from her people . . . It was and is the Jews who bring negroes to the Rhineland, always with the same ulterior motive and clear aim of ruining the hated white race by the bastardization that inevitably results, dashing it from its cultural and political eminence and themselves rising to become its masters.'[47]

Hitler's youthful relations with the opposite sex stopped short at the adolescent stage. Once across the threshold between adolescence and manhood, he fled from this problem, as from others, into the realm of fantasy. He tried to explain away his inability to sustain an easy relationship with women just as he blinded himself to his general incapacity for social contact. The solution was simple but convenient.

His world was a world of fighters, a man's world divided into masters and servants according to racial quality. Women were by nature excluded from this world. They could not fight; the most they could do, if their pedigree permitted, was bring fighters into the world. That was their function, but it was also the extent of their role. They were not only subordinate to man but of minor importance altogether. A man had to prove himself among men.

That relegated Hitler's personal problem, his flawed relationship with woman in her capacity as a sexual antipole, to the background. He solved it completely in the course of his political career by convincing himself that Providence had destined him for higher things, that he must never squander his vital forces on a woman.

On the other hand, he had an incessant craving for approbation, that of the opposite sex included. This he needed as much at his mass rallies as he did in personal intercourse. It very soon dawned on him that he could appeal to women's emotions and arouse their admiration, indeed, fervour. The initial liability of his immature personal relations with women, inhibitions and all, turned into an asset when it came to posing as a charismatic hero. Hitler later declared that women had played a 'not unimportant' role in his political career. For once, this was an understatement.

Hitler had not long made his mark as a Party orator when a whole series of women, all of mature years, took him under their wing. They ranged from Carola ('Hitler's Mummy') Hoffman, the widow of a schoolmaster, to Gertrud von Seydlitz, the widow of a Baltic German officer. Like others of their sex, they assisted the young agitator financially, and it was their backing which enabled him to purchase the *Völkischer Beobachter*.

Despite his rather unappealing background and manner, 'the coming Messiah' – as he was christened by Countess Reventlov during his early days in Munich – found a remarkable degree of favour with members of the upper middle class. Elsa Bruckmann, wife of a Munich publisher and daughter of a noble house, provided him with a useful entrée. The strange outsider became a favourite guest at her parties and did full justice to the role expected of him. Hitler had a talent for varying his performance. He tended to turn up late, a tactical device which suited his tribune-of-the-people act and heightened its dramatic impact. His formal suit was not quite *comme il faut*, nor was his spray of flowers for the hostess. He kissed hands a trifle too obsequiously in the traditional Austrian manner, or, alternatively, startled the company from time to time by clicking his heels. However, all this merely seemed to enhance the ladies' delight at his clumsy manners.

Prominent among those who furthered Hitler's social education and connections, apart from Elsa Bruckmann, was Helene Bechstein, the wife of the piano manufacturer. The Party matador was first introduced to her holiday home on the Obersalzberg by Party bard Dietrich Eckart. In 1925, when he rented Wachenfeld, the house which later grew into the Berghof in accordance with his own bombastic designs, Helene Bechstein helped to equip his bachelor home. She was not alone: Winifred Wagner sent china, kitchen utensils, table-linen, pictures and books from Bayreuth. Even more important than this good neighbour-liness were the social and political contacts which Frau Bechstein was able to procure for her protégé in Berlin. The influential manufacturer's wife willingly introduced Hitler, during his sojourns in the capital, to politicians whom it paid him to know. The efforts made by the Austrian from Munich and his Brownshirt party to acquire prestige in Berlin circles derived additional and vigorous support from Victoria von Dircksen, whose distinguished circle met at the Hotel Kaiserhof, later to become one of Hitler's regular haunts.

Otto Strasser, joint leader with his brother Gregor of the Party's North German wing, described Helene Bechstein's relationship with Hitler as 'an ecstatic and faintly maternal devotion'.[48] He backed this statement with a spiteful picture of the incongruous pair: 'When they were alone, or occasionally in front of friends, he would sit at his hostess's feet, lay his head on her opulent bosom and close his eyes, while her beautiful white hand caressed her big baby's head, ruffling the historic forelock on the future dictator's brow. "Wölfchen," she murmured tenderly, "mein Wölfchen" ("Little wolf, my little wolf ").'[49]

Even allowing for exaggeration – one cannot quite imagine the wolf-cub behaving with such drawing-room docility – Hitler's erstwhile associate did put his finger on one undoubted truth: that Hitler possessed a remarkable magnetism for women of mature years and knew how to make the most of it. He was as ready to simulate depend-ence in private as he was to play the masterful human dynamo in public. According to one witness, he 'systematically' tailored himself to the taste of his female listeners when making a speech. He had a familiar psychological formula for this: women's emotions are gov-erned by an indefinable and instinctive craving for complementary strength; like the masses, they yield most readily to the strong – the leader among men. There was no room for women as individuals in their own right, each with a differently moulded disposition. Hitler's gamble on woman's capacity for devotion and desire for domination was a huge success, particularly in the turbulent circumstances of the period. His conception of mass psychology proved correct.

Women hung eagerly on every word of his speeches as he made arbitrary assertions and swept away objections with emotionally charged rhetorical arguments until he was finally assured of rapturous approval – an approval which turned into frenzy. It was sexual excitement which he knew how to kindle, especially among his female listeners, just as it was an erotic affinity with all the elements of passion and ecstasy which characterized his relationship with the masses – whom he in any case identified with womankind. The course and effect of Hitler's speeches can, with significant ease, be described in sexual terms, a fact which fascinated critical observers. The author René Schickele remarked of Hitler's speeches that they were 'like sex murders'. Hermann Rauschning said that 'anyone looking down from the platform on those front-seat women and watching their expression of rapturous self-surrender, their moist and glistening eyes, could not doubt the character of their enthusiasm'.[50] One of Hitler's addresses, delivered before 20,000 women at the Party rally of 1937, culminated in the words: 'What have I given you? What has National Socialism given you? We have given you Man.'[51] Otto Strasser described the women's reaction to this pronouncement as a rapturous delirium comparable only with an orgasm.

In 1932 Guida Diehl spoke for many early female supporters of National Socialism when she declared: 'And so the Führer stands before us: upright, honest, thoroughgoing, God-fearing and heroic – a truly German man of the kind we women yearn for and demand in the Fatherland's hour of direst need.'[52] Adolf Hitler owed such encomiums not only to ludicrous excesses of hero-worship but also, and in equal measure, to his powers of suggestion.

As his confidence and self-assurance grew, so Hitler came to appreciate female company in private life as well. Women stimulated him, but not to convivial conversation, still less intellectual debate. Their presence raised his spirits, but he appreciated them primarily in the role of admiring or long-suffering listeners. Intelligence was not required, and he never tolerated contradiction from a member of the opposite sex. He relished feminine adulation during his palmy years, for instance at the tea parties for young actresses which Magda Goebbels arranged at his suggestion. On these occasions the Reich Chancellor would turn up with flowers and chocolates, doing his best to exude charm and gallantry for the benefit of the artistic fraternity of which he secretly claimed membership. Later on, as failure set in, he preferred a patient audience for his continual essays in self-justification and tedious monologues, a role that fell to his secretaries.

Hitler, we are informed by his jovial court photographer Heinrich Hoffmann, had no preference for any particular female type. He probably made it a rule not to commit himself for fear of damaging his appeal to millions of women. He had a lasting dread of being gossiped about in connection with a woman, which was one of his grounds for rejecting the idea of marriage. 'It's perfectly true that I love flowers, but that's no reason why I should become a gardener.'[53] Although this quotation sounds more typical of Hoffmann's man-of-the-world approach than of Hitler's temperament, the basic idea squares with the 'sales psychology' of the Führer, who spoke ardently of being married to Germany.

There were, however, plenty of gossips who categorically disputed his fitness or even capacity for marriage. Frau von Pfeffer, the wife of his SA chief of staff, got the impression that he was afraid of women. Henriette von Schirach, wife of the Reich Youth Leader and daughter of Heinrich Hoffmann, was convinced that he was no great lover, to say the least. Frau Hanfstaengl pronounced him a neuter, and her art-dealer husband 'Putzi', Hitler's first press chief, concurred in thinking the Führer impotent. Finally, there was a persistent rumour that Hitler had suffered from syphilis ever since his years in Vienna.

These secret whispers eventually broke surface in the form of a popular lampoon:

> He who rules in the Russian manner,
> dresses his hair in the French style,
> trims his moustache English-fashion
> and wasn't born in Germany himself,
> who teaches us the Roman salute,
> asks our wives for lots of children
> but can't produce any himself –
> he is the leader of Germany.[54]

(The shorthand typist Else W., who had entertained her office colleagues by reciting this piece of doggerel, was in 1943 charged under the Heimtückegesetz, or law of malicious denigration, and sentenced to two years' imprisonment by a special tribunal at Frankfurt. The public prosecutor had asked for twelve months.)

In 1925, when Hitler rented the house on the Obersalzberg, he invited his widowed step-sister Angelika Raubal, the daughter of Alois Hitler's second marriage to Franziska Matzelsberger, to come and keep house for him. She moved in with her two daughters, Geli and Friedl. Geli, a fresh and uncomplicated seventeen-year-old with a pretty face and an agreeable singing-voice, found favour with her uncle. It seems unlikely that she set her cap at the older man, who was twenty years her senior, but it must certainly have flattered the unsophisticated girl to receive her famous uncle's attentions and be escorted to the theatre, cinema or shops by him. If we are to believe Hoffmann, Hitler blossomed in her company. He would do anything for her, even break his golden rule and be seen alone with her in public or indulge in the Arcadian pleasures of picnicking. In 1929, when he rented his big nine-roomed apartment at 16 Prinzregentenplatz, Geli moved in too. The vivacious girl had to pay for this privilege by submitting to her uncle's jealous and suspicious guardianship. She was only permitted to attend dances, which he frowned on, until 11 p.m., and then under the surveillance of his crony Hoffmann or his former sergeant-major Max Amann. On 17th September 1931 Hitler travelled to Bayreuth with Hoffmann. He dashed back into the apartment just before leaving, having evidently quarrelled with Geli. Just beyond Nuremberg news reached him that she had shot herself. He turned back immediately.

The motive for her suicide can only be guessed at. One theory is that she was in love with someone else and could no longer tolerate Hitler's tyranny, another that she loved him but became disenchanted. The whole of their six-year relationship is shrouded in the same uncertainty. Did Hitler adore and spoil the girl because he voluntarily remained at arm's length or because he was kept there willy-nilly?

The answers to these questions are wild conjectures for which no solid evidence is forthcoming, but the outcome of the relationship can be gauged. Hitler had failed in what was probably his sole – and certainly his most serious – attempt to get close to a woman and win her heart. He seems, though this is guesswork, to have built up a tension which defied his efforts to resolve it and finally broke her spirit. His reaction to Geli's death was too exceptional for one to doubt its sincerity, even taking into account his flair for self-dramatization. With

Hoffmann as his companion and witness, he withdrew to a remote country house beside the Tegernsee, where he gave himself over to dull despair. He secretly travelled to Vienna to visit Geli's grave. Her rooms at Prinzregentenplatz and at the Berghof remained untouched, and Hitler's intimates testify that he became even more unsociable from then on.

All observers of the 'Greater Germanic Reich' and its truly world-wide effects have been repeatedly struck by the narrow horizons of its ruling clique. If anything, this applied more to the Führer himself than to his lieutenants. Until his final years, when he completely isolated himself in his headquarters and bomb-proof command posts, his favourite company consisted of fellow-veterans of the 'time of struggle', docile and intellectually limited aides and servants, secretaries and immediate subordinates. Not only in spirit but physically as well, Hitler never left the circle in which he had felt at home as a political pseudo-Bohemian and small-time agitator. His background, too, clove to him. It is noteworthy that, like his forebears from the Waldviertel and his own father, he found his strongest emotional tie – his niece Geli – among the members of his immediate family. With the significant exception of his youthful passion for Stefanie, Hitler's few manifestations of emotional attachment never transcended the confines of his given circle of intimates. His second close relationship likewise blossomed inside his own 'court': Eva Braun worked as an assistant in the photographic studio of his friend Hoffmann, at whose home the dictator could behave like a member of the family.

Hitler had known the pretty blue-eyed blonde for a considerable time. He may have flirted with her on his visits to the Hoffmann household, brought her the occasional bunch of flowers or included the pleasant, good-natured girl in his guest-list when planning an excursion. Eva Braun's interest in Hitler went beyond such trifling courtesies, however, and she managed to secure his closer attention. In summer 1932 she attempted suicide on his account. A scandal was the last thing he could afford on the threshold of his political destination. What was more, he seemed personally smitten and dismayed. Eva got her way, and he accepted her as his mistress.

She had, of course, to remain strictly in the background and was never allowed to appear in public. She moved into his Munich apartment and accompanied him on visits to his house at Berchtesgaden, though always at a proper distance: for purposes of camouflage, she travelled in the Führer's cortège with two of his secretaries. There were inevitable clashes at Wachenfeld with Frau Raubal, who resented her daughter's successor. In 1936 Hitler's half-sister retired from the fray and Eva Braun took her place as his housekeeper. At table, in the tea-house and during the tediously protracted evenings round the Berghof fireplace, she sat on Hitler's left. He treated her amiably, more like a member of the family than a mistress, though her status was no secret to his intimate circle. Before the Obersalzberg residence was rebuilt, she lived in the small house with Hitler, his aide and his personal valet. Later, she was given a bedroom beside the Führer's. Her departure for bed was a signal to his exhausted guests that their host would soon follow her example.

Eva was seldom permitted to visit Berlin. Not until 1939 was an adjoining bedroom prepared for her at his Berlin apartment, where she led an extremely sheltered existence. Even on the Obersalzberg she was confined to quarters before the arrival of guests who were not members of the Führer's old inner circle – Göring and his wife included. The situation eased somewhat during the war, when Eva's sister Gretl married Hermann Fegelein, Himmler's SS representative at Hitler's head-quarters, because Eva could now be introduced as Frau Fegelein's sister.

It was an extremely thankless role for a vivacious young woman to play, and to sustain it must have required a considerable measure of self-effacement and adaptability. Although neither calculating nor individualistic, Eva Braun was certainly not the dumb blonde she has so often been painted. A young woman of humble background, she gave Hitler a touching devotion and loyalty from which she derived scant personal benefit. Her 'privileged status' consisted, at most, in having to conform even more closely than other people to Hitler's petty notions of propriety. She was a keen dancer, but she lived in constant dread lest he learn of the gay soirées in which she indulged during his frequent absences, innocently but with an aching conscience. She thought it chic to smoke, but had to conceal it from the Führer. She was athletic and a good skier, but her activities in this field, too, were severely curtailed by Hitler's disapproval. Films were the one passion she could gratify because he liked to stew in front of the flickering screen for hours every evening. As the idol of a million women once told his close associate Albert Speer, unblushingly and in Eva's presence: 'A highly intelligent man should take a primitive and stupid woman. Imagine if on top of everything else I had a woman who interfered with my work! In my leisure time I want to have peace . . .'[55]

And peace was what Eva Braun could offer. Her company was

intended as an aid to relaxation, the prime requirements being patience and passivity. Eva could entertain no hopes of marriage and was probably intelligent enough to realize it. We do not even know whether Hitler's loyal friend became his mistress. The stage management of the Third Reich proved its excellence yet again. Eva Braun's existence remained hidden from the nation whose devout belief it was that the Führer had sacrificed his private life for the common good. To quote Hitler: 'Lots of women are attracted to me because I am unmarried. That was especially useful during our days of struggle. It's the same with a film star; when he marries he loses a certain something for the women who adore him. Then he is no longer their idol as he was before.'[56] To the denizens of the Obersalzberg menagerie, by contrast, their master's discreet companion was a familiar figure. Yet, even to Hitler's immediate circle, his behaviour towards Eva Braun was too indifferent and his private life too unfathomable to convey the certainty of a sexual relationship between them. In Hitler's case, not even the most natural thing in the world could be taken for granted.

Hitler, whose prudish sensibilities were offended by suggestive allusions and crude jokes alike, nonetheless posed as a free-thinking pioneer of natural sexual relations throughout his political career. He was fond of pillorying the moral hypocrisy of certain circles: 'I love to see this display of health around me. The opposite would make me misanthropic. And I'd really become so, if all I had to look at were the spectacle of the ten thousand so-called élite. Luckily for me, I've always retained contact with the people. Amongst the people, moral health is obligatory.'[57]

The examples he quoted to illustrate the false morality of the 'so-called élite' are remarkable, and serve to reveal the confusion in his own mind. For instance, he inveighed against men who objected to marital infidelity in others when they themselves had married divorcées. The moral undertone in his indignation is not fortuitous, for such an attitude can only be called hypocritical if one believes in the indissolubility of marriage. Hitler did not, hence the revealing nature of his mental blank: it indicates the lingering but unrecognized influence of Catholic dogmas and shows how muddled and nonsensical a conception of 'healthy moral instincts' reigned inside the Führer's head.

Such examples had nothing at all to do with the moral condition and problems of the twentieth century and very little bearing on the double standards of middle-class society. They seem rather to be in direct line of descent from the slushy novels of E. P. Marlitt or Hedwig Courths-Mahler, who might easily have written the following mawkish effusion: 'Is there a more lovely consecration of love, pray, than the birth of a handsome babe, glowing with health? . . . it is obvious to the eyes of any reasonable person that nature blesses the love of two beings by giving them a child . . .'[58]

This was the point on which the supreme moral arbiter liked best to dwell, because here at last his assault on the middle-class moral code acquired a firm popular basis. He fulminated against the 'ridiculous blockheads' who accepted the paramount importance of a government stamp – the marriage licence – and branded unmarried mothers and illegitimate children with the stain of dishonour. What could be more ideal than that two people should expect a child? The birth-rate had to be boosted. Marriages were justified by children alone, so couples should ensure in advance that children would spring from their loins. What was more, the children must be racially unobjectionable and of Nordic stock – a contribution to the reservoir of national strength. In all these moralizings about middle-class discrimination against pre- and extra-conjugal conception, therefore, the moral and ethical element had no significance whatever. It was overriden by the dictates of a higher birth-rate and selective breeding. Hitler took this monomaniac requirement for granted – so much for granted that he could not perceive that it conflicted in any way with his self-righteous diatribes against the narrow-mindedness of 'ridiculous blockheads'. He was concerned, not with social morality and still less with healthy sexual morality, but with the mass production of offspring. Hitler's assessment of children – the finest 'consecration of love' – is epitomized by one of his more macabre war-time utterances. When someone drew his attention to the heavy casualty rate among young officers, he retorted: 'But then, that's what young men are there for.'[59] Just as young women were there to breed and rear them.

The fanatical exponent of racial breeding did, simultaneously and in all seriousness, espouse views on the nature of marriage whose triviality and naïvety would be hard to surpass. Nature, so he proclaimed to his intimate circle, had intended marriage to be the fulfilment of life's greatest yearning, and the union of two people who belonged together by nature was the acme of happiness. They should see their bond, not as an institution for mutual entertainment, but as 'a mission in which it is the husband's task to fight for a livelihood and the wife's to manage the home in its capacity as the fortress from which the struggle for existence is waged'.[60] In this militant alliance against an environment which was evidently construed as hostile, the wife's organizing function assumed a relatively pacific form: her job was to maintain 'a certain cultural standard' and look after the practical running of the household.

The picture changed considerably when it came to men of high intelligence and true distinction. It was not really enough for them to take a simple and unintelligent wife as an antidote to affairs of state. Wives require their husbands to live for them, but a husband is the slave of his ideas, his duties and obligations. 'That's the worst of marriage – it creates legal claims! By far the best policy is to have a mistress. The burden lifts and everything remains a boon.'[61] But there was a second important reason why a great man like himself should remain celibate. What if he had children! The sons of great men were seldom great themselves – 'Consider Goethe's son, a completely worthless person!'[62] – because they inherited their mother's characteristics. It was Hitler's waking nightmare that such a son might be appointed to succeed him.

Eva Braun's steadfast devotion endured to the last. She was one of the few people who remained loyal to Hitler in defeat and the only one who did so without compulsion or self-interest. He married her during the night of 29 April 1945. Shortly afterwards he signed a personal will and testament in which he gave his reasons for this decision: 'Although I did not think I could undertake the responsibility of contracting a marriage during these past years of conflict, I have resolved, before terminating my mortal existence, to take as my wife the woman who, after many years of loyal friendship, of her own free will entered this city when it was virtually besieged in order to share my fate. At her own wish, she accompanies me into death as my wife. This will compensate us for what we have both been deprived of by my labours in the service of my people.'[63]

Some have discerned a hint of gratitude in the above. If there at all, it is overlaid by a melodramatic assumption of self-sacrifice and rectitude which fails to conceal the cynicism of Hitler's conduct. It was not a woman with whom he wished to be united at the eleventh hour; it was a last loyal retainer, obediently escorting him into the hereafter.

On the morning of 30 April 1945, Hitler had his faithful dog Blondi killed. That afternoon his faithful companion Eva took poison. The Führer shot himself.

2 The Handmaid of the Lord

WOMAN IN THE NATIONAL SOCIALIST IMAGE

'THE wonderful thing about Nature and Providence,' Hitler rhapsodized to himself and the National Socialist Women's Association at the Nuremberg Rally in 1934, 'is that no conflict between the sexes can occur as long as each party performs the function prescribed for it by Nature.'[64] Providence, he declared in explanation of this beauteous harmony, had allotted the wife a world of her very own: her husband, her family, her children, her household. It was a perfect division of labour in which male and female complemented one another smoothly – just as long as women stuck to their own field of operations and made full use of their inherent gifts. What counted in the world of men – politics and society – was insight, toughness, decision-making and a readiness to act. Woman had always respected the bold, courageous and resolute man, just as man showed a never-waning admiration and predilection for the 'womanly wife' who demonstrated her womanliness by strength of character and spiritual fortitude.

The limitations imposed on a woman were narrow and constricting. They unequivocally confined her activities to home and hearth, but the Führer knew how to render such an admonition palatable to his millions of female supporters. Never once, when appearing in public before a female audience, did he forget to extol the outstanding importance of women during the Movement's time of struggle. They had fought shoulder to shoulder with their embattled menfolk, steadfastly loyal even when pessimistic know-alls gave vent to defeatist sentiments and fortune frowned on the cause. Their profound power of perception, born of an unspoilt character, instinctively went straight to the heart of things. 'The power of instinct so clearly demonstrated its superior strength and accuracy. It turned out that the over-subtle mind can only too easily be misled, that men of uncertain intellectual discernment can be swayed by seemingly intellectual arguments, and that it is just at such periods that there awakes in woman her inherent instinct for self- and national preservation. Woman proved to us in those days that her aim is sure!'[65]

The fire-power of the wooden spoon

The ecstatic admiration and rapturous approval that gripped the Führer's female listeners during his personal appearances, which were staged with practised brilliance, concealed the vacuity of such statements and definitions. Hitler's appointment of woman to be the guardian and sustainer of true values did not fail in its effect. Less weight attached to his simultaneous denial of her intellectual endowments. After all, National Socialism conceived of reason and intellect as qualities which were not only secondary but positively suspect. Party ideologists gave scant indication in their public utterances of the factors which really determined the nature of woman. Instead, they competed with each other in devising formulas of maximum obscurity and unintelligibility. Alfred Rosenberg, the Party's official supervisor of ideological instruction, won first prize. Nature, he philosophized profoundly, decrees that man's approach to life should be architectural and woman's lyrical. What this statement lacked in meaning it made up for in method. Women had been given notice not to participate or interfere in the world of men. Any resentment they might have felt at this loss of status was assuaged with high-flown declarations which impressed on them that they dwelt at the roots of existence, the well of eternal truth. This line was pursued not only in emotionally charged speeches to mass audiences and flatulent ideological treatises but also in practical Party field-work. In 1934 the female members of the National Socialist Teachers' Association (NSLB) conferred at Alexisbad in the Harz Mountains. Their task was to develop the intellectual gifts of young girls. Auguste Reber-Gruber, the NSLB's senior authority on female education, told the assembled schoolmarms how to tackle this problem. 'The female mind differs in its approach to mundane occurrences from the male mind, which excludes inward involvement and takes a coolly businesslike pride in its "objective" attitude. Owing to her natural disposition, her greater reverence for life, woman has the capacity for that inner devotion which more deeply fathoms the nature of things and perceives their true value and substance by means of loving absorption.'[66]

Euphonious terms such as reverence, devotion and absorption were an elegant way of defining what was expected of woman, namely, obedience. Lydia Gottschewsky, a female champion of the brown-shirted league of males, hailed this demand for submission with ecstatic approval. The new women's movement, she enthused, claimed but one right, 'the right to be permitted to serve, to be willingly allocated a place in the national community which accords with our own specific laws'.[67] Gertrud Scholtz-Klink, chieftainess of the Women's Association, put it a little less brutally. Speaking at the Party Conference of 1934, she exhibited a fluent and pious capacity for presenting the stylized Party line: 'The German woman must be such that she does, and does gladly, all that is required of her. In short, she must be able to think politically – not politically in the sense of a conflict with other nations, but politically in such a way that she feels, thinks and sacrifices herself in concert with the entire nation, proud, poised and self-assured.'[68]

If the nature of woman was hard to define in National Socialist terminology, her function was less so. She was, to quote that exponent of the architectural approach to life, Adolf Hitler, 'built into' the struggle waged by the folkish community. Rather than attend to her rights, she must concern herself with the duties which Nature had laid upon her in the interests of communal survival. That was a plain and straightforward function. All that remained was to paraphrase it in lofty and warlike terms. Hitler did so at the 1939 Party Rally, in the following words: 'What man sacrifices in his nation's struggle, woman sacrifices in the struggle to preserve that nation on the individual plane. What man contributes in heroic courage on the battlefield, woman contributes in ever-patient devotion, in ever-patient suffering and endurance. Every child she brings into the world is a battle which she wages for the survival or extinction of her people.'[69]

Comical offshoots sprouted from the quasi-military jargon then in vogue. Gertrud Scholtz-Klink, also known as the 'Reich Mother-in-Chief', heroically proclaimed during her speech at the 1937 Party Rally: 'Though our weapon be but the wooden spoon, its impact must be no less than that of other weapons!'[70] The authoress Kuni Tremel-Eggert, who was much read at the time, approached the subject more like a sports commentator. Her best-seller, *Barb, der Roman einer deutschen Frau*, spiritedly described the emotions of a pregnant working woman: 'She did not know what mattered most – what it was, this thing full of deliverance and promise; she only felt its deep, deep contentment, and it lent wings to her legs – the long, tough, muscular legs of the mother who hurries home to tend her brood and go on tending it with a love that never fails.'[71]

Underlying this absurd blend of naïvety and fervour, these only apparent aberrations, was something deadly serious. Woman was committed to the 'battlefield of life'. Her contribution was an ability to bear children, her mark of achievement the frequency with which she did so. National Socialism, exulted Paula Siber, had rediscovered the German woman who was rooted in her native soil, the ever 'enduring' (the German word, *tragend*, connotes child-bearing as well), ever self-sacrificing mother of the nation, and was supporting her in her battle for deliverance. A senior adviser on women's affairs at the Reich Ministry of the Interior, Frau Siber went on to declare that women's deliverance consisted in the Party avowal 'that in her womb reposes the people's future and in her soul the heart of a nation'.[72] This official declaration likewise exemplifies the coupling of maternal function with praise of inner qualities. Even Richard Walther Darré, the agricultural expert who became the Third Reich's 'blood and soil' ideologist, observed the same tactical precept. To quote one of his racist maxims: 'Not only the womb of woman but also her mode of thought and character play a larger part in the ebb and flow of generations, the ebb and flow of the State, than the capacities and incapacities of men.'[73] Should that womb prove infertile, of course, the woman in question must suffer the consequences. Rosenberg had already proclaimed in his *Myth of the 20th Century* that the childless woman was not a fully paid-up member of the national community. He envisaged a legal application of this principle: should the husband of a barren wife form an extra-marital liaison which produced a child, he was not to be charged with adultery but merely obliged to pay maintenance. Hitler had promoted the same principle to form part of his programme in *Mein Kampf*, and it was also – subject to cautious extension – official policy in the National Socialist Women's Association. 'Citizenship of the future Third Reich shall belong to every German woman who devotes her entire vital energy to people and Fatherland, either as a mother and wife or as a working *Volksgenossin* ("People's Comrade").'[74] From the outset, therefore, married women were tolerated on the assumption that marriage implied a readiness to bear children, working women for their contribution to the national economy. Most assiduously cultivated of all, however, was the image of the young mother. Unqualified Nazi tributes to womanhood were reserved for her, and her alone.

Das Schwarze Korps, the official organ of the SS High Command, displayed this journalistic technique to perfection. Wilhelm Stapel, for decades the champion of a conservative folkish ideal, had declared war on the 'neo-pagan' quality of German nudism in his just-tolerated periodical *Deutsches Volkstum*. In so doing, he had attacked the official *Farming Calendar for 1935*, with its nude illustrations of stalwart young Germans. Among them was a monochrome drawing entitled *Mother and Child* by Wolfgang Willrich. This showed a sturdy full-bosomed young woman gazing down contentedly at the child she was suckling. *Das Schwarze Korps* seized upon Stapel's criticism as a welcome occasion to protest against false puritanism, against 'the degradation of the German human being and systematic destruction of all that is beautiful and noble'.[75] Only a 'depraved sensualist' could take exception to this German mother. The thrust was skilfully aimed at two targets simultaneously: first at the 'Semitic wire-pullers' who never portrayed the noble human body in its natural form, who had not – unlike Willrich – sensed 'the majesty of young motherhood'; and, secondly, at 'alien teachings' – namely, those of the Church – which had 'broken our women's pride' by characterizing woman as a sinner and seductress – the servant of man, no less – and a creature of impure body and sinful soul. In radiant contrast to this debasement of womanhood stood the noble image of woman under National Socialism: 'Woman is sacred to us in her naturally predestined role, and every man has reverence for her vocation. She is the guardianess of the German race, and pure by nature. She is not the servant of the German male but his comrade and companion in life. No less a person than our Führer has restored the German woman to this most worthy and befitting place in the nation!'[76]

The modification of Hitler's original text is slight but not without significance. He had declared that woman was 'at all times the helper of man and thus his truest friend', while man was 'also at all times the protector of his spouse and thus her best friend'.[77] This set the record straight. Woman was man's subordinate 'helper', not the 'companion' who marched beside him on equal terms.

The craze for equality

National Socialists considered it undignified for a woman to participate in politics because her essential purity would be bound to suffer in consequence. Hitler strongly opposed the idea of admitting women to parliament so that they could 'ennoble' it. His retort: 'I don't believe people should ennoble what is bad in itself; so far from ennobling parliament, the woman who engages in parliamentary activity will be violated by that activity.'[78] The word 'violate' speaks volumes in this context, and not only about Hitler's conception of the 'Jewified system' – for it is this subconscious link which explains his use of a metaphor from the sexual domain. Over and above this, Hitler clearly conveyed that equal participation by women in public life transcended his powers of imagination. To him, their allotted role and function was that of the solicitous wife and fertile mother. His campaign against the Weimar Republic, i.e. against the democratic principle, was thus a firm rejection of equal rights for women.

The phrase 'emancipation of women' was in Hitler's view a product of the Jewish mind. 'In the truly good old days of German existence',[79] women had stood in no need of emancipation. The truly good old days . . . To the National Socialist, this meant a pre-industrial age during which, in accordance with the Blood and Soil myths, woman had tended hearth, home and children while her rustic spouse tilled the fields with measured tread. It was a swift and nimble step from these bucolic genre pictures, which wielded a strong educational impact in all traditional school-books, to the Germanic days of yore. The phrase 'plough and sword' acquired ideological force. Women, too, were susceptible of inclusion in the concept of warlike vassalage, and the renewed demand for their subordination was obscured by such heroic ideals. Nazi propagandist Guida Diehl borrowed from the same store of imagery when she declared that 'The truly Germanic woman is a fighter, and fights from mother-love'.[80] She fought for the family, for people and nation, and there were no doubts about her equality in that role. Adolf Hitler: 'The equality of woman consists in her receiving, in those spheres of life allotted her by Nature, the esteem which is her due.'[81]

This natural esteem for woman 'as the mother of the sons and daughters of a nation'[82] constituted her supreme ennoblement. When liberalism was fighting for the quality of the German woman, asserted the Führer, her countenance was 'despairing, glum and sorrowful'.[83] Woman had been made rootless and unstable by the feminist movement, snorted the fanatical Guida Diehl: 'And so we women were cheated out of our right to womanly esteem, feminine nobility and maternal dignity, because, with our hands tied, we were compelled to witness every shamelessness and every manifestation of national debasement, down to and including complete cultural bolshevism and

Godless propaganda.'[84] Now, however, 'countless radiant and laughing faces'[85] had reappeared because the future of the nation was assured and the dignity of woman secured by National Socialism.

Needless to say, this answer to the problem of women's rights was not universally hailed as a deliverance, even in National Socialist quarters. A number of dissentients rallied round the feminist Sophie Rogge-Börner and voiced their opposition – as late as 1933 – in a memorandum entitled *German Women to Adolf Hitler*. In so doing, they displayed tactical skill of a high order. Irmgard Reichenau quoted a Hitlerian pronouncement to the effect that the best form of government was that which assigned paramount importance to the best brains in the national community. Her inference was that gifted and able women should likewise be incorporated in the political organism, indeed, 'in all its various domains'.[86]

While subscribing to a folkish and Nordic outlook, these feminine individualists showed courage and critical resolve in their campaign against 'unilateral male domination'.[87] It was not enough, declared Irmgard Reichenau, to accuse them of being still enmeshed in liberalism, of failing to comprehend National Socialism – not enough to dismiss them with the strange term of abuse 'feminists'. They did not seek women's rights, merely human rights of the most natural kind.

Lenore Kühn left no doubt as to what was meant by this. Cunningly, she insinuated that the National Socialist revolution was betraying its aims and lapsing into democratic egalitarianism. 'Natural aristocratism' was being eroded by a new two-tier class system consisting of man and woman. 'A positively democratic craze for equality deludes each of these members of the male class into claiming the right of such dominion over the "second class", and a further craze for equality regards this "female class" as the universally inferior object of such intellectual leadership in all spheres of life. The class State is dead, long live the class State . . .'[88]

It was a well-directed attack. These women had taken at its face value the élitist Nazi avowal that genuinely gifted people alone were destined to rule the State and occupy senior positions within it. During the intoxicating heyday of the time of struggle, they had been permitted to assume without contradiction that this applied to women as well. They were swiftly disabused once the Party seized power. Women were systematically ousted from all senior posts and their chances of promotion curtailed. Sophie Rogge-Börner: 'It is no use all professions being open to women on paper when every government authority and all official professional associations deny them employment.'[89]

The consequences of official policy were only too apparent. Under the quota system introduced for female students, their numbers were not allowed to exceed 10 per cent of the student population. The new civil service law contained special provisions whose practical effect was to exclude women from jobs in government. In the labour market, attempts were made to reduce female employment, partly on principle and partly to create vacancies for millions of unemployed males. Women were encouraged to give up their jobs by means of marriage loans and family allowances, and the introduction of a year's unpaid domestic work was intended to retard the flow of female job applicants. Women could discern their loss of status even in that much-vaunted gem of National Socialist legislation, the Hereditary Farm Law, under which the daughter of a deceased farmer came fourth in line of inheritance after his son, father and brother. It was here that the gulf between Nazi propaganda and reality showed up most of all. Heroic or cosy visions of bonds with the soil and the simple joys of peasant life might stir the hearts of urban Party officials, folkish romantics and youthful idealists; they held few charms for those directly affected, country girls in particular. Young farmers had considerable difficulty in getting married. In one Swabian farming community, for example, only 8 of the 32 marriages contracted between 1932 and 1939 involved farmers. The flight from the land persisted in the face of all ideological prohibitions. Farmers' daughters aspired to marry parsons or schoolmasters, labourers or serving soldiers – anyone but a farmer. Their parents thought much the same. To quote a farmer's wife from the Tübingen district: 'I'd sooner pack my daughters off than let them take a farmer. I've slaved all my life for nothing – my daughters are going to do better for themselves.'[90] In agricultural work, women really did assume the vital role for which National Socialism commended them so highly, and it was quite absurd to reward them for bearing this burden by stripping away still more of their rights.

There was no essential difference between curtailing the female right of inheritance, refusing girls higher education or barring women from access to senior professional posts. All these restrictive measures were born of the same fundamental attitude, one which Irmgard Reichenau bluntly defined as follows: 'By excluding women from all influential and intellectually demanding posts, one automatically brands her as something inferior and of minor status. No amount of glorification can disguise that . . .'[91]

The beauty of labour

In January 1936, Hitler granted an interview to a woman reporter from *Paris-Soir*. Professional curiosity apart, Madame Titayna had a personal and very feminine interest in discovering what *he* was like – what could account for *his* extraordinary power. 'The Führer comes to greet me with outstretched hand. I am surprised and astonished by the blue of his eyes, which look brown in photographs, and I prefer the reality – the face that brims with intelligence and energy and lights up when he speaks. At this moment, I comprehend the magical influence wielded by this leader of men and his power over the masses.'[92] The French-woman's reaction exemplifies yet again how readily Hitler could ingratiate himself with the opposite sex when he chose to. She almost forgot to ask how he assessed the role of women and whether he really believed that their sole *raison d'être* was to be given children by men. The Führer chuckled. 'I grant women the same right as men, but I don't think they're identical. Woman is man's companion in life. She shouldn't be burdened with the tasks for which man was created. I don't envisage any women's battalions – in my view, women are better suited to social work. But in any case, unmarried women – and we have many of them in Germany because we don't have enough men – are entitled to earn a living just as men are.'[93]

The same old basic line was unmistakable, yet Hitler's remarks betrayed a considerable shift of accent. Less definite emphasis was laid on the natural differences between man and woman, and explicit sanction was given to female employment in the Third Reich. Hitler supported this statement with a seemingly cogent allusion to the fact that a woman – Leni Riefenstahl – was to direct the film of the 1936 Olympic Games in Berlin. His remarks were not merely off-hand or destined for consumption by critical foreigners. They were in keeping with the change of tack that had been forced on the National Socialist leadership after its initial campaign against the employment of women. Reality had very swiftly shown that the economy could no longer dispense with female labour.

This is substantiated by statistics. The proportion of women employed in the economy at first declined from 29.3 per cent (1933) to 24.7 per cent (1936). It then rose again, reaching 25 per cent in 1938. These

figures are deceptive, however, because they only reflect an improvement and consolidation of economic conditions in general. The 6
million unemployed of 1932 had by 1936 been reabsorbed into the
labour process, and it was not until the ensuing period that the increase
in female labour found due expression. The absolute figures illustrate
this development. The number of female employees in industry, trade
and commerce rose from 4.24 million in 1933 to 4.52 million in 1936
and 5.2 million in 1938, by which time industry alone employed one-
and-a-half times as many women as in 1933. If we include female
workers in agriculture and forestry, public and domestic service, we
obtain a total for the base-year (1933) of 11.48 million employed
women. By 1936 the figure was nearly 11.7 million, and by 1939 –
inclusive of Austria and the Sudetenland – 12.7 million. Thus the proportion of female labour had risen from 35 per cent in the year of the
National Socialist seizure of power to more than 37 per cent in the year
war broke out. The programmatic objectives of Party ideologists had
surrendered to the realities of economic compulsion: more and more
women were engaged in the modern industrial process.

All the mellifluous speeches about 'womanly' work were quickly
revealed as hot air. In 1936 the Women's Bureau of the German
Labour Front (DAF) published a report handsomely entitled *The
Daily Toil and Leisure of the German Working Woman*.[94] This confirmed,
by authorization of the Reich Women's Leader, that there was no
objection in principle to the gainful employment of eleven-and-a-half
million women. It was simply that they must be fitted into the world
of employment 'purposefully, with due regard for their aptitudes and
organic strength'.[95]

Attention was drawn to the success of efforts to fulfil this aim:
certain occupations of a physically taxing nature were now barred to
women for their own protection. Johannes Schunke[96] extolled these
protective ordinances in *Women and the Law*. It was forbidden to employ
women in (a) mining below ground or loading and transportation on
the surface; (b) coking-plants and the transportation of building
materials; and (c) night-work between 8 p.m. and 6 a.m.

A directive issued by the Reich Ministry of Labour on 30 November
1940 shows how little guarantee women were given against injurious
physical strain by these sparse provisions. Women, the Ministry decreed,
were not to be employed as drivers of locomotives, buses and motor-
lorries with a load capacity exceeding 1.5 tons. Every rule had its
exception, however. In an emergency – and what wasn't an emergency

in the second year of the war? – women were permitted to drive trams and omnibuses.

The DAF also lauded certain improvements in women's working conditions. These were mainly theoretical. Under the programme entitled 'Beauty of Labour', shabby factory workshops were given a lick of paint, potted plants installed on window-sills and yards embellished with a few benches and patches of grass. On these, workers were permitted to indulge in sun-drenched relaxation during the lunch-hour break, providing a favourite subject for illustrations in the propaganda booklets issued by the Labour Front. Women were supposed to have a midday break of at least an hour-and-a-half. Those with homes to run were also permitted to stop work thirty minutes early 'on request'.

The Women's Bureau's essay in self-justification had much to say about the German woman's daily toil and nothing at all about her leisure activities. It was clearly aimed at convincing still more women of the 'beauty of labour'. At the same time, it naïvely rebutted its own claims about specifically feminine occupations. Sixteen economic groups were examined and summarized with the proud comment: 'This breakdown illustrates the utilization of women in all sectors of employment.'[97] 70,000 women were employed in welfare work and social services, 345,000 in public health and hygiene – in other words, barely 4 per cent of the female labour force came into Hitler's 'social work' category. What was more, the 'organic strength' of the female sex was highly rated by the DAF. The caption beneath a photograph of happy women tram-cleaners: 'A physically demanding job.'[98] Beneath a telephonist joyously wielding her plugs: 'Plenty of patience and strong nerves.'[99] And beneath a sturdy textile worker: 'Some 600,000 women work amid the din that reigns in the factories of the textile industry . . .'[100]

The Führer had promised women the same rights as men. The Labour Front boasted that women were doing light work instead of heavy labour and earning the same wage. True, the wages of female workers rose even faster than those of men, but women still earned one-third less than their male workmates and a skilled female worker less than an unskilled male.

Given the folkish system's mania for procreation, every woman was enjoined to biological piece-work by a supreme commandment designed to raise the birth-rate. In accordance with this principle, most attention was devoted to the welfare of mothers and mothers-to-be. Pregnant women could stop work if a doctor certified that their baby was due in six weeks' time. This regulation did not apply to the agricultural, forestry and domestic sectors, where the ministerial view was that discretion might be exercised in individual cases and pregnant women assigned to lighter duties. New mothers were allowed six weeks off work, a period which also applied – plus or minus the confinement itself – to protection against dismissal. Expectant and nursing mothers could not be employed for longer than eight hours a day, and the latter were granted two periods of thirty minutes or an hour as paid 'nursing breaks', every day for six months after giving birth.

This all sounds very pretty and corresponds in outline with mothercare legislation in force today, but it cannot be ignored that the regulations in question were discretionary. The national interest required that women waive such reliefs and facilities, and waive them they did. Incessant appeals were made to public spirit, not only by senior Party officials and labour leaders but also by junior functionaries and Nazi 'block wardens'. Could a woman worker really presume to demand an extra half-hour off because she had a household to run? How much could an office worker do for her baby during a brief nursing break in the middle of working hours?

Pregnant women were additionally chained to their places of work by purely economic factors. They worked for a living, not for the public weal or their own amusement. If they stopped work six weeks before their confinement they received 75 per cent of their wages. If they stayed at work they received 100 per cent plus 50 per cent sickness benefit – evidently an alluring prospect, for many of them remained in employment. Party propaganda had it that their places were regularly filled by student volunteers who deputized for expectant mothers without pay, but the estimated annual total of 15,000 student-hours makes nonsense of this claim. It would barely have covered the woman-hours lost as a result of three dozen births. Female labour was essential to a booming industry stimulated by the arms drive, so there was a tacit understanding that no one should claim such entitlements.

Any lingering doubts on this score were dispelled by the establishment and function of the Reich Labour Service (RAD). The RAD's field of operations had a close bearing on developments in agriculture, where women represented half the available labour force. Although 75 per cent of them had family ties with the farm-yard, they deserted it in droves, sick of working an average of eleven hours a day seven days a week. The number of non-family female farm-workers fell by 20–30 per cent. This flight from the land was naturally decked out in ideological trappings and blamed on the cinema, the aping of fashion, the temptations of urban life. But the young women's patently under-developed sense of Blood and Soil was more than an ideological fiasco – more than mere confirmation of the stupidity of experiments in agricultural self-sufficiency. In practical terms, agriculture became afflicted by a labour shortage. The RAD's job was to fill the breach.

Steps towards the establishment of a State-sponsored labour service had already been taken by the Weimar Republic with a view to solving the problem of unemployment. The National Socialists acclaimed this institution – like the plans for motorway construction lifted from the files of the last democratic Chancellor, Heinrich Brüning – as a brain-wave of their own. In 1936 a voluntary labour service was established for girls as well, known in the abbreviated jargon of the Nazi system as WRAD. Only 1,000 girls volunteered. This figure is indicative of various things: first, the extent of full employment in the female labour market; second, the exiguous impact of stern Party appeals; and, third and most important, that what now mattered was to procure badly needed female labour, not to find jobs for unemployed workers. In January 1939 the 'voluntary' façade was dropped and twelve months' national labour service declared compulsory for all women under 25. Officially, they were to be trained in womanly duties. Actually, since all Germans were expected to toil for the common good, it was per-missible to add that they would 'supply the labour required in agricul-ture and the household, particularly by overworked farmers' wives and mothers of large families'.[101] 90 per cent of recruits were employed as land-girls. These, who in 1940 numbered 200,000, were the dumb ones. The remaining 10 per cent ended up as 'domestic help' or 'nurse-maids' in the homes of friends and relatives who swapped their daughters by private arrangement.

Fritz Sauckel, whose official title was Plenipotentiary-General for the Utilization of Labour, proceeded to give the screw another turn by decreeing that only a certificate of pregnancy could exempt women from employment. The products of this directive were popularly known as 'Sauckel children'.

Childbirth requires a minimum of intellect

In January 1939 Ilse Buresch-Riebe, an official of the National Socialist Women's Association, took stock of the situation in the *Völkischer Beobachter*: 'Owing to force of circumstance, industry is falling back more and more on female co-operation, and there are signs which lead one to conclude that whole sectors of industry, hitherto regarded by men as their own preserve, should be declared female spheres of employment. It is nonetheless difficult to predict the extent which the demand for female labour will assume in coming decades.'[102] This sober assessment demonstrated the continuing fruitlessness of ideological intentions. Woman's role in the economic life of the Third Reich had become just as well established as it was in other modern economic systems. The conservative revolution whose espousal gained the National Socialists such wide support in reactionary circles, among agriculturalists and the middle class, had utterly failed. Official Party glorification of the industrious farmer's wife and the health-giving properties of a countrified existence proved unable to stem the rising tide of urbanization and rural depopulation. The female right to vote remained untouched, being anyway limited in the case of all 'People's Comrades' to a plebiscitary and exultant '*Ja!*' whose extent could be predicted in advance. The female student quota was also quietly abolished. In the summer semester of 1939, their share of the student population was 11.2 per cent. The influence of National Socialist principles was undoubtedly apparent in their choice of courses, though even here contradictions arose. The proportion of women studying law and political science fell from 10.2 per cent (1932) to 8.3 per cent (1939). Women could not become judges or attorneys, though they were admitted to the two junior legal grades in the government service. Their representation in the faculties of general medicine and dentistry also declined from 15.8 per cent to 11.2 per cent, but the number of practising women doctors rose nonetheless. The number of female arts and sciences students likewise declined from 33.4 per cent to 31.7 per cent and from 18.8 per cent to 9.4 per cent respectively, though it was certainly not the aim of Party educationists that the number of women teachers at girls' schools should also decline. Rapid increases were registered by the proportion of female students in pharmacy (from 28.1 to 38.5 per cent), physical education (from 22.8 to 52.2 per cent) and journalism (from 20.7 to 27.9 per cent). Only one inference can be drawn from these percentage shifts: that girls were simply yielding to massive pressure and choosing courses of study which offered the swiftest access to a career.

Contrary to original intentions, the scope for female employment in industry, trade and commerce continued to expand steadily. In the public service, too, the authorities soon confined themselves to excluding women from senior positions only. This accorded with general practice: their chances of promotion were slender and their salaries did not match those of their male colleagues. To that extent, the Nazi rulers stuck to their guns, but their attitude was not specifically National Socialist. The economic exploitation of women, coupled with social and political underprivilege, can be found in all modern industrial societies and is only gradually being overcome.

The war years proved, once and for all, the emptiness and futility of National Socialism's lofty image of womanhood. In May 1941, Hitler decreed wider utilization of women in the munitions industry and the national war effort as a whole: 'I believe that the German girl and German woman, in particular, can render an additional contribution. Millions of German women are in action on the land and are having to replace men in work of the most arduous nature. Millions of German women and girls are working in factories, workshops and offices, where they likewise replace their menfolk. It is not unfair for us to demand that many more hundreds of thousands model themselves on these millions of productive German women comrades.'[103] The man who claimed to want no women's battalions employed whole divisions of women on the heaviest manual labour in munitions factories. As for 'social work', they were privileged to carry it out as uniformed women auxiliaries in the armed forces.

Writing in the *Frankfurter Zeitung* in 1931, the author Fritz von Unruh warned that 'A minimum of intellect and a maximum of physical aptitude are required to make woman what she is intended to be: the womb of the Third Reich.'[104] The dig was apt but inadequate. National Socialism exploited female labour ruthlessly and with no ideological qualms whatsoever.

Joseph Goebbels: The unscratchable itch

'Every woman attracts me like blazes. I prowl around like a ravening wolf, yet I'm as bashful as a boy. I can hardly understand myself, sometimes. I ought to get married and become a solid citizen – and then hang myself after a week!'[105] It is not difficult to recognize the Third Reich's greatest propagandist in this piece of self-dramatization, for Goebbels was his own greatest propagandist as well, and these few words undeniably convey some of his most salient characteristics. Goaded by an insatiable urge to prove himself to himself, he never missed an opportunity to conquer an attractive woman, though he could never grasp why full satisfaction eluded him. It was certainly not because the lower-middle-class youth from Rheydt lacked a tendency towards solid citizenship, but rather because it was his burning ambition to dissociate himself from the bourgeoisie, to be different, to be superior – to indulge a craving for recognition which, if not triggered by his physical disability (Goebbels had been afflicted with a short left leg since childhood), was undoubtedly sharpened by it.

While still an impoverished and conspicuously ugly student of German language and literature, Joseph Goebbels had his first taste of love – though not his first experience of sex – with a pretty fellow-student of good family whom he met at Freiburg in summer 1918. The affair lasted quite a while and did not end until the winter term of 1919–20, when Goebbels was studying in Munich. His sweetheart, Anka, became engaged to a lawyer. It was a blow to his self-esteem, and he seems to have revenged himself for it in the bombastic autobiographical novel *Michael*, which he wrote in 1923. In it, a girl character named Hertha Holk (= Anka) assured the hero: 'You're one of the few people who discern the reality behind outward appearances. You think in associations – organically, so to speak.' Her reward for this glowing tribute was a homily: 'It's a woman's job to look beautiful and bring children into the world. That isn't half as crude and old-fashioned as it sounds. The female bird preens herself for the male and hatches out eggs for him. In return, the male provides food. The rest of the time he stands guard and repels enemies.'[106] Minister Goebbels was clearly cock-a-hoop when he eased his youthful flame, since divorced, into a

69

job with a woman's magazine: 'What an ass she was! Today, she'd be the wife of the Minister of Propaganda. How she must be kicking herself!'[107]

Late in 1921 Goebbels graduated from Heidelberg. He then retired to his parental home and tried to market his literary efforts. Vainly, because – in his view – the Jews who dominated cultural life refused to let him make good.

A school friend named Prang introduced him to Else Janke, a young schoolmistress. Else got him a job with the Dresdner Bank, calling out prices at the Cologne Stock Exchange. He worked there for nine months, then unsuccessfully hawked his services as an editor and dramatic adviser. In 1924 his friend Prang introduced him to politics. Goebbels started to write anti-Semitic articles for the *Völkische Freiheit*, became a friend of Karl Kaufmann, and in September 1925 was appointed regional manager of the NSDAP for North Rhineland. As editor of *Nationalsozialistische Briefe*, he passed in Strasser's anti-capitalist wing of the Party for an opponent of the 'Munich bosses'. Goebbels's diary for this period reflects his superheated love-life:

'I'm on tenterhooks for a sign of life from little Else. Why doesn't the girl write? She knows how impatient I am.'[108] But his thoughts were not confined to his betrothed. Two days later: 'Alma wrote me a card from Bad Harzburg. The first sign of life since that night. Mischievous, enchanting Alma! I'm really fond of the girl. Else's first letter from Switzerland. Only little Else can write that way.'[109] Alma, be it noted, was the girl-friend of his friend Prang, and it was through her that he had met Else. But yet another fond memory rears its head: 'I think so often of Anka these days. Why just now? Because it's the holiday season? What a wonderful travelling-companion she was! What a magnificent creature! I yearn for little Else!'[110]

'Elisabeth Gensicke writes from Lugau. Between the lines a mute indictment. Why did it all have to happen? Why do I have to hurt Else so much? Why did Anka have to leave me alone for so long? Was it a breach of faith? Hers or mine? I mustn't think of these things. Work is my only salvation.'[111] But there were pleasanter forms of salvation, some of them provided by Else. 'A delicious night. She's so sweet and good to me. I hurt her so bitterly sometimes. What a budding, bursting night of love. I am loved! Why complain?'[112] He complained because he derived pleasure from lamentation, from self-pity as much as from magnanimous gestures of sympathy. Six weeks later, in December 1926, the affair was off again and he received a farewell letter from Else. At once, he itched for a reunion. 'Else arrives, plunged in sorrow. We try to part. She weeps and implores. Hours of torment until we rediscover one another. The same old story! What am I to do? I have to have someone. She is perfectly happy. And I? The less said about me the better! It has to be, I suppose. There's a curse on me and women.'[113]

It was a curse to be relished, for in all the ups and downs, tos and fros of his waning affair, the assiduous lover never overlooked temptations by the wayside. 'Christmas party. A dark, dainty girl from Franconia. Just my type. Escorted her home in a rainstorm.'[114] He travelled from Hamburg to Rendsburg: 'A glorious woman sitting in my compartment. You gorgeous creature!'[115] On to Bamberg: 'Opposite me, a magnificent figure of a woman asleep on the cushions. I long for her!'[116]

And so on – page after page devoted to the irrepressible outpourings of a man ungovernably obsessed with sex. He eventually parted from Else, who was half-Jewish, but not without difficulty. For the moment, he continued in the same vein: 'My dear Else! Life is a farce, and we all join in. Must things be this way? Why don't we tell the truth? Man! Scoundrel!'[117]

Meanwhile, flattered and delighted by Hitler's deft manipulation of his psyche, and responding to him with fervent devotion, the 'scoundrel' had transferred his allegiance from Strasser's socio-revolutionary faction to the bigger battalions grouped round Hitler. In November 1926 Hitler sent him to the capital as Gauleiter to construct a Party bastion mid-way between the rival groups centred on Strasser and Daluege. Goebbels did so with bravura, demagogy and downright infamy. He scored an overwhelming success.

In 1931, regional Party headquarters in Hedemannstrasse received a visit from a woman who must have stood out among the common run of Party worthies like a swan in a flock of geese. Née Johanna Maria Magdalena Behrend, the lady who offered her services to the Movement had been born on 11 November 1901 and was the child of an unmarried maidservant, Auguste Behrend. Her mother later married a Jewish businessman named Friedländer, and in 1920 the girl was legitimized by her putative father, Oskar Ritschel. This was a few months before her marriage. Early in 1921 the textile manufacturer Günther Quandt married her straight out of her boarding school at Goslar. The same year she gave birth to a son whom she named Harald. Her marriage to Quandt, who was twenty years older, headed for the rocks and was finally dissolved in 1929, after Magda had gone off with a young student. With a luxuriously appointed flat at 2 Reich-Strasse and a 4,000-mark allowance, she was reasonably well provided for but bored. She heard Goebbels speak at the Sportpalast, developed a sudden interest in politics, and joined the NSDAP.

Goebbels was fascinated by the attractive young woman. For her part, Magda was enthralled by the Gauleiter's superior intelligence and persuasive charm. On 19 December 1931, her ex-husband magnanimously made arrangements for their wedding at Severin, his country seat. Hitler and Ritter von Epp acted as witnesses.

For Goebbels, marriage to 'Engelchen' (little angel) meant promotion to the Führer's innermost circle, quite apart from social advancement. Magda's luxury apartment became Hitler's favourite port of call when he visited the capital.

'The importance of the family cannot be overestimated,'[118] the newly appointed Reich Minister declared when inaugurating the exhibition Die Frau in March 1933. The family was certainly of importance to his career. Goebbels set the public a shining example on behalf of his fellow-potentates. Magda produced no less than six children (though only one boy) between 1932 and 1940, and was duly invested with the Mutterkreuz on Mother's Day 1939.

Making up for the deprivations of his earlier years, Goebbels began to collect houses appropriate to his status. His official residence in Budapester Strasse, later renamed Hermann-Göring-Strasse, did not satisfy him. In 1938–39, with Hitler's approval, he had it remodelled from top to bottom. This little whim cost three-and-a-half million marks, and not even the war quenched his ambitious plans for structural improvement. Understandably eager to possess a little place of his very own, he built himself a luxurious seat on Schwanenwerder, an island in the Havel. Main house, guest annexe and outbuildings, also the trim yacht Baldur moored alongside his private landing-stage – but that was only a start. There was also the neighbouring property, which he converted into a more intimate abode. He was vain enough to display himself in this dream setting, complete with children and ponies, for the benefit of journalists and newsreel cameras. 'Men of great creative drive need relaxation to help them recoup their energies. Dr Goebbels derives his capacity for work from the family, that fount of youth and eternal nucleus of the nation.'[119] This was a misconception, or Goebbels would hardly have built himself a week-end retreat next door – one which was strictly out of bounds to his family. A similar aid to relaxation was the romantic little lakeside cabin near Lanke, presented to its Gauleiter by the grateful municipality of Berlin in 1936. A plain log-cabin being too modest for him, he erected a stately home on the far shore equipped with technical gadgets of every kind. The log-cabin's open fireplace was nice, but even nicer was a cocktail bar which sank into the floor at the touch of a button. The German film industry financed this particular little folly to the tune of 2.7 million marks.

Goebbels was wholly indifferent to the publicity or notoriety of his amours as long as they did not jeopardize his position. 'Affairs of the heart are the least dangerous because they're the most natural.'[120] Gossip flourished and venomous rumours proliferated in the higher reaches of the Party, but Goebbels's career and his standing with the Führer remained intact – and that was all that mattered. 'I have no need to bow down before false bourgeois morality.'[121]

Lida Baarova, a stylish young Czech actress, had been a rising star ever since making the film *Barcarole* in 1934. Her name was intimately linked with that of her leading man in *Barcarole*, Gustav Fröhlich, who lived near Goebbels on Schwanenwerder. It was only natural, in view of the Minister's physical proximity and official connection with the German film industry, that the trio should have become acquainted.

One winter's night in 1937, Baarova relates, she returned to Schwanenwerder after attending a film première. Fröhlich had not yet reached home. She was on her way to meet him when she saw a big Mercedes travelling in the opposite direction. She waved under the impression that it was Fröhlich, but out stepped his distinguished neighbour the Reich Minister, who greeted her with polished courtesy.

Goebbels laid siege to the young film star. He courted her and pampered her, and this time the affair was not a fleeting one. It developed into a protracted relationship. 'Sometimes he played the piano for hours, and I listened to him. No man ever brought me such a feeling of undiluted romance and fascination.'[122] And so it continued until summer 1938, when Goebbels told Lida that he was 'going to get a divorce and resign'.[123] It may also be that his wife wanted to divorce him, but they had both reckoned without Hitler. He had heard of the disquieting developments in the Goebbels *ménage* and was adamant: divorce and resignation were out of the question. He, Hitler, could not afford such a scandal in his immediate circle.

Summoned to give an account of himself, Goebbels did a unique thing – he stubbornly resisted the Führer's demands and applied for a posting as ambassador to Japan. Hitler refused to budge, and that settled it. The prospect of ending his career and abandoning the Führer proved too much for Goebbels. He agreed to sever relations with Lida Baarova for a trial period of twelve months. At the end of the year, she was packed off to Prague.

'With women, Goebbels is a cynic'[124] was Hitler's comment on the nature of the reconciliation which he had imposed on his lieutenant. Faced with the choice between deserting Lida and abandoning his career and beloved Führer, Goebbels plumped for the Führer. His life, which he had meant to risk for the sake of a grand passion, was not then at stake. That he abandoned later as his master's sole remaining confederate, accompanied by his wife and six children – voluntarily.

3 Mundane Pleasures

PERMITTED VICES

MORE morality, less hypocrisy! With this slogan, vintage January 1934, Joseph Goebbels gave yet another demonstration of his psychological expertise and talent for propaganda. The Reich Minister of Public Enlightenment conceded that every revolution had its vices. In his view, one of the vices of the current National Socialist revolution was a mischievous claim on the part of a few officious and misguided people 'not only to stipulate and determine the great moral principles governing our national life, but, over and above that, to dictate the private individual's code of purely personal views'.[125]

By publishing this attack in *Der Angriff*, the press organ of his own Berlin Gau, Goebbels made himself a champion of progressive sexual morality and the scourge of 'unnatural people' whose moral concepts might, at a pinch, govern 'community life in a nunnery' but were utterly out of place in a 'modern civilized State'. Every inch the enlightened revolutionary, he poured scorn on the moral snoopers who would have liked nothing better than to set up 'chastity committees' in town and country and transform the new Germany into a wilderness of carping and hypocrisy. Characterizing this behaviour as *Bettschnüffelei* (bed-sniffing), he went on to accuse those who claimed a lien on morality – 'the under-endowed' whose aim it was to supervise the sex-life of Müller and Schulze (Smith and Jones) as well as the morally harmful activities of dancers and stage stars – of contemptible hypocrisy and specious prudishness. No self-respecting German woman should venture forth unescorted, smoke, drink, dress up or wear her hair bobbed: these were rules of decorum advocated by mean-minded bigots and arrogant arbiters of morality.

The 'little Doctor' obviously revelled in this tirade. He could scarcely be suspected of prudishness himself. On the other hand, he could – at this stage – lay claim to an exemplary family life of his own. His timing was perfect in three respects. The sally against so-called moral crusaders gave the Party a veneer of broadmindedness and reassured those who had good reason to fear the extension of Nazi regimentation to their private lives. Secondly, it defended one or two liberties in which the country's new masters indulged and to which respectable citizens might have taken exception. Last of all, it enabled the Gauleiter of Berlin to take a gleeful poke at some of his bigoted rivals from Party Head-quarters in Munich, notably Rosenberg and Hess.

In so doing, Goebbels posed as the better revolutionary. He did not omit to enlist economic factors or the concept of wholesome national existence in his array of arguments. One should naturally be above suspicion of barren pomp and provocative splendour, but how many people would lose their livelihood if no more cars were bought, no new suits sported and no theatres or cinemas frequented? Wasn't National Socialism on the side of life and didn't it aim to infect the nation with optimism and *joie de vivre*? It was and did. 'That is why we bring our people into the theatres. That is why we give the worker, too, a chance to dress festively on festive occasions. That is why we purvey strength through joy. And that is why we brush aside the agents of prudish hypocrisy and refuse to let them spoil, with their everlasting and spiteful pedantries, the pleasures that are so essential a counterpart to the troubles, cares and privations of mundane existence for a decent nation which has every reason to draw strength for its arduous fight for survival from an ever-renewed and deliberate affirmation of life.'[126]

Graceful as the Balinese

The pedantries of National Socialism did, however, include precepts such as: the German woman does not smoke, does not drink, does not paint her face and disdains fashionable fripperies. One apostle of this morality, Curt Rosten, spelt out the *ABC of National Socialism* in 1933. With exemplary racial awareness, he claimed that German men wanted German women, 'not an irresponsible toy which superficially aspires to pleasure alone, adorns itself with baubles and finery, and resembles a glittering husk whose interior is void and bare'.[127] He even attired his message in poetic garb:

> Retain your honour, nor become
> the sport and toy of alien stock.

The nation shall stay pure and clean:
such is the Führer's lofty aim.

Certainly the nation was to stay clean, and on no account were
German women to become the prey of lustful foreigners – that was
the official and unyielding Party line. Whether women were to be
denied their trivial pleasures and forbidden their feminine vanities was
another matter, and one on which the Party leaders were far from
unanimous. Each was swayed to a varying extent by personal inclination, tactical considerations or ideological rigidity. In this as in other
things, they all took their cue from one man, Adolf Hitler. But Hitler
stuck to his proven tactic of playing one off against the other and never
committing himself. By so doing he brought off a triple feat: some felt
reassured that their puritanical ideals were desirable, others that their
totalitarian code was the ultimate goal, and others that their easy-
going attitude was the sensible one to adopt.

What mattered to Hitler was that an attitude should bear fruit. A
fruitful attitude merited a modicum of consideration, at least initially.
During the Party's early days, members had debated whether women
with the outlawed Eton crop should be admitted to their meetings.
Hitler's conservative opponents said no; he said yes. He had nothing
against lipstick and nail-varnish provided their users kept faith with
him. Besides, he may have felt obliged, as a frustrated artist, to pay
homage to beauty. He condemned the first uniforms of the German
Girls' League (BdM) as 'old sacks' and ordered them to be redesigned.
As late as 1937, the Führer boasted to an audience of district Party
chiefs at the Vogelsang Ordensburg that he had always resisted the
introduction of unduly puritanical uniforms for the BdM. The girls
should look attractive and healthy, but not err on the 'primitive' side:
'You cannot suddenly revert to the Stone Age in matters of dress.'[128]
Hitler wanted his Nazi maidens to look pretty and well dressed.

In the same speech, he called for greater courtesy towards women
on the part of men and young people. He must have had his reasons
for this. One of them he voiced himself: it was a way of diverting
women 'from male concerns'. So feminine influence was not as easy to
eradicate from the National Socialist system as the reactionary league
of males had imagined. Equally, the rough good-fellowship prevailing
among Party members had engendered an attitude towards women
which fell mid-way between unadulterated arrogance and clumsy
camaraderie, and was hardly beneficial to the folkish community.

Speaking at the Führer's headquarters in 1942, Reichsleiter Rosenberg lectured his listeners 'in that spirited way of his' on the essence of feminine refinement. He drew a sweeping comparison in terms of cultural groups: 'The European woman, painted, bedizened and gesticulating; the refined woman of India with no false colour on her face, simply but stylishly dressed, her deportment the epitome of dignified poise. The female European hopping as she dances, courting attention and craving applause; the Indian woman, and notably the Balinese, performing every movement of the dance from a position of repose, full of genuine fervour and, thus, perfection.'[129]

Rosenberg erred. The island of Bali is inhabited by Malays, who are generally classed as members of the yellow-skinned race. But never mind: the German woman was – Balinese-fashion – to display grace, poise and genuinely feminine perfection. As a European, she was too noisy, too flashy, too undignified for Rosenberg's taste.

The pragmatic Goebbels argued from a diametrically opposite standpoint. Still in 1942, he wondered whether female dancers ought to be inducted into the Labour Service, where they would only become 'fat and ungainly'. With the Führer's approval, he found a way of giving them the requisite political education without impairing their balletic grace. Special training courses were devised for them, but Goebbels was just as opposed in principle to the idea of teaching competent wives and mothers how to march in step. 'It is surely a sad state of affairs when actresses, dancers and singers have to be released from the Labour Service by special order of the Führer, so as to create, at least in the domain of the fine arts in Germany, a sort of enclave in which feminine grace and beauty, unimperilled by the quasi-officially encouraged brutalization and masculinization of our womenfolk, can pursue a modest but secure existence.'[130] To a visionary like Rosenberg, this view was doubtless embedded too deeply in the mundane lowlands of everyday life, but Goebbels had put his finger on a sore point. Harnessed to the Third Reich's battle order and armaments programme, German women were losing more of their 'true femininity' than was privately agreeable to the arbiters of Party opinion.

Fashion is the foe of regional dress

Of course, only the most exalted members of the Party hierarchy could afford to deliver lofty lectures on the nature of feminine grace or criticize the system's masculinization of womanhood, and then only in private. The lower ranks strictly implemented what they took to be official Party policy and the ABC of National Socialist decorum. Junior functionaries conscientiously toed the line that had been drawn by those on high, and many of them won credit for overstepping the mark.

A few weeks after the outbreak of war, the ministerial ban on dancing was lifted in principle. The regional director of propaganda and cultural supervisor at Koblenz took the occasion to draft a circular addressed to district Party chiefs. Local authorities were to ensure that 'swing' dancing and similar contortions did not take place. Although prohibitive notices were to be avoided, dance-halls could be adorned with broad hints, e.g. 'Enjoyment does not preclude poise and dignity!'[131]

In many towns, police chiefs made restaurants display notices to the effect that persons of the female sex were forbidden to smoke. The police commissioner at Erfurt was even more zealous. He called upon the inhabitants to 'remind women whom they meet smoking on the streets of their duty as German wives and mothers'.[132]

These tighter restrictions were indicative of the extreme vagueness that surrounded Party promulgations from above. Despite general pronouncements on the dignity of the German woman, her simple appearance and behaviour, her abhorrence of trinkets and finery, her natural and maternal grace, no precise rules of conduct were laid down and no unequivocal statements made. A behaviour pattern grew up notwithstanding, and policy-interpreters in the middle and lower ranks of the Party seized upon it with alacrity.

Constant changes of fashion, as Teutomaniac cultural pessimists had demonstrated beyond doubt, were the product of a degenerate and destructive urban civilization. The new rulers of Germany began by approaching this subject with restraint. They had more important things on their plate, foremost among them the co-ordination of government and Party. But the petty apostles of folkish salvation, borne up by the crystalline waters of national revival, floated to the surface. No matter that they were merely welcome and useful bits of flotsam swept along by the Brown flood. All that weighed with them was the result, the chance to present themselves as guardians of the supreme national virtues.

The Reverend Kurt Engelbrecht instantly aligned his traditional prejudices with the new trend. Ostentation at any price was the slogan in women's fashions. But behind this urge, thundered the worthy cleric, lurked the vilest sensuality, the most brazen eroticism and unbridled animal lust. The noble German woman should dress nobly, with simple refinement. Garish colours and materials she 'leaves to whores'. And now came the small but crucial step which brought the old philistine into line with the new reactionaries: it was the *Parisian* prostitute who dictated fashions to *German* women in league with *Jewish* clothing manufacturers! It was an outrage and a disgrace, a debasement and degradation of German taste. Under the sign of the crooked cross, however, all would – God be praised! – turn out for the best. 'German community spirit in the new Total State can indeed stir, even in the German "lady" who purchases a hat! Either that, or the Total State must forcibly intervene here too, in this subsidiary but vital field of cultural taste.'[133] State intervention was unnecessary. The dictatorship of taste could safely be entrusted to puritanical philistines without the Party and bigoted petty bourgeois within – innocuous-seeming individuals like the novelist Kuni Tremel-Eggert. Her auth-entically German heroine 'Barb' rejected powder and make-up as a matter of course, in deference to the wishes of her husband, whom she invariably addressed by his surname. The sanitary Barb dismissed cosmetics with a scornful laugh, though she was a regular customer of Lanolin-Industrie and Haus 4711 – German firms both. 'I've got a nice big tin of face-cream, a litre bottle of Eau de Cologne, and my shower – full stop! That's all I need . . .'[134]

The undertone is unmistakable. These ideological – or rather, chauvinistic – calls to arms against changes in fashion and feminine titivation concealed a number of vested economic interests. The Party was active on this front. In 1939 the Reich Director of Organization, Robert Ley, opened the 'House of Beauty Culture' in Berlin. There was no general objection to beauty as such, but Ley's inaugural address made a point of differentiating between 'beautiful' and 'new'. They were not, he stressed, synonymous.

Ley could have quoted one of his Führer's speeches at Nuremberg. Referring to art in the Third Reich at the 1933 Rally, Hitler had declared that 'unprecedentedness' was no evidence of an achievement's quality but might just as easily prove its 'unprecedented inferiority'.[135] *Das Schwarze Korps* dismissed rapid changes of fashion as a craze for novelty and railed at such aberrations of taste as milliners' confections adorned with artificial Brazilian plovers or miniature Australian storks. It was an appeal to the purchaser's purse as well as her better judgement. Indignation was levelled not only at the exorbitant prices charged for such models but at fashion dictatorship in general: under this disgraceful and materialistic system, cost became the criterion of beauty.

None of this prevented the outraged arbiters of taste from thinking in highly materialistic terms themselves. Hugo Kaiser, the editor of *Notes for German girls who plan to become housewives and mothers*, was a case in point. Ninety-nine out of a hundred German women needed no make-up, he flatteringly proclaimed. Furthermore, no German women needed the cosmetic products of Germany's hereditary foe because the German chemical industry maintained an equally high standard. It was a crime against German national resources if, as in the year 1932, 8 million German marks were paid to France for such commodities.

Seven years later there was more at stake than the ideal of economic self-sufficiency. Industry was working flat out to produce guns, explosives and uniform cloth, not butter, face-cream and dress-lengths. In 1939, Robert Ley again rejected the fashion concept which equated beauty with novelty. His reason: it led to the pointless consumption of textiles and militated against economic planning. The Party press took up the same cry and publicized a national 'War on Waste'. Fashion dictatorship was not only a violation of German good taste but a crime against national resources.

Few arguments were neglected which could help to justify ever more vehement attacks on the great 'fashion fraud'. The new Germany had reasserted the timeless beauty of motherhood, whereas the so-called humanitarian democracies judged their beauty-queens by degree of nudity and circumference of thigh. Again, who was responsible for creating modish novelties? Mannequins and bachelor-girl types who were as alien to the German woman's biological function as they were to her labours in the service of the nation. Wasn't that a clear enough indication of the *demi-mondain* nature of this ideal of beauty, with its latent image of the prostitute? Behind it lurked nothing less than the pestilential Jewish spirit. The language of the fashion ad – 'cute, smart, extravagant' – was proof enough of that.

In face of these insidious arguments, opposition was dangerous. Nobody could fail to detect a note of menace when *Das Schwarze Korps*, the official organ of the SS, continued in an apparently indulgent vein: 'These remarks are not meant to be taken as an all-out attack on lipstick, powder and silk stockings – quite the reverse. They are merely a modest reminder that, as soon as they begin to stifle a woman's inherent worth, these beauty-aids – which are far from objectionable in themselves – create a danger that emphases will be wrongly distributed and real values take second place to a materialistic veneer.'[136] Yes indeed, but who could estimate when the needle of the gauge stopped pointing at inner values and swung towards Jewish-materialistic superficialities? Only the Party or someone who made himself the mouthpiece of official dogma. . . .

The inanity of such standards became wholly manifest during the war. By autumn 1941, German troops had firmly established themselves in occupied France. Their most sought-after presents to those back home – quite as eagerly coveted by private soldiers' wives as by the spouses of government ministers and senior civil servants – were nylon stockings, women's underwear and perfumes from Paris. At the same time, an expert from the Reich Press Office declared in the periodical *Die Mode* that the New Order in Europe would present the German fashion industry with problems of the utmost magnitude.[137] Though sober enough at first glance, the article soon struck a rich vein of comedy. Its author, Ernst Herbert Lehmann, went on to assert that countries like France and England had used fashion to enhance their geopolitical power. All of a sudden, the side-issue 'fashion' was metamorphosed into a cultural factor of the first order and credited with vast political importance. Germany must no longer be patronized in matters of fashion nor forced to speak a foreign fashion-idiom. So far from being an 'unpolitical' matter, fashion was an instrument of imperialist policy and must now be utilized as such by the Greater German Reich.

Even where fashion was concerned, the National Socialist approach was still determined by a totalitarian claim to authority. The higher consumption of clothing entailed by fashion's law of change was a drain on economic resources which the State planned to put to better use elsewhere, in the interests of greater industrial and military strength. Slogans such as 'Fashion is the foe of regional dress' concealed their ulterior purpose but poorly. How many of the Third Reich's urbanized inhabitants, most of whom worked in factories, offices and government departments, were keen to wear regional costume? A few countryfolk, perhaps, but that was all. The National Socialist call for practical and durable clothing embodied an economic commandment as well as an unmistakable desire for uniformity. What could be more practical and durable than the outfit issued to every German boy and girl in the 'Young Folk', and what finer feat of Party organization than to ensure that they never stepped out of such uniforms again? Hitler Youth, Labour Service, National Socialist Students' Association, National

Socialist Women's Association – to every citizen his, or her, proud livery of national service.

These dull forms of attire had little in common with the colourful gaiety of German regional costumes, but the planned devastation of feminine finery was justified by a solemn slogan: Faith and Beauty. Authentic manifestations of this ideal could often be observed at Party functions, when young BdM girls with their blonde hair plaited or braided and their bodies swathed in flowing white shifts pranced demurely – and where possible bare-footed – through the measures of a round-dance.

The Party's idea of how German females ought to dress was exemplified by gatherings of Women's Association members at the Nuremberg Rallies. The *Frankfurter Zeitung* correspondent ironically described one such parade in 1938: 'Quite a few women turned up in the costumes of their native districts, which were situated in every part of the Reich and beyond the German frontiers as well. They appeared in sparkling coifs and colourful kerchiefs, in black velvet jackets and silken aprons, in red bodices and with ribbons woven into their hair.' After the old style, the new: 'The girls of the Labour Service wore their uniforms, the girl students their new, simple, standardized costume consisting of a dark-blue skirt and jacket over a white blouse, very similar to the new costume of the BdM and the junior sections of the Women's Association. Girls in peasant costume, a few hundred female youth leaders, Labour Service leaders and representatives of the Working Women's Groups (in a sort of pale-blue porter's smock over a white blouse), seen here for the first time, entered in a long procession down the central aisle of the hall. . . .'[138] The opening phrase from Beethoven's Fifth Symphony provided an uplifting background: the sound of destiny knocking at the portal. . . .

Even in the field of feminine aesthetics, however, tactical requirements ultimately prevailed over the Party's planned objectives. In 1943 Goebbels's propaganda batteries began to zero in on the 'total war' target. The man who had tended to poke fun at puritanism suddenly declared the feminine 'cult of beauty' pernicious. Women should scrimp for final victory. Better to wear darned dresses for a year or two, ran the new tactical line, than wander around in rags for centuries. But Goebbels's new-found sense of realism proved too much for his Führer, who was loath to put excessive pressure on the female citizen. 'Lift a finger against beauty culture,' he told his Propaganda Minister, 'and you make an enemy of her.'[139] Goebbels obediently corrected himself: 'Total war is not a play-ground for plebeian instincts. There is no need for a young woman to make herself look ugly.'[140]

The *Völkischer Beobachter* published tips on how to make old clothes look fashionable. The settlement of the fashion question was relegated to the period after final victory.

German lady, chew!

In 1934, Goebbels heaped scorn on the moral arbiters who wanted to stop women smoking. He was a trifle precipitate. Himself a heavy cigarette-smoker, he had noted melodramatically during the arduous years of struggle: 'Smoking is my last remaining pleasure. That's why I find it so hard to stop.'[141] As a government minister, he once tried to give up the habit for reasons of policy, but it proved too much for him. His consumption rose during the war to thirty cigarettes a day, but he took care to conceal the blue haze from other people and only smoked when he was alone.

There were two associated reasons for this. In the first place, there was the view – unofficial but effective up to a point – that no German worth his salt was a slave to nicotine and alcohol. The limping little Doctor, whose love affairs and large family were ample demonstration of his virility, found it opportune to set a resolute example in this respect. In the second place, smoking was disapproved of by the Führer, Goebbels's idol and protector. Again, Hitler was a vegetarian. Goebbels followed that particular lead with ease. The fare at his table was scanty and unappetizing, and he made sure that it included nothing surplus to the daily quota imposed by the ration card. Finally, Hitler was a teetotaller, and here too his lieutenant could conform without too much difficulty.

The Führer's aversion to meat, liquor and tobacco was firm and categorical. Very few of his associates practised such abstinence voluntarily, but they were careful not to smoke in his presence or drink as their inclination took them. They often made up for lost time when he finally departed after one of his long and nerve-fraying nocturnal sessions. This was another reason why membership of Hitler's private circle held few attractions, even for old and obsequious comrades-in-arms. The fanatical abstainer sometimes gave it as his strange belief that meat-eating paved the way for drinking and smoking in a sort of vicious chain reaction. His dream was to convert all People's Comrades to a vegetarian diet after the war: 'The society of the future will lead a vegetarian existence.'[142] He also held that smoking should be banned by the State for health reasons and planned to prohibit the consumption of alcohol at Party gatherings.

The Führer's attitude, being sufficiently well known, was grist to the mill of crusading health-faddists and hidebound fanatics of decorum alike. They condemned alcohol as a source of mental debility and criminality, sexual impairment and hereditary degeneration. Nicotine they denounced as a cause of premature senility, a nerve and gland poison. In his outspoken primer on sex education, the popular educationist Reinhard Gerhard Ritter went so far as to assert that smokers became frigid, impotent and ultimately infertile. Women smokers were threatened with particularly dire consequences: atrophy of the ovaries, poisoning of the breast-fed infant, and loss of personal freshness, beauty and youthfulness. Their complexion acquired 'a peculiar grey, sometimes dull yellow tinge'.[143]

Robert Ley, head of the largest National Socialist organization, the Labour Front, made smoking and drinking the touchstone of male will-power. In the Ordensburgen or training centres whose appointed task was to mould the political executives of the Party, both vices were sometimes banned for one week as a 'disciplinary exercise'. Generously, Ley conceded that 'Any man may smoke and drink as much as he can tolerate, as long as it does not harm his body and hamper his work.' On the other hand, 'Anyone who aspires to be a real man must be able to control himself, in other words, have command of himself...'[144] Strong stuff, especially from the mouth of a Reichsleiter whose nickname was 'Reich Boozer'. His worthy fellow-fighter in the cause of self-discipline and decorum was the expert pornographer and Gauleiter of Franconia, Julius Streicher, who preached a ban on smoking for German women.

The success of such campaigns was minimal, of course. They did result in some harassment of women who dared to smoke in public, but their lack of support can be deduced from this cheeky little jingle by the popular Fred Endrikat, who entitled it *Hypocrisy*:

> German woman, please behave
> as it behoves you to.
> German housewife, do not smoke.
> German lady, chew.

Strength through joy

The petty vices of the National Socialist citizen were hard to cure. The man in the street kicked like a mule when his modest love of fashionable elegance, tobacco-smoke or a convivial glass was suddenly branded an un-German vice. Supporters of the system soon realized that it was wiser to hang fire for a while, but their system eventually staked a claim to the whole human being. It was the mighty soul of the nation that counted, after all, not the paltry soul of the individual. In order to bring that home to the entire nation, the individual's spare time had to be 'taken in hand' (one of the régime's pet phrases). If moral precepts wouldn't work, remedies must be sought in legislation. One remedy, and probably the most successful, went by the name of Strength through Joy (KdF).

It was Robert Ley, the Party's Director of Organization and head of the German Labour Front (DAF), who built up the Strength through Joy association. 'See to it,' ran the Führer's brief, 'that leisure and recreation keep the nerves of the toiling masses sound and strong enough to facilitate a vigorous policy.'[145] There was no attempt to gloss over the truth. The citizens of the Third Reich, now fully employed, were to be kept physically fit and strong-nerved enough to serve as chips in the Führer's geopolitical poker-game.

Ley duly organized the leisure of the masses. His KdF bureaux had nothing to fear in the way of financial problems. Not only could they call on the sequestrated funds of the old trade unions, but the whole undertaking was backed by enormous State subsidies. Appropriately enough, its 'Theatre of the People' opened in January 1934 with Schiller's *Die Räuber* (The Thieves).

The 'Leisure Bureau' arranged cheap-rate theatre shows and concerts, films, exhibitions and 'socials'. No less than 38 million people attended 117,000 such functions in 1937 alone. Even the remotest village was catered for by KdF. Officials ensured that the atmosphere was decorous and refined, for dance bands, cabaret dancers and smutty comedians had no place in the leisure activities of German countryfolk. The 'German Popular Education Service', which exploited and developed the prestige of the old German adult education movement along Party lines, absorbed 16.5 million people into its 'national-politically' stream-lined framework. The 'Sports Bureau' boasted nearly 10 million participants in its first four years of existence. In December 1936 the authorities publicly declared athletics an aid to pre-military training and racial improvement, and introduced sport at factory level. Reich Director of Sport Hans von Tschammer und Osten devised the ingenious term 'political physical training' to cover these activities. The International Olympic Committee paid tribute to the KdF organization in 1938 by awarding it an Olympic cup for special achievements in the field of sport.

However, the jewel of the Party's welfare system was its 'Travel and Tourism Bureau'. KdF mass tourism was liberally exploited as an advertisement for National Socialism. It also had some extremely gratifying economic side-effects. German State Railways did well out of the subsidized mass-travel bureau: its share in 1934 was approximately 7 million marks out of a total KdF tourism turn-over of 45 million. In the following year, the figures were 3 million tourists and 68 million marks. These sums were carefully channelled into rural development areas. It was a shrewd piece of arithmetic: health-giving holidays among simple countryfolk, cheap accommodation in depressed rural areas, and economic aid to the latter supplied by the tourist industry. Week-end excursions and holidays in Germany were not all, however. The real show-piece consisted of spectacular cruises to Norway or the Mediterranean. Of the 10 million people who went on KdF holiday trips up to the outbreak of war, 500,000 travelled abroad. KdF built a dozen splendid snow-white ships for this purpose – a wise investment because their 200,000-ton capacity came in useful for transporting troops at a later stage. They proved their military value in 1939 when the Condor Legion had to be withdrawn from Spain (the transportation charges of 209,000 marks being paid for, incidentally, out of DAF dues). The development of a KdF car was backed by the same well-capitalized organization. Although originally built as an all-purpose military vehicle, it also became an effective social symbol under the name Volkswagen, or People's Car. The KdF vacation centre at Rügen on the Baltic was likewise built with a timely eye to subsequent military use, and the skeleton of this gigantic project served as a hospital when war came.

KdF tours were unbeatable value. A week's trip from Berlin to the Baltic cost 32 marks and a trip to Italy 155 marks. In 1935 the average worker's income was approximately 120 marks a month, and he was the official beneficiary of the new arrangement. There were persistent complaints, nonetheless, that these holiday offers were reserved for well-heeled citizens rather than the ordinary worker. Robert Ley responded with some statistical data: one-third of KdF holiday-makers earned less than 100 marks monthly, one-third between 100 and 150 marks, and only 6 per cent more than 250 marks. But even the official figures were a vindication of the critics. There is no doubt that the tourist who could afford the coveted trips abroad belonged to the higher income-groups.

In 1937 a French correspondent joined one of the Norwegian cruises and analysed the status of his 939 fellow-passengers. 217 were workers, 249 white-collar workers and craftsmen, 202 women employees, 187 accompanying wives and 28 self-employed persons. 56 passengers would not disclose their occupation or profession. In other words, barely a quarter belonged to the working class proper.

But KdF had a ready explanation for this too. Workers were not to be found in factories and mines alone: DAF looked upon every employed German as a worker, and the word was an honorific title. The effective aim of these tours was to iron out class differences, for the whole vast undertaking naturally had an ideological purpose as well.

Those for whom a KdF holiday represented their first real glimpse of the Fatherland were meant to be reinforced in their patriotism and national pride, elbow to elbow with other loyal citizens. Politically trained tour organizers ensured that their sense of togetherness burgeoned into Party loyalty. The so-called foreign tours were ideal for this purpose. For weeks on end, passengers on the *Wilhelm Gustloff* or *Robert Ley* cruised off foreign shores in a well-supervised mood of holiday cheer. Shore excursions were rare, however, and they saw little of foreign countries. A comprehensive shipboard programme, ranging from matutinal callisthenics to the nightly singing of folk-songs, kept them community-minded. Experienced officials and officious fellow-passengers made sure that no one failed to engage in communal jollifications and acts of patriotic reverence. Moreover, passenger-lists regularly included a brace of Security Service agents whose job it was to maintain an unobtrusive watch on the attitude and behaviour of crew and passengers and transmit reports on the subject. Uninfected by their surroundings, KdF liners ploughed the seas like microcosmic repositories of German nationhood.

Gerhard Starcke, press secretary to the DAF, was quite frank about the purpose of these social achievements: 'We did not send our workers vacationing on their own ships or build them seaside resorts for our own amusement or that of the individual who can make use of such amenities. We did so merely so as to maintain the individual's capacity for work and return him to his place of employment invigorated and re-equipped. KdF does, in a sense, overhaul every worker from time to time, just as the engine of a motor vehicle has to be overhauled after it has done a certain number of kilometres.'[146]

Robert Ley put it even more bluntly: 'We have no private individuals any more. Gone are the days when everyone could do as he pleased.'[147] Even the Party's Director of Organization admitted that sleep was a private matter, but in other respects the eye of Big Brother was all-seeing. Leisure time had to be regimented, and the Party's brainwaves in this field ranged from the KdF holiday to block alerts supervised by local air-raid wardens. Most remarkable of all, however, was National Socialism's talent for celebrating its own existence and involving the entire population in patriotic revelry. National Socialist festivals were dotted throughout the calendar.

The sequence began on 15 January with a minor commemoration of the Nazis' early successes in the Landtag election at Lippe-Detmold in 1933. 30 January was known as Accession Day (strictly, 'Day of the Seizure of Power') and marked by huge torchlight processions and fervent speeches about Germany's awakening and the Thousand-Year Reich to come. The next anniversary followed swiftly on 24 February, the date on which the Party programme had been published in 1920. The Day of National Mourning, which fell in March, was systematically remodelled so as to invest it with heroic lustre. Renamed 'Heroes' Remembrance Day', it was signalized on 16 March 1935 by the re-introduction of universal conscription. This made it clear that the day was one on which to prepare for sacrifices in future wars rather than mourn those of the past. Finally, in February 1939, Hitler proclaimed 16 March – or the preceding Sunday – to be the 'Day of Armed Freedom'.

20 April was the Führer's birthday. This was celebrated like the Kaiser's birthday, though far more extravagantly and with increasing ritual. Representatives of the youth organizations solemnly pledged their allegiance to the Führer, delegations from all over the country brought him gifts, and the armed forces paraded before him in his capacity as Führer, Reich Chancellor, and – ultimately – Supreme Commander.

In 1933, Hitler boldly proclaimed 1 May to be National Labour Day. The trade unions were smashed in the name of National Socialism, and the DAF, the Party's coercive labour organization, assumed control of

25 million 'soldiers of labour', consisting of employers and employed alike. According to the national-community doctrine, this rape upon the working class meant that it had been 'regained for the nation'. In place of banners proclaiming the socialist class struggle, government-authorized processions now brandished uncontroversial and fraternal slogans such as 'Strength through joy and joy through strength. Hail to the German working class.'

Mother's Day on the second Sunday in May had been invented by the flower trade to boost its turn-over. National Socialism sanctified this profane institution. BdM girls and members of their junior branch, the Jungmädel, provided a gay but symbolic background for ceremonies at which the Party bestowed Mother's Crosses on the dutiful and prolific.

Strenuous efforts were made to introduce the 'German Solstice' in June and the 'Germanic Yule Festival' in December. The enthusiasm of the young could certainly be kindled by the academic or romantic symbolism of fire-wheels, stirring speeches and blazing bonfires, but even the Germanically oriented SS treated these occasions with little reverence. The pagan masquerade was too showy and hollow, Christian usage too deeply ingrained.

National Labour Day had its agricultural counterpart in 'German Farmers' Day', a harvest festival held on the Sunday after Michaelmas. This was when folkish agrarian romanticism and the myth of blood and soil celebrated their triumphs. On 1 October 1933, 500,000 farmers and farm-workers from every Gau in Germany were herded together on the Bückeberg near Hamlin, 700,000 in the following year and 1 million the year after that. The racial ideologist Walther Darré hailed the Reich's agriculturalists as the 'biological blood-renewal source of the body politic', and Hitler also regarded them as 'the future of the nation itself'. The gigantic mass demonstration terminated in an impressive ceremony and was crowned by an hours-long display of modern German armed might. After all, even the Germanic peasant of yore had carried a sword at his side for the defence of blood and soil.

Every year, on 9 November, sombre pageantry lent mythical status to the abortive Munich putsch of 1923. The 'Day of Remembrance for the Movement's Dead' developed into a folkish day of remembrance on which the 'martyrs' of the Party were honoured for their self-sacrifice in the German cause. In 1935 the mortal remains of the putsch's 16 fatal casualties were transferred with impressive ritual to the National Socialist Valhalla, the Ehrentempel in Munich's Königlicher Platz. There was symbolic significance in this too: commemoration of the past with an eye to the future. Far from fortuitously, this was also the day on which SS recruits were administered the oath of allegiance and reminded by the Führer of their duty to die for him if need be.

The *pièce de résistance* of the annual cycle was the Party Rally held at Nuremberg in the first half of September. For a full week, the régime displayed its immense talent for rousing huge masses of humanity to organized jubilation in its own honour. Scenic aids ranged from the homely German backcloth provided by Nuremberg's medieval architecture to the pan-Germanic megalomania of gigantic new Party buildings, from the visual impact of high-precision parades and forests of all-enveloping banners to the magical enchantment of a luminous dome erected in the night sky by more than a hundred searchlights.

Although designed as instruments of self-corroboration, these spectacles were not pure show or an end in themselves. This applied as much to the incredible expenditure of effort and financial outlay as it did to the almost unbroken sequence of national festivities. The 'stage management' of public life in the Third Reich, as the modern historian Karlheinz Schmeer has called it, was designed to give real expression to the ideal of 'national community', if only temporarily and by emotional means. The individual was meant to feel fused with the mass, hence the eminent suitability of mass suggestion, mass performances, mass demonstrations, mass settings; also slogans, readily intelligible and oft-reiterated formulas delivered by demagogues who were in command of their well-drilled audiences and had an equal command of mass psychology.

The festal cycle of the National Socialist year was nothing more nor less than an application of this recipe. The more frequently slogans and clichés were repeated and the more systematically these so-called communal experiences were strung together, the more strongly they imprinted themselves and the more effectively they quelled critical objections and individual resistance. Mature personalities and those who opposed the régime on principle were not, of course, open to such persuasion. This was one of the main reasons why intellectuals were so fiercely attacked and older people so contemptuously brushed aside. But the younger generation, Germany's future, could indeed be impressed and have its enthusiasm kindled by just such means – likewise 'the nation'. The latter was an uncertain quantity, an alleged totality whose actual existence was rendered no more credible by overwhelming Party victories at the polls. There was, however, an impressive substitute to hand: deputizing for the nation's will were the huge crowds of people who attended public ceremonies and were seduced into wild ovations.

The gamble on the masses paid off. Not even sceptical observers were immune to the magic of such occasions. André François-Poncet, then French ambassador in Berlin, had long declined to attend any of the Nuremberg Rallies. What he saw when he finally did so evoked more than mere astonishment. His reaction was, in fact, precisely illustrative of the true purpose underlying these national celebrations: 'Stranger still and difficult to describe was the atmosphere of collective enthusiasm that permeated the ancient city, the singular exaltation that seized hundreds of thousands of men and women, the romantic fever and the mystic ecstasy and the sacred delirium, as it were, that possessed them! Seven days yearly Nuremberg was a city devoted to revelry and madness, almost a city of convulsionaries . . .'[148]

The days when everyone could do as he pleased were over – Robert Ley had said so. They were now to be banished for ever by the introduction of a collective phase in which the wishes of the individual followed a prescribed course. Personal awareness was to be effaced by national anaesthesia.

Pages and Amazons

François-Poncet went on to note that 'The surroundings, the beauty of the spectacles presented, and the luxury of the hospitality offered exerted a strong influence upon the foreigners whom the Nazi Government was careful to invite annually. Many visitors, dazzled by Nazi display, were infected by the virus of Nazism. They returned home convinced by the doctrine and filled with admiration for the performance. Heedless of the sinister realities lurking beneath the deceptive pomp of these prodigious shows, they were ripe for collaboration.'[149]

The Nazi régime did its utmost to impress foreigners with the grandeur and success of its ideas. For years it made every effort to win over foreign visitors with specious courtesy and solicitude. This was more than political calculation. It was an endeavour by a pushful upstart of humble origins to gain diplomatic and social recognition in the *grand monde* of international relations. This being so, ideological ballast had to be jettisoned and lip-service paid to the rules of high society.

The 1936 Olympic Games, which were held in Berlin, provided the

Third Reich with a welcome opportunity to display its might and glamour to the world at large. German athletes won more medals than their fellow-competitors and visitors from all over the world were astonished and impressed by the perfect arrangements and extremely handsome setting. The organizers were, after all, experts in mass enchantment.

The Games afforded a politically valid pretext for entertaining on the highest social plane. Goebbels's 'Italian Soirée' on the Pfaueninsel passed swiftly, though with many distortions, into the realm of legend. Over a thousand people were invited, including Olympic dignitaries, foreign guests of honour and diplomats, big names in the Party and government. Decorations were flown in, trees converted into glittering candelabra. Army engineers erected a pontoon bridge and lined it with oars at the 'present'. Girls in white pages' costumes of the Renaissance period ushered guests in the direction of champagne and beer, bar and cold buffet. The *corps de ballet* of the Deutsches Opernhaus went through their paces, a dazzling firework display was mounted at midnight – 'one got the impression of a huge artillery bombardment,' wrote François-Poncet – and dancing continued into the small hours under the baton of Paul Lincke, the popular composer of operettas.

Hermann Göring, ever eager for self-advertisement and entertainment on a lavish scale, threw an Olympic party of his own on 13 August, two days before the 'Italian Soirée'. The last Renaissance Man – his favourite term for himself – had devised an elaborate attraction in the grounds of his Ministry: a miniature village in eighteenth-century style, 'fashioned by the tribes of Germany' and complete with inn, post-house, bakery, craftsmen's shops and country fair. The corpulent Marshal lived up to his reputation for gay conviviality and demonstrated his sunny nature for the benefit of illustrious guests by riding a merry-go-round until his breath gave out. The same night, he showed that he could move with equal ease in the rarefied atmosphere of high society. The Berlin Staatsoper was taken over for a banquet followed by a grand ball. Here too, the décor was suitably extravagant. Every wall was draped in cream-coloured silk, and an intermediate platform linked the stage with the auditorium. Red-liveried lackeys with powdered wigs were stationed in the aisles as lantern-bearers.

What was sauce for the first flight of Nazi potentates was sauce for the second, whether they were actuated by a desire to demonstrate their own importance, like Ribbentrop the former wine salesman, or whether they had a genuine taste for pleasure, like the ex-bouncer

Christian Weber. Hitler appointed Joachim von Ribbentrop ambassador in London during the Olympic Games. Despite his scorn for diplomatic conventions, Ribbentrop deemed this an occasion worth celebrating. He invited seven hundred people to pay homage to him in a huge marquee erected in the garden of his Dahlem villa. There were no pages or lackeys, but quite enough servants to ply the guests liberally with Pommery, which, although a French champagne, was choicer than the German version marketed by Ribbentrop's father-in-law. Besides, the Foreign Minister had long acted for Pommery as well as Henkell.

The festivities organized by Christian Weber, the veteran Nazi from Munich, were less insipid. Weber had an effortless mastery of the entire festive scale, from the stag drinking-session, with or without ladies of easy virtue, to the glittering gala occasion for which female extras were provided by the Reich Labour Service (Women's Division), the municipal department of physical education, and sundry ballet schools. An erstwhile beer-hall bouncer, Weber had been one of Hitler's bodyguards and cronies during the time of struggle. The Führer later cooled towards his old comrade-in-arms, whose unsavoury reputation disqualified him from high office. Weber none the less carved out a sphere of influence for himself in Munich, capital of the Movement and headquarters of Gauleiter Adolf Wagner, his faithful boon-companion. Popularly nicknamed 'the Stallion of Riem', Weber distinguished himself as president of the Riem International Race Meetings. He not only instituted the 'Brown Ribbon of Germany' prize for flat racing but became famous for his exuberant parties. In 1938, for example, the horse-fancier organized a 'Night of the Amazons'. The grounds of Schloss Nymphenburg provided a harmonious setting for this 'grandiose spectacle from the world of courtly chivalry', as the *Münchner Beobachter* described the 'social high-spot of the current year'.[150]

From Göring's theatrical appearances at his country seat, Schorfheide, attired in a fanciful hunting costume and carrying a huge Germanic spear, to the sparsely clad *Birth of Aphrodite* in Munich's gala show marking National Art Day, or from SA chief Viktor Lutze's boozing sessions to the strait-laced receptions at the Chancellery, the party manners of the Nazi potentates were neither highly ideological nor specially unconventional, neither unduly extravagant nor particularly decorous. Their amusements were – to modify Bert Brecht – a three-penny operetta at most. In short, they were as sumptuous as only the lower-middle-class mind could devise.

For example, Ernst Röhm: A taste for men

Words such as civilian, bourgeois or philistine, which he often used in conjunction, were terms of abuse much favoured by Ernst Röhm, the scion of a long line of Bavarian public servants. His homosexual proclivities had little bearing on this hostile attitude, though they naturally intensified it. Ernst Röhm's world and elixir of life lay far beyond the scope of civilian concepts and bourgeois standards. His autobiography, published in 1928, was grandly entitled *Story of a Traitor*, and even after the seizure of power, when Party bigwigs were striving to convey at least a semblance of personal propriety, he declared to a foreign diplomat, with the air of a condottiere, that he would 'rather come to terms with an enemy soldier than a German civilian, because the latter's a swine and I don't speak his language.'[151]

For Captain Röhm, to whom compromise was a dirty word, the war never ended. This was one reason why the Führer had to jettison him on the last stage of his ascent to absolute power, having previously made the fullest use of his organizing skill, unquenchable drive and complete lack of scruple, personal and official.

Röhm, who joined battle with the Weimar Republic as a Free Corps and Reichswehr officer in 1919, was instrumental in bringing home to Hitler, a minor agent working for the army's Political Department, the full extent of his abilities as an agitator. He helped the aspiring politician by putting him in touch with those officers in the seething Bavarian capital who were smarting under the ignominy of national defeat. By establishing secret ammunition dumps and co-ordinating armed bands of right-wing revolutionaries, he paved the way for the attempted putsch of 1923. Above all, he converted the Party leader's squad of shirt-sleeved stewards into a useful private army which became the executive instrument of Nazi intimidation.

The first estrangement between these oddly assorted confederates occurred during Hitler's imprisonment at Landsberg. Röhm, the ruthless mercenary type, could not conceive of any means to power other than naked force and armed conflict. Hitler, still under the impact of the abortive putsch, favoured the 'legal' method of infiltrating and undermining the democratic system, and there was no room in that scheme of things for an uncompromising fire-eater like Röhm. There had already been numerous accusations and complaints about wild drinking-orgies and debauchery, corruption and low behaviour in the SA chief's immediate circle. The Brownshirt militia, which consisted largely of rootless ex-soldiers, undisciplined irregulars and the semi-criminal dregs of the urban slums, regarded such conduct as natural rather than reprehensible. The SA was hardly a prudish outfit, and the weapons used by its storm-troopers – knuckle-dusters, rubber truncheons ('india-rubbers'), iron chains, jemmies, knives and revolvers ('lighters') – belonged to the arsenal of the criminal fraternity. Röhm's SA proved an effective and successful force in assembly-room and street battles, and to the Party leaders that was the sole factor of any importance.

Röhm never worried much about his reputation. His homosexual leanings were brought to the notice of the authorities in consequence of a case – reference number 197D 18/25 – heard at Berlin's Central District Court. Röhm had preferred charges of theft against a seventeen-year-old male prostitute by the resounding name of Hermann Siegesmund. In January 1925, he invited the youth first to a beer and then to his hotel room. When Röhm 'asked me to engage in an abhorrent form of sexual intercourse, to which I could not agree',[152] the bashful catamite took to his heels. Quite by chance – so he testified – young Hermann found that he had taken a left-luggage ticket which he promptly exchanged for a suitcase belonging to Röhm. The case contained some compromising letters, and Röhm called in the police.

In May 1932, General Ludendorff, Hitler's erstwhile political associate, wrote: 'I have in my possession documentary evidence that Herr Hitler was acquainted, as early as 1927, with grave abuses inside the organization stemming from the homosexual proclivities of his subordinates Röhm and Heines, and, in particular, with the corruption of the Hitler Youth by Heines. Herr Hitler flatly refused, at first, to dismiss the said persons.'[153] Hitler declined to dismiss the pair, but not only 'at first'. He merely suspended them temporarily from duty, but that had nothing to do with their homosexual leanings. Edmund Heines he fired in May 1927 because he was undisciplined and insubordinate. He recalled him four years later after the 1931 putsch, when he needed a keen and energetic successor to replace Stennes, the repudiated SA leader. As for Röhm, he was an obstacle to the new SA scheme which Franz Pfeffer von Salomon was to put into effect, but this did nothing to impair the friendly relations between Hitler and Röhm.

Not long afterwards the ex-Reichswehr captain found himself a
lieutenant-colonel on the general staff of the Bolivian army. Hitler had
not simply got rid of him, as Ludendorff claimed. Röhm had gone
willingly to South America in quest of an unhoped-for reputation as a
military instructor: 'It will enable me to check whether my mind is
still receptive or not.'[154] Röhm was pleased with his work as a military
adviser but tormented by the sexual privations of Bolivia, where 'my
favourite form of activity' seemed to be unknown. The following
lament from afar was addressed to a Dr Heimsoth, who shared his
tastes: 'So here I am, poor fool, not knowing what to do with myself.
I think back sadly to beautiful Berlin, where a man can be so happy.'[155]
He also recalled his correspondent's 'enchantingly lovely collection of
pictures' and begged him to forward a few copies.

Röhm did not have to pine much longer. In autumn 1930 Hitler
dismissed his SA chief, Pfeffer von Salomon, and appointed himself
OSAF instead. His homosexual henchman in La Paz now seemed the
perfect type to smarten up and reorganize the 100,000-strong army
which had fallen into disarray. Hitler reminded his dear Ernst of past
loyalties, and in January 1931 Röhm reassumed the post of SA chief
of staff. The novel feature of the situation was that Hitler now out-
ranked him as the SA's supreme commander.

On 3 February 1931, the new OSAF smoothed Röhm's path with
an official statement whose phraseology could not have been more
explicit:

'The Supreme Command of the SA has considered a number of
reports and charges levelled at SA officers and men, most of them
embodying accusations in respect of their personal conduct.

'It emerges from an examination of these matters that most of them
fall entirely outside the scope of SA service. In many cases, attacks by
political or personal opponents have been taken on trust.

'Some people expect SA commanders of high and senior rank to
take decisions on these matters, which belong purely to the private
domain. I reject this presumption categorically and with all the force
at my command.

'Quite apart from the waste of time which could be better employed
in the fight for freedom, I am bound to state that the SA is a body of
men formed for a specific political purpose. It is not an institute for
the moral education of genteel young ladies, but a formation of
seasoned fighters. The sole purpose of any inquiry must be to ascertain
whether or not the SA officer or other rank is performing his official

duties within the SA. His private life cannot be an object of scrutiny unless it conflicts with basic principles of National Socialist ideology.'[156]

Obviously, this did not apply in Röhm's case. Hitler further threatened that it would in future be necessary to check whether the author of a denunciation should himself be called to account for sowing discontent among his seasoned fellow-warriors.

Armed with this blank cheque from the Führer, Röhm not only reorganized the SA to Hitler's entire satisfaction but rebuilt his personal life along lines entirely satisfactory to himself. His old clique once more congregated regularly at the *Bratwurstglöckl* in Munich. Edmund Heines was back in evidence, and Karl Ernst turned up from Berlin with many a new SA commander who owed his rank primarily to homosexual achievement. Fierce indignation was voiced in the Party, but Hitler turned a deaf ear.

When Röhm's plaintive letters from Bolivia were published in March 1932 – leaked to the press by an unknown informant – Walter Buch, the senior Party judge, complained of treason and homosexual intrigues inside the Party to Emil Traugott Danzeisen, an old crony from his early days in the SA. He also named names. Danzeisen got the point and organized an *ad hoc* extermination squad under the command of Karl Horn, a bankrupt architect. Its assignment: to slug one Georg Bell with a hammer and string him up, then do the same to Stabsführer Uhl and finally Röhm himself. First, though, the assassins were to deal with Count Du Moulin-Eckart, an old friend of Röhm and chief of SA Intelligence. Instead of sending the Count to eternity by faking a car accident, however, Horn went to him and talked. Buch's authorship came out, and Himmler summoned him for an interview.

But the affair did not remain secret, and not only because Du Moulin and his colleague Count Spreti denounced Party Judge Buch and associates to an ordinary court of law. (Danzeisen, who was the only one to draw a sentence, got six months for incitement to murder in October 1932.) Röhm and his henchman Georg Bell also took fright and fled for their lives.

Bell, who also worked as an informer for the Social Democrats, had been dispatched by Röhm to see an old Reichswehr comrade, Major Karl Mayr, when the troublesome letters began to appear. Mayr now belonged to the Republican Reichsbanner organization and was thus in the enemy camp. It was he, of all people, whom Röhm asked to guarantee that no more of his letters would be published in the SPD press. Worse still, it was he to whom Röhm and Bell fled on April

1932 with a request for evidence against fellow-SA man Paul Schulz, whom they suspected of being the prime mover in the conspiracy. A few days later Bell actually called on the Social Democrat newspaper *Vorwärts* and blackened the Brownshirt leaders so that, in the event of his death, everyone would know who was responsible.

This was going too far. Buch's son-in-law, Martin Bormann, fired off an outraged letter to his boss Rudolf Hess, who was holidaying in Dachau: 'I have nothing against Röhm as a person. As far as I'm concerned, a man can fancy elephants in Indo-China and kangaroos in Australia – I couldn't care less.' But: 'It is drummed into every SA man and every ordinary Party member – and this was particularly important in Röhm's case – that he must back his comrades and leaders to the hilt, even when blunders occur. And now the most prominent SA commander goes slandering and denouncing people in this blatant manner. If the Führer hangs on to the man after this business, I can't fathom him any longer, like countless others . . .'[157] Hitler hung on to the man, nothing daunted, and Bormann came to understand his Führer better in the fullness of time.

If 'Party treason' did not put paid to Hitler's old friend, his homosexual streak was still less of a threat. On 4 April 1932, Röhm sought a temporary injunction against the publication of further intimate disclosures. It was refused because he did not deny authorship of the letters in question. Two days later, Hitler put his name to a leaflet defending the honour of his SA commander: 'Röhm remains my chief of staff, both now and after the elections. Nothing will alter this fact, not even the filthiest and most loathsome smear campaign, which does not shrink from falsifications, illegalities and abuses of authority, and which will make due atonement under the law.'[158] So much for Hitler's way of interpreting an incontestable statement of fact and the refusal of an injunction.

Röhm's renewed application to another court, Landgericht München I, three weeks later, failed on the same grounds. Munich's Oberlandesgericht instituted a hearing to consider the second plea and on 20 July again refused a temporary injunction. Röhm lodged an appeal and withdrew it on 7 September, but not promptly enough. Oberlandesgerichtsrat Dr Kemmer testified under oath that Röhm had confirmed the authenticity of the three letters.

The SA chief of staff could hardly have advertised his homosexual leanings in a more foolish or blatant manner. The situation gradually became too much even for his old friends in the Party. J. F. Lehmann, the ultra-reactionary publisher and long-time promoter of Hitler, sent a letter complaining that Röhm was damaging the Party's reputation from every angle. The Führer should prevail on him to resign quietly because he was filling senior posts in the SA and SS according to his personal inclinations. 'The fish stinks from the head downwards . . .'[159]

The stench did not worry the Party leader. He needed his able mercenary commander and could not afford to imperil the efficiency of his smoothly functioning private army because of moral scruples. Even when he became Reich Chancellor, Hitler was worried more by rival claims to authority on the part of his chief of staff, now Reich Minister Röhm, who was always sounding off about the 'second revolution', than by the moral stench that emanated from him. A political strong-man in command of a 500,000-strong army which even the Reichswehr had reason to fear, Röhm drafted an order of the day designed to show these 'civilian swine' once and for all:

'I take advantage of the prevalence of these often absurd excrescences of prudishness, and worse, to make it clear that the German Revolution has been won, not by philistines, bigots and sermonizers, but by revolutionary fighters who will secure that revolution and that alone. It is the SA's task, not to keep watch on the attire, complexion and chastity of others, but to haul Germany to its feet by dint of their free and revolutionary fighting spirit.

'I therefore forbid all officers and men of the SA and SS to employ their activities in this field and allow themselves to become the stooges of perverse moral aesthetes. This applies also, and in particular, to those SA and SS officers whom I have appointed to police commissionerships or other government posts. Röhm, Chief of Staff.'[160]

The chief of staff spent happy days and nights in his beloved Berlin, sampling the delights of the *Kleist-Kasino*, the *Silhouette* and the Turkish baths. He also held boisterous banquets and orgies at his head-quarters. 'Chief of Staff Ernst Röhm requests the pleasure of the company of Brigadeführer Adolf Kob to a Punch Evening on Thursday, 17 May, at 9 p.m.'

Six weeks later Röhm was dead. Hitler had him killed because he was an obstacle to his compromise with the Reichswehr, which he needed if he were to assume the Presidency after Hindenburg's imminent demise. Himmler and Göring staged the Röhm Putsch, as the bloodbath of 30 June became known, in order to destroy a powerful rival, eliminate numerous conservative opponents, and settle a long tally of old scores.

No preparations for an SA coup were ever made. Hitler may have chosen to believe the insinuations of his two lieutenants for a brief period, but that was not the reason for Röhm's murder. The Reich Press Office announced: 'His notorious and unfortunate proclivity gradually became such an intolerable burden that the Leader of the Movement and Supreme Commander of the SA was himself forced into the gravest conflicts of conscience.'[161]

This was even further from the truth. Hitler was wholly indifferent to the homosexual leanings and intrigues of his erstwhile friend and associate. As long as he had a use for Röhm he shielded him from attack with every ounce of authority he possessed.

4 Warriors and Mothers

EDUCATION IN THE TOTALITARIAN STATE

'TODAY, we no longer see the ideal of the German nation in the ultra-bourgeois of yore, but in men and girls who are taut-limbed and sound as a bell. What we require of our young Germans is something other than the past required.'[162] Such was Hitler's call to a parade of 54,000 Hitler Youth members at the Nuremberg Rally of 1935. Addressing students in 1927, he had already pilloried the stolid dependability of the veteran student as a false ideal for the young German to pursue. And, now as then, though omitting the compliment to his steel magnate backer, he proclaimed his celebrated definition of what German youths should be: 'Nimble as greyhounds, tough as leather and hard as [Krupp] steel.'

The Führer's definition of the German girl was just as readily intelligible. School text-books, calendars and posters everywhere blazoned forth his injunction: 'German girl, remember that you are destined to become a German mother! In my State, the mother will be the most important woman citizen!'

It seemed a modest enough educational assignment for the younger generation to tackle in its capacity as the nation's future, but that was its full extent: children were required to become efficient soldiers and diligent mothers for the sake of Fatherland and Führer. Since writing *Mein Kampf*, Hitler had never tired of stressing the evils of intellectual instruction. 'Knowledge is power' he assailed as a formula for common-or-garden decadence. Lecturing his Danzig henchman Hermann Rauschning in 1932, the Führer explained how vital it was to abolish what was known as universal education. He went on to outline his barbarous formula: 'Universal education is the most corrosive and disintegrative poison ever devised by liberalism for its own destruction. There can be only one education for each class and each separate grade within it. Complete freedom of education is the prerogative of the élite and of those whom it specially admits. All learning must be subject to continuous supervision and selection. Knowledge is an aid to life, not its central purpose. And so, being consistent, we shall bestow upon the broad mass of the lowest class the blessings of illiteracy.'[163] Even if this policy could not be put into effect quite as stringently as Hitler would have wished, he had at least prescribed its direction.

The first step was to inculcate discipline and good order in general, and submit young people to strict National Socialist schooling. Liberalism was a thing of the past, and so were the days when all could do as they pleased. Service to the nation far transcended personal interests. The totalitarian claims of the Führer-State took cover behind terms such as national rejuvenation and folkish community. Into whom could this attitude be dinned more readily and with better hope of success than a susceptible younger generation? That was one of the principal reasons why the Thousand-Year Reich gambled on youth, repository of the national future. It also explains why the Führer could bluntly declare to 'his' young people at the 1935 Party Rally: 'In future, the young man will be promoted from one school to the next. The story opens with the child and ends with the veteran fighter. None shall say that there is a period during which he can be left entirely to his own devices.'[164]

Believe, obey, fight

The new masters certainly showed consistency in applying themselves promptly and expressly to school policy and education when they assumed power in 1933. Their method was the usual one – 'co-ordination' – and their reasons were self-explanatory: 'National Socialism is an ideology which makes a total claim to validity and refuses to be a matter for random opinion-formation. The means wherewith to impose this claim is called education.'[165] Numerous members of the teaching profession who had entertained no liking for the democratic principles of the Weimar Republic acceded voluntarily to this demand. School authorities made a prompt start on their own national-political re-education. Courses were hurriedly established at which 'educators' – to use the preferred term – received enlightenment on the importance to State education of genealogy, genetics and racial theory. Later on, the powerful National Socialist Teachers' Association (NSLB) took charge of this service to the teaching profession. By 1939, its 41 training camps had prepared 215,000 members for their educational tasks by means of ideological instruction, para-military physical training and field sports. Examination statutes for entry to the teaching profession followed the same line. Candidates had to prove that they were steeped in the 'spirit of National Socialism', and their political attitude had a bearing on examination results. Further professional training was supplemented by courses, conferences, group travel and special literature of the sort published by the 'German Central Institute of Education and Instruction'. The ideologically slanted curriculum was dominated by subjects such as German Prehistory, The Racial Study of History, Folk Art, Popular Art Education, Music and Games, Para-Military Training, and The Educational Role of Women.

Curricula of this type indicate what was required of education by National Socialist ideology. It was hard to devise a methodical programme because the outlines of that ideology were far too indistinct. Even Professor Ernst Krieck, a leading authority on folkish education, was vague in his terms of reference: 'Race, blood, nationality and natural and historical situation are supernatural forces as crucial to every view of the world as they are to the life of those who espouse it.'[166] Only one thing was clear, and that was the rejection of liberalism and materialism, scientific objectivity and 'intellectualism'. Instead, every individual had to regard himself first and foremost as a component of the people and derive his education in the 'essential harmony of body-mind-soul' from ties of blood and folkish coexistence.

What this educational programme lacked in logical cogency it more than made up for in clarity of aim: the creation of fighting spirit and physical efficiency coupled with racial qualities which had to be nurtured by selection.

The educational and cultural authorities, their key-posts occupied by new men, steered for this objective by issuing new directives, courses of study and time-tables. The first subject to be remodelled was history. Pupils had to be coached in the history of the 'National Revolution' and its official Party interpretation, which naturally assigned a central role to Adolf Hitler, who had saved the nation from peril and servitude. Later, the conception was expanded. The whole of history was construed from the aspect of the Nordic race as a success story made possible by the Germanic peoples and men endowed with outstanding qualities of leadership. Terms such as 'Lebensraum', 'hereditary foe' and 'dagger-thrust of 1918' were indicative of how these historical findings could be applied in practice.

German lessons, too, became an ideological branch of instruction designed to cultivate 'German awareness'. The teaching of German covered 'national literature', 'native grammar' and essay subjects such as 'The German "policy of fulfilment" prior to the National Socialist Revolution and German peace policy thereafter' (1935). What was demanded of the German teacher applied to other educators as well: 'The merely contemplative, critico-scientific, historical and aesthetic outlook is being replaced by the appraising, creative and militant approach.'[167]

The nation-to-be

Biology lessons afforded the best opportunity to preach the supreme importance of ethnology to the future of the Reich. The laws of heredity, racial breeding and selection were given exhaustive treatment. Hitler had himself pointed the way: 'No boy or girl shall leave school without having been fully instructed in the need for and nature of racial purity. This will create the prerequisite for the racial foundations of our nationhood and, in turn, provide a secure grounding for later cultural development.'[168] These words appeared as a motto in the *Rassenhygienische Fibel* (Primer of Racial Hygiene) – one of many – which Emil Jörns and Julius Schwab wrote 'for the benefit of young Germans'. In the spirit of National Socialism, children of all age-groups were instructed in the great value of the national heritage and the importance of genealogy, in racial hygiene and racial improvement, in Nordification and selective breeding, in natural and unnatural selection and the folkish campaign for population growth. It had to be impressed on every boy and girl that they stood 'at the loom'[169] of their nation and that no mistakes in weaving were permitted. In this way, children were not only attuned to National Socialist racial legislation and the cultivation of hereditary health but taught to make a correct choice of spouse and have large families.

In geography, ideological training continued by way of geopolitical and racial theories which justified Hitler's aggressive expansionist policy and stressed the national need for Lebensraum. A lyrical backcloth was provided by artistic activities such as communal dancing in regional costume. The same Arcadian diversions were envisaged for the yeoman-warriors of the SS in their fortified villages just west of the Urals, once the Reich's pacification policy had secured these territories for the master race.

Foreign languages and mathematics were exempt from the dictates of ideology. There was a simple reason for this. Goethe the many-sided cosmopolitan could be transmogrified into a national poet, and

Frederick the Great, that wavering supporter of the Enlightenment, into a materialistic Fridericus Rex; the monk Mendel could serve as a theoretician of human breeding and the geopolitician Haushofer as a champion of folkish territorial claims. None of these distortions affected the nation's assets, but the Third Reich also needed efficient administrators, competent technicians, experienced economists and a horde of ancillary workers who were capable of solving accurately defined problems with precision. Germany had urgent need of such experts if it was to satisfy its craving for power. That was why two 2s continued to make 4, and why 'German physics', as devised by Nobel Prize-winner Johannes Stark, never amounted to more than a scientific gaffe of marginal importance.

Religious instruction was first encouraged and then curtailed. The Nazis initially supported it with an eye to the concordat which was intended to bring their régime its first international recognition. Moreover, there were idealistic elements inside the Party which aimed at coexistence with the Christian churches. The wind soon veered, however. Clerics were removed from school boards and odd hours selected for religious instruction so as to encourage truancy among pupils and make it easier for parents to withdraw their children from Bible classes as the Party desired. The establishment of undenominational schools was another anti-clerical measure, its ultimate purpose being to replace religious instruction with National Socialist indoctrination.

In accordance with the Führer's will, the folkish State had to focus its educative endeavours on the 'rearing of healthy bodies' rather than the 'injection of pure knowledge'.[170] Racial enlightenment was supplemented by physical training, and the previous underemphasis on physical education was reversed. In schools, the number of weekly PE classes was raised to three, then five. Boxing and field sports helped to vary the programme. School reports attached more and more weight to athletic prowess. Pupils with severe physical disabilities and a consistent record of failure in PE were barred from admission to centres of higher education. A demand was even voiced at the Reich Ministry of Education that sports masters should automatically be appointed assistant-principals. This overemphasis on PE had as little in common with the *frisch, fromm, fröhlich, frei* (lively, devout, blithe, free) preached by Friedrich Ludwig Jahn, the father of German popular physical education, as it did with the moderate humanistic ideal of *mens sana in corpore sano*. Sport had an ideological and selective function: its purpose was to instil corporate spirit and corporal vigour.

These educative principles were perfectly exemplified by two institutions, the Landjahr, or year of national service on the land, and the National Socialist élite schools.

By introducing the Landjahr, Reich Minister of Education Bernhard Rust combined the economically useful with the ideologically desirable. From the economic aspect, the labour market was swamped and required disburdening, whereas agriculture lacked labour because of continuing rural depopulation; ideologically, the National Socialist training of children could be accomplished far more effectively if they were herded together in communal camps under the aegis of the Party. Rust's original intention was that all State school pupils should be obliged to do one year's agricultural service after completing the 9th grade, but his plan proved unworkable, mainly for financial reasons. Of 360,000 Prussian school-leavers, for example, only 20,000 could be recruited for this form of national service in Easter 1934 and 30,000 every year thereafter until the outbreak of war. Great store was set by the recruitment of children from families considered to be 'hygienically and politically at risk'.[171] These were mainly the offspring of lower-class parents who, being hard hit by unemployment and a superabundance of children, tended to welcome such an easing of their financial burdens. More prosperous families often declined to entrust their children to the Party pedagogues of the Hitler Youth for so long a period. Thus the Landjahr precisely encompassed those sections of the population on whom Hitler had promised to bestow the blessings of illiteracy.

The fourteen-year-old boys and girls were sent for nine months to communal camps in the country. Parental visits were forbidden and no leave was granted. The youngsters worked for farmers in the morning and devoted their afternoons to classes in ethnology, the racial study of history, and the history of the Movement. The Hitler Youth soon came to dominate these isolated communal centres, which bore no relation to many a new recruit's dreams of a romantic campfire existence in the style of the old German Youth Movement. The young people were sternly drilled in National Socialism and systematically turned against their parents. One youth leader reported proudly: 'The life was utterly new to thousands of German girls, most of whom had yet to join the BdM and found it hard, at first, on account of other and somewhat obsolete educational principles deriving from their parental home, to endure this life of self-trial and comradeship. The boys, too, embarked on their year's service with prejudices stemming from home and Church, with ideologically warped and preconceived opinions and attitudes.'[172] Their attitudes were adjusted by the Hitler Youth leaders who recruited new members in these camps. Catholic priests were quicker to respond to this threat than parents. The local government authority and Gestapo headquarters at Aachen reported that problems had arisen from Church propaganda against the Landjahr. Priests were trying to dissuade parents from sending their children to camps by alluding to the religious neglect that reigned there. The authorities reacted promptly by threatening to suspend religious instruction altogether. When the diocesan journal mildly objected that the Landjahr's interdenominational mixture was aimed at effacing denominational differences, the relevant edition was hurriedly impounded on the grounds that it would mislead the public.

Sound instincts make sound fellows

Hitler did more than declare that the masses must be protected from the corrosive effects of intellectual instruction. He also expounded his personal vision of how the élite should be educated. He planned to establish Junker schools in which the future ruling class would learn 'the gospel of the free man', that is to say, freedom from preconceptions in the arts and sciences: 'My system of education is a harsh one. Weakness must be stamped out. The world will shrink in trepidation from the youngsters who grow up in my Ordensburgen. A violent, masterful, dauntless, cruel younger generation – that is my aim. There must be nothing weak and tender about it. Its eyes must glow once more with the freedom and splendour of the beast of prey. I want my young people to be strong and beautiful. I want them trained in every form of physical exercise. I want them to be athletic – that is the prime and paramount requirement . . . I want no intellectual instruction. Knowledge spells perdition to my young people. I would prefer them to be taught only what they will learn voluntarily by pursuing their instinct for play. But they must learn self-command. I want them to learn to conquer the fear of death by undergoing the severest ordeals. That is the heroic stage of youth.'[173] Such was the basic pattern underlying the National Socialist élite schools: the National-Political Institutes of Education, the National Socialist German Secondary School, the Adolf Hitler Schools, and the Ordensburgen.

   The first three National-Political Institutes of Education – known as Napolas – were a birthday present to the Führer from Education

Minister Rust in 1933. They were the former Prussian cadet schools at Potsdam, Plön and Köslin. The Napolas multiplied fairly rapidly. There were 15 two years later and 21 in 1938, four of them in Austria and one in the Sudetenland. Their numbers reached a peak of 39 in 1943, though the original plan envisaged 100 of them by 1945. Initially run by the Reich Ministry of Education, they were taken over in 1936 by Obergruppenführer Dr August Heissmeyer, who headed the SS 'controlling authority for institutes of political education'. Soon afterwards, the Napolas passed completely under the authority of Himmler's élite Order, which had already exercised a controlling influence.

Being élite schools for the future ruling class, the National-Political Institutes of Education had to develop a pattern for National Socialist education in general. Their principals were mostly veteran members of the SA and SS, their teaching staff young, unmarried, and specially picked for their ideological reliability. Instructors from the Hitler Youth and SS were responsible for administering the Napolas' programme, which borrowed heavily from the normal type of camp education. In addition, engineers and officers were available to instruct pupils in technical and military subjects.

The Napolas selected their 'Jungmannen', or cadets, from intellectually able, physically fit and politically promising boys of the 3rd and 4th primary-school grades. Napolas were officially open to all qualified youngsters regardless of social origin, the decisive factors being blood and race. Statistics show that the sons of civil servants (26 per cent), salaried employees (22 per cent) and officers (5.6 per cent) predominated. Preliminary tests and a one-week trial were held to examine candidates in respect of character, physique and intelligence – in that order. Athletic prowess and tests of courage weighed as heavily as academic knowledge, bespectacled boys were excluded and the sons of Party veterans or war-dead given preference. Ernst Krieck verbosely outlined the purpose of national-political education. It embraced purely folkish and racial values and demanded an absolute allegiance which no transcendent moral standards could be allowed to disrupt: 'The politically supportive élite class of the folkish total State will from the very outset be firmly defined: subject to strict discipline, aligned with the communal and binding folkish ideology, attuned to honour, truth, allegiance, readiness for service and self-sacrifice, devotion to the whole, a disciplined way of life and austere conduct, to the values of folkish, military and political life: soldierly in public life and the conduct thereof. Compliance and obedience to one's leaders, valour and courage, straightforwardness, veracity and justice, a sense of community, militant strength of will and arm – those are the characteristics and values to be bred, the collective and binding political order.'[174]

The curriculum was designed accordingly. Five subjects remained obligatory throughout a pupil's school career: German, history, geography, ethnology and biology – precisely the subjects predestined for ideological instruction. From the Untersekunda or lower-fifth stage onwards, when mathematics could be dropped, two hours a week were devoted to 'national-political instruction'. In accordance with the scheme for all-round education in the Nazi sense, deliberate attempts were made to ideologize the boys' spiritual resources, aesthetic inclinations and irrational desires. Art education, drawing, handicrafts, music and amateur dramatics – artistic subjects for which considerable time was allowed – provided ample opportunity to do this with due nationalistic emphasis. Eminently suited to the same purpose was a whole range of ceremonial functions, so designed as to display strongly ritual features and make a romantic impact on youthful participants. A cadet from the Stuhm Napola describes how he and his comrades gathered round the camp fire after being presented with their dirks, a sort of coming-of-age ceremony which was accompanied by fanfares and injunctions to fight for Fatherland and Führer: 'The Principal stood there alone with his collar turned up and his back to the river. He stood there in silence for a long time. And then he started to speak. He spoke gravely of the Northern Lights, of how young Germans of bygone days were admitted to the warrior class of their tribe or clan, of the problems a young warrior had to surmount. The unyielding Germanic conception of honour and loyalty must be our constant example, he said. That was why we received a ceremonial dirk, as a token of our ability to bear arms. And finally he voiced the thoughts that had particularly stirred us that evening: the duty to fight, to do battle for our nation, the duty to give our last ounce of strength and energy in that cause.'[175]

On 9 November, the day sacred to the 'March on the Feldherrnhalle' and its dead, the presentation of dirks at the Ballenstedt Napola was accompanied by a rhythmical alternation of voices. One of the cadets led the chant as follows:

'We aim to forge a path for freedom,
though foreign nations howl with rage.
Devoutly we already sense it:

we see the German strong and free!
Let this an aim be in our struggle,
though still from our young lives remote.
We shall triumph, and we know it:
a nation free, we stand prepared.'[176]

Songs such as *Wo wir stehen, steht die Treue* (Where we stand, stands loyalty) and *Lever dod as Slav* (Better dead than enslaved), passages from the *Edda* and music by Händel accompanied these occasions, and over all loomed the motto of the Institute: Believe, Obey, Fight. The youngsters' esprit de corps was invoked and strengthened at innumerable ceremonies: trooping the colour, Führer's parades, dirk presentations, German Solstice, and the whole gamut of National Socialist ritual from the Führer's birthday to harvest festival.

The object was to fashion a political human being who, as the Stuhm commemorative booklet of 1938 put it, 'will later be capable, thanks to his faith in National Socialism and his knowledge, of correct political judgement and action even under difficult circumstances'.[177] Applied to the education of warriors, this meant that, in addition to sound political convictions and a sense of community, they must above all possess the fighting efficiency with which – in the words of Education Minister Rust – 'to survive the contest of life'.[178]

'Education from and through the body' was what gave life at the Napolas its shape and provided the chief attraction for many of the boys who competed for admission to these exclusive establishments. The high priority assigned to physical training is evident from a glance at the daily routine. Morning classes were interspersed with gymnastics, athletics, swimming and ball-games, which together with field sports constituted the basic forms of physical exercise. The lion's share of the afternoon schedule was devoted to specialized sports such as rowing, riding, driving, fencing and boxing. The boys also went sailing and gliding, activities to which importance was attached by the navy and air force respectively. Field exercises, manoeuvres, route marches and group excursions were arranged to familiarize them with rifle, compass and map-case, because the army and Waffen-SS, or military arm of the SS, vied with each other in recruiting officer material from the Napolas. Graduates were technically free to choose their own careers. Very many of them opted for civil engineering, many for teaching and medicine. After the outbreak of war, the principle of physical education – hitherto interpreted as an aid to character-building – stood revealed with increasing clarity as a form of pre-military training. 75 per cent of ex-Napola pupils reported for service as officer cadets and nearly 20 per cent planned to become regulars. Although their initial preference was for the army, most of them eventually joined the Waffen-SS, which suited their inbred sense of élitism. The others favoured the air force rather than the army or navy.

Success attended this educational policy designed to produce a 'splendid beast of prey' unencumbered by humane prejudices. In 1942 an upper-fourth-form Jungmann doing agricultural service in the Warthegau noted: 'I have to keep the Poles on their toes and make sure they don't pinch anything. Most of them are illiterate and far from intelligent. Their living-quarters are indescribable compared with O. They're Poles, that's all, and inferior. Enough said.'[179] A classmate gave apt expression to his feelings of superiority: 'Poles and Jews are still needed here as labour. They're very subservient, but they'd love to hit us over the head with the nearest iron bar, given half a chance, as the Principal so admirably put it when posting us to Posen.'[180]

Hitler's young heroes also learnt to conquer the fear of death. Early in 1944, Heissmeyer praised the heroism of Napola graduates in a report addressed to Reichsführer Himmler. 1,226 of them were already reported dead or missing. They had gone to their deaths as full of faith and free from frailty as their beloved Führer could have wished. The last will and testament of an ex-Jungmann who had been killed in action is a further tribute to this successful form of educational perversion:

'Should fate ordain that I fail to return from this great war, it is my wish

1. that the event should be seen for what it is in reality: a necessary sacrifice in the cause of German victory, willingly made by me in fulfilment of my life as a soldier;

2. that my beloved wife and revered parents strive to convince themselves that they, too, have gladly made this sacrifice on the altar of the Fatherland;

3. that my obituary notice shall contain no reference to divine ordinances, God, sorrow, deep mourning, or the like. I want it signed as follows: For Germany's victory, we are ready to give our all. In proud remembrance . . .

6. that, should I have no son, my brother G. take notice that he is the sole bearer of our name;

7. that my wife shall not remain a widow, and that, being a healthy woman, she shall heed the duty she must perform for the perpetuation of our Reich;

8. that, should I have a son, he shall always bear my name and be brought up to become a healthy, honourable, clean, self-denying and courageous man with an unshakable faith in Germany;

9. that, should I have a daughter, she shall grow into a healthy German woman fully cognizant of her duties toward Germany . . .

Napola K.! I spent three years with you. They were the best years of my life. You lent clear shape to my idealism. You taught me to believe in the eternal Reich of the Germans. You gave my life its direction. You became a second home to me. No one who was one of your cadets will ever be able to forget you. You enjoin everyone to hard and unremitting toil on Germany's behalf. The words "Believe, obey, fight!" have never left me. . . .

Your former cadet greets you, believing in victory and the perpetuity of the Reich.'[181]

Neither of the Reich's other two schools for the élite attained anything like the importance or status enjoyed by the National-Political Institutes of Education, for which Himmler took the precaution of reserving the title 'Reich Schools'. The National Socialist German Secondary School at Feldafing on the Starnberger See was founded in 1933 by SA chief of staff Ernst Röhm as a sort of cadet school for his Brownshirt army, its pupils being the sons of veteran SA men. The National Socialist Teachers' Association took it over in 1936 but was obliged to relinquish it to the Party during the war. Its main educational aims went without saying: ideological reliability and physical fitness. Its standard of education was, however, pitiable. It even proved difficult to find enough pupils, although their path to matriculation could not have been made easier. The final examinations consisted of essays on optional subjects and an oral test by members of the teaching staff. 15 of the 37 graduates in 1939 became officials in the Party service.

More ambitious were the Adolf Hitler Schools (AHS), the first of which was opened at Krössinsee in 1937 – once again on the Führer's birthday – by the Party's Director of Organization, Robert Ley, and Reich Youth Leader Baldur von Schirach. Having long sought to gain control of Rust's Napolas – vainly, because Rust favoured the SS – Ley proceeded to open his own élite academies with Hitler's blessing. The Minister of Education was taken aback, but Ley gleefully and rudely rejected Rust's attempts to trespass on his new preserve: 'The Adolf Hitler Schools are absolutely none of your business . . .'[182]

In December 1936 the Hitler Youth was declared the national youth organization and thus forfeited its role as a Party breeding-ground for the élite. It was intended that this loss should be more than offset by the establishment of special six-form boarding schools. Provided with curricula and teaching aids of their own, the AHS were expressly designed as leadership schools for the Party and Hitler Youth. Each Gau was supposed to have its own Adolf Hitler School, but the expense proved too big a drain on Party funds, and Party Treasurer Franz Xaver Schwarz jibbed. There was also a shortage of teaching staff, so the Hitler Youth maxim 'Youth must be led by youth' was applied even more radically than Party educationists found agreeable: the Jungzüge, or junior forms, were supervised by pupils from the more senior forms (Scharen). Only eleven Adolf Hitler Schools were in existence by 1942, and seven of them were accommodated in the Ordensburg at Sonthofen.

Gauleiters were responsible for the supervision of AHS and the appointment of teachers, also the selection of pupils, who were chosen from among the brightest twelve-year-olds in the local Young Folk. Although a smart bearing, athletic prowess and pure ancestry were again more important than scholastic achievement, it proved difficult to muster 600 suitable candidates in the first few years. Their fathers included a high proportion of tradesmen and shopkeepers, also white-collar workers. Two-thirds of the boys came from smallish communities and rural areas, and barely half had previously attended the equivalent of grammar school. These figures correspond with a fair degree of accuracy to the petty bourgeois and provincial lower middle class from which the Party's early supporters had been recruited, then moulded into a bloc. Even though free education in the Adolf Hitler Schools held a special attraction for such families, it is none the less remarkable that the budding Party and administrative élite should still have been drawn from the very class which helped the Nazi movement to victory. There were no reports or downgradings in the AHS, partly because the boys' previous schooling was too disparate to permit the imposition of satisfactory standards. Instead, class and school competitions were held in the course of a so-called 'performance week'. The inventors of the system preened themselves on educational innovations such as study syndicates, a comradely teacher–pupil relationship, and a new method of debate known as the Kampfgespräch or 'battle-discourse'. Here again the emphasis was on 'folklore', a new collective term covering the five ideological subjects, together with pre-military training and service within the community. The propaganda organ *Das Reich* boasted: 'The work schedule of the Adolf Hitler Schools hardly differs in appearance from a day's schedule in the Labour Service or armed forces. All that counts is the spirit that must permeate all soldierly convention and render it a matter of course.'[183]

Not even the leaving certificate awarded any marks for individual subjects. In 1942 the members of the first year's intake received their diplomas from the Reich Director of Youth Education in the NSDAP – another of Schirach's titles. Each certificate confirmed, by order of the Führer, that the graduate had been awarded the diploma. The criterion governing this singular testimonial was 'predominantly political, though this should be interpreted in comprehensive, human terms'.[184] Although AHS graduates were certified as being up to university standard, two-thirds of the first 230 obediently settled on a career in the Party.

For aspirants to this career, Director of Organization Ley had devised a dream-route which would help the Party to build up the élite it so badly needed. It already had more than 200,000 functionaries in 1935, but many of these were parvenus and petty careerists of varying respectability who wanted payment for services rendered and had been rewarded with an ingenious diversity of uniforms and titles. They certainly did not constitute an effective and smooth-running Party cadre of the sort required to handle the organization and improvement of the National Socialist super-State of the future. Ley consequently urged that, from now on, no political leader should be appointed to a Party or government post who had not passed through the 'school of the Movement' in its entirety.

This schooling was deemed to begin when the proven twelve-year-old Pimpf (member of the junior youth organization for boys) went to his AHS. At eighteen he received his diploma and did a spell in the Labour Service and armed forces. He could then study for a profession, marry and beget children. If his political reports were favourable, he was then, at the age of twenty-five, sent to a Party Ordensburg. After another four years, the most able Ordensjunker would be admitted to the 'High School', a monstrous Party university which Alfred Rosenberg was planning to erect on the shores of the Chiemsee. The High School barely got beyond the committee stage, like all Rosenberg's schemes, but Ley built his Ordensburgen. He wanted to turn NSDAP officials into *the* National Socialist élite Order, just as Himmler was determined to do with the SS.

In Pomerania (Krössinsee), Upper Bavaria (Sonthofen) and the Eifel (Vogelsang), three colossal and Teutonic-looking Nazi castles were grafted on to the inoffensive landscape. Each Ordensburg (literally 'castle of a knightly order') was to accommodate 1,000 Junker, or cadets. The qualifications required of applicants from the Party membership were modest in the extreme: they must be 25–30 years old and have practical experience of Party organization. 'Sound fellows' was how Ley, who undertook their selection in company with regional and district Party chiefs, chose to describe them. 'We aim to govern and take pleasure in governing, not so as to become despots or pay homage to a sadistic tyranny, but because it is our unshakable conviction that only one man can lead and one man bear the responsibility in all things.'[185] Ley had no need to ask more of his future leaders because the available places were hard enough to fill as it was. (According to some estimates, half of them remained vacant.) The Ordensjunker were of humble origin, most of them being the sons of Party officials, farmers and artisans. They were also of limited intelligence. Very few had matriculated and scarcely any had attended university, nor did three-and-a-half years at an Ordensburg greatly improve their education. Ordensburg graduates cannot have acquired many qualities of leadership either, or they would hardly have been ridiculed as 'golden pheasants' (a jibe at their brown uniforms) at home, in the Eastern territories and at the front.

Ideological education based on National Socialist principles functioned with notable success when, as at the Napolas, it was linked with military traditions and appealed to the pugnacious élitism of the young. In the hands of Party organizers like Ley and Party ideologists like Rosenberg, by contrast, it failed miserably. It became obvious that a purely Party career held few attractions for a bright boy or his parents, so there was an enforced lowering of standards. Although extolled as a token of National Socialist progress, the humble background of most Party students brought problems in its train. One is tempted to suspect that the Party leadership was less interested in well-educated and fervent National Socialists – in the 'self-fashioned god-man' whom Hitler proclaimed to be the educational objective of the Ordensburgen – than in well-drilled functionaries and docile executive agents. The martial spirit which genuinely pervaded the Napolas was more of a garnish or veneer at Party-run educational establishments.

Sparta was the title of the military-style manual used at the Adolf Hitler Schools, though its subtitle – true to the ideological view of history – told of the exemplary 'life-struggle of a Nordic race'. For all its discipline and good order, however, school life was not unmitigatedly Spartan. Shoe-cleaning, bed-making and room-sweeping – these chores the political soldier had to do for himself, but budding aspirants to the élite were served at their snowy dining-tables by a 'swarm of waitresses under the supervision of a steward'.[186] Even in 1942, at the height of the war, the Spartan life-style entailed a knowledge of which cutlery to use with which course and which glass went with which wine. The finer points of social etiquette were cultivated still more assiduously at the Ordensburgen. Senior Party officials had exalted social obligations to fulfil; therefore, they deserved to be suitably distinguished from the common herd. The 1,000 Junker at the Ordensburgen were attended by a staff of no less than 500, comprising instructors, cooks, porters, orderlies and other personnel.

The rules governing sex education were, on the face of it, strict: the problem of adolescence had to be solved by self-restraint. Albert Müller defined the attitude of the Reich Department of Youth Leadership as follows: 'It goes without saying that self-denial leads also to the outright rejection of sexual gratification.'[187] All that was necessary was to appeal to the 'positive forces' in boys and girls, to self-control, willpower and discipline. Should this method fail, however, an ideological net was spread to catch the transgressor. Any such cases were subject to a dictum enunciated by the old folkish prophet Julius Langbehn: 'To fall is no disgrace, only to remain lying.' This exonerated the girl – she had, after all, presented the nation with a child – and absolved the boy from petty extremes of self-discipline.

Besides, the call for asceticism was not taken too literally, even at the Reich Department of Youth Leadership. As late as 1944, Schirach's successor Arthur Axmann held parties at the RJF's Gatow guest-house which were noted for more than their Lucullan delicacies and alcoholic excesses. Fastidious Hitler Youth leaders supplemented the company of fun-loving BdM girls with that of film starlets whose personal charms were doubtless even greater. According to Melitta Maschmann, who once joined this circle as an idealistic young BdM leader, it consisted of 'a positively classic assortment of superficial dazzlers and approbation-seeking egoists'.[188] Somewhat more liberal standards were applied to the 'noble majority of young people' – another of Langbehn's phrases. Self-discipline was not to be confused with the 'pettifogging morality of yore', with the religiously tinged appeals for self-denial made by bourgeois society. 'Instead of being directed along natural channels, the healthy instincts stirring inside a young man are here condemned and described as vile. The result is that, unless his character is strong enough simply to rise above it, the young person joins battle with the hypothetical enemy inside himself and only too often lapses into aberrations which cannot be termed wholesome, still less normal. And all this because, instead of supporting natural development, people seek to warp it with an upbringing which is biologically absurd.'[189] That was how *Das Schwarze Korps* saw the problem. But the SS correspondent envisaged a far worse danger than intercourse between boys and girls. 'A clean and wholesome upbringing' should be directed primarily against homosexual and 'biologically absurd' aberrations. Educational work in the National Socialist State was sex-oriented, declared the writer, so care must be taken that it did not breed an undesirable 'arrogance towards the opposite sex'. The implication was that, as a soldier and warrior, the young man should joyfully acknowledge his sound instincts and practise self-control from 'a sense of duty to the folkish community' rather than from ethical and moral considerations.

Given that the folkish community aimed to combat the declining birth-rate, this was more of an invitation than a limitation. Before yielding to homosexual blandishments, therefore, the adolescent boy would do better – or so the 'sensible' National Socialist philosophy tacitly conceded – to practise a little sexual indiscipline in female company.

Baldur von Schirach applied this educational formula to the Hitler Youth. His policy was to establish 'harmless contacts'[190] between youths and girls, and he felt convinced that he had cured the Hitler Youth of the homosexual symptoms so often attributed to it. Comparison soon reveals that his method was inefficient and his confidence unfounded.

In 1934, when it was still empowered to cover shortcomings inside Party organizations, the Gestapo reported approximately 40 cases of suspected homosexual relations in the Hitlerjugend-Oberbann Aachen. The cases that came to the notice of the courts in 1941 were little different. Philipp E. from Mannheim-Käfertal, a thirty-one-year-old flying instructor who had for eight years belonged to the 80th Regiment of the National Socialist Flying Corps (NSFK), was sentenced to three years and three months' penal servitude for at least ten cases of homosexuality with student pilots of the Hitler Youth. In the same jurisdictional area, sixteen Hitler Youth members were denounced for violations of Paragraph 175. Proceedings were instituted at Munich against a twenty-year-old man named Anton A., who had been dismissed from the Hitler Youth in 1938 for indecent conduct and embezzlement. The NSFK at Augsburg nonetheless accepted A. and promoted him sergeant. He supervised work by members of the Hitler Youth gliding association and was eventually detailed to help with physical check-ups – a grievous temptation. He promptly fell from grace once more, but was not dismissed from the NSFK. The affair did not become public until some boys reported him to the authorities. At the district court in Mainz, Werner C. and Edgar I., a student teacher and student respectively, were sentenced to a total of four years seven months' penal servitude. As district youth leaders, they had committed twenty-eight proven acts of indecency with twenty boys at Hitler Youth and Young Folk camps where candidates were selected for admission to Adolf Hitler Schools.

These cases were only the tip of an iceberg, for few misdemeanours within the Party became public in later years and even fewer came to trial. It is indicative that two men like Schirach and Himmler should both have attached such importance to the pedagogic argument that homosexual dangers can be combated by bringing the sexes together. One a romantic idealist of upper-middle-class background and the other a fanatical petty bourgeois moralist, they coincided in their prejudices and problems – one of them being how to organize élite communities which would be proof against the homosexual liaisons that inevitably arose from their all-male composition.

Robert Ley did not indulge in such circuities. To someone who had run through four wives in quick succession, the problem was quite straightforward: a real man needs a woman. He duly declared, with the common touch so dear to him, that a National Socialist cadet should stand with his feet firmly planted in the midst of life, not languish in 'monastic seclusion from the world . . . That is why I am particularly keen for these men to remain in constant touch with their environment, also with the opposite sex. I therefore recommend, wherever possible, that they should preferably be married when they come to the Ordensburg.'[191] It was a sign of diffidence and indecision, he added coaxingly, if a man of twenty-five was still unmarried. Ley's mask of bluff sincerity almost concealed his underlying interest in population growth. There were, after all, a few intermediate stages between 'preferably married' and 'in touch with the opposite sex'.

But the real author of all such part-concessions and semi-invitations was – yet again – Adolf Hitler. His dream-nation required flawless youths for fabulously beautiful maidens. The National Socialist movement was to bring the two together by fostering 'mutual esteem'. Lecturing Party officials at the Vogelsang Ordensburg in 1937, the Führer said: 'The Movement must not allow itself to be somehow dissuaded by those who suddenly invoke morality in opposing such a natural and wholesome delight in existence. We must build a nation healthy to the core, robust in its menfolk and absolutely feminine in its women; that is our aim.'[192] Hitler waxed even more explicit in private conversation.[193] Uninhibited by moral qualms, he expounded his ideas freely: a rigorous upbringing – for that alone could produce the type of warrior he needed – was impracticable unless one provided it with the safety-valve known as a 'wholesome delight in existence'. As he explained to his table-companions, only the man who was permitted to love unreservedly would be ready to die unquestioningly. 'Love and war go together, after all. The whining philistine can think himself lucky to get what's left over.'[194] All that remained of woman, the female of the species, was her sexual function. Her education was designed accordingly.

Paddocks for pedigree cows

If women existed solely to be mothers or objects of unreserved love for unquestioning warriors – and even official pronouncements demanded little more of them than that – there was no need to lavish any special care on their academic training when young. Minister of the Interior Wilhelm Frick, who was also responsible for educational policy during the first year of the 'new era', defined the utilization of the female sex in the Third Reich as follows: 'The mother shall be enabled to devote herself exclusively to her children and family, the wife to her husband, and the unmarried girl shall be assigned only to those occupations which suit the feminine disposition.'[195] This clearly established the female pecking-order and sequence of development. The girl had to serve the nation by working for it, the wife her husband by obeying him, the mother her children by caring for them.

Girls' education was geared to these requirements. Friederike Matthias, an official in the Reich department for secondary schools, explained its basic principles: 'The prerequisite for future mothers of the nation must be sound physical training during their girlhood. The undue accumulation of academic knowledge must be curtailed in favour of a girl's healthy growth. This can be effected by biological instruction, gymnastics, athletics and walking tours – all subject to close liaison between the school and the BdM.'[196] Steps were promptly taken to introduce sound measures of educational reform.

Demolition began at the top. The quota for female students was fixed at 10 per cent. Their numbers, which had been rising steadily for two decades, fell 50 per cent by 1936. Higher education for girls was not only unfeminine but a wasted investment. According to Elisabeth Lenz of the Reich department for primary schools, the 'supreme intellectual capacity' required of a woman found supreme expression in the so-called mental attributes 'perception and wisdom'. She had no need to add that, in a woman, intellectualism was unwholesome and misguided. It was obvious. No woman required academic instruction to mother healthy German males. Accordingly, only two of the forty-two exclusive Napolas – Hubertendorf/Türnitz and Colmar-Berg – were allocated to girls, and these were former girls' colleges which could not immediately be converted for use by male pupils. No girls were admitted to the Adolf Hitler Schools.

The bewildering multiplicity of the school system under the Weimar Republic had offered girls no less than ten different routes to a higher education. Since all of them – to quote Nazi educationist Franz Kade[197] – were modelled on boys' schools, however, the result had been a suppression of 'natural femininity' and 'belittlement of womanhood and motherhood'. There was now to be a unification and accentuation of 'what makes a woman a woman'. Girls received special lessons in handicrafts, biology and gymnastics which would satisfy 'the elementary requirements of female education'.

The same subjects were given prominence at the new unified secondary schools for girls. Fifth-formers could choose whether they wanted to perfect their linguistic training or their housewifely skills. Those who decided on domestic science could also qualify to study at university, so many girls opted for what was popularly known as 'pudding matriculation'.

Logically enough, this anti-intellectual bias was even more pronounced at primary school level. 'Superfluous' subjects were drastically pruned. 'It is sufficient for a girl to be familiarized with her immediate environment. Natural history, too, contains much material which can only retard a girl. Let everything be so arranged as to create scope and opportunity for rousing her to an adequate awareness of the meaning and purpose of her own and her nation's existence. Physical culture, care of the body and hygiene, social work, the theory of heredity, ethnology and genealogy, etc., are the subjects which should entirely occupy natural history lessons in the final school-year . . .'[198] On that basis, girls at primary school were to be taught only what lay between the poles of bed and bath, hearth and home, and could be put to immediate practical use by those whose literacy was minimal.

Of course, there were plenty of female Nazi zealots who wanted to extend the idea of political soldiership and pre-military training to the education of girls. One such was Ilse Gadow, who urged that a soldierly outlook and folkish spirit of military preparedness be fostered by instruction in practical and theoretical aspects of military science. The form of military instruction which she advocated in the periodical *Deutsche Volkserziehung* (1937) set itself three tasks. First, girls must have a full and complete grasp of the nation's military requirements and the need for military training, or they would not, if the worst came to the worst, be equipped to lend moral support at home to the fighting men at the front. Secondly, they must learn map-reading, fieldcraft, directional hearing, judgement of distances and similar para-military skills so as to be able to appreciate the front-line soldier's achievements. Finally, women must be trained to take the place of men in the armaments industry in case of emergency, i.e. in the event of their utilization in war.

Whatever the ideological perception and practical wisdom of this sabre-rattling contribution to educational theory, its author was wide of the mark in two respects. In the first place, she disregarded Hitler's official peace policy, which, coupled with his boundless overestimation of German military strength, meant that the economic resources of the Reich were not focused on war requirements until a very late stage. The employment of women in munitions factories was still unthinkable in 1937. It would have been a grave violation of Hitler's avowal that he never proposed to tolerate a women's battalion in Germany.

In the second place, Ilse Gadow's recommendations conflicted with the principle that woman's supreme intellectual capacity should be developed exclusively for the requirements of hearth and home. Physical education for girls was not intended as a form of pre-military training. Indian clubs were swung and girlish knees flexed in pre-paration for the childbed, not the fox-hole.

In 1934, girls were jointly called upon to do a 'Domestic Service Year' by the National Socialist Women's Association, the German

Women's Service, the Department of Youth Leadership and the Reich Bureau of Employment and Unemployment Insurance. The reason was quite simple. 625,000 girls left school at Easter of that year and the overburdened labour market could not absorb them. They were therefore requested in the name of duty and patriotism to work for their keep in other people's homes. This, it was said, would help to train them for their domestic and maternal obligations in years to come.

Plenty of ideological justifications were produced, no matter how absurd. Hedwig Förster, Director of Studies at the Reich Ministry of Education, impressed on teachers and pupils alike that it was far from immaterial whether or not a fish was cooked à la National Socialist. Home ties and service to the nation, a feeling for political economy and family care – these were what endowed every domestic activity with its 'scope and dedication'[199] – and, presumably, every lump of cod with its correct ideological flavour.

The success of the campaign was predictably meagre. Four years later this voluntary form of national service became obligatory. Hermann Göring, who was in charge of the Four-Year Plan, ordained a 'Compulsory Domestic Service Year'. Secondary school-leavers did not receive their certificates and primary school-leavers their record books until they had submitted proof of such service.

These coercive measures brought public resentment to a head. The girls were officially supposed to ease the burdens of large families and farmers' wives by acting as unpaid help, their keep being subsidized by tax concessions. Parents were understandably reluctant to see their daughters exploited in this way, but Party authorities sought to appease them by lauding the compulsory year's service as an educational measure: 'A practical continuation of domestic life as it is known to the girl school-leaver from experience of her own home, and – as doctors repeatedly affirm – a proper aid to physical and mental development. The young child, with its increasing responsibilities, grows involuntarily into adult life. A wholesome ambition to do well in a strange family and a consequent increase in conscientiousness sharpen its faculties, enhance its power of decision and perseverance at work – qualities which are of such value to occupational training at a later stage!'[200] In these untypically dulcet and humanitarian tones, the Völkischer Beobachter confirmed that the scheme was a flop.

It could hardly have succeeded in the teeth of parental opposition. Mothers – especially better-class mothers – strove to place their daughters with relatives, acquaintances or friends. Reich Women's

Leader Gertrud Scholtz-Klink raised an indignant cry at the Nuremberg
Party Rally in 1938: 'One thing must be said to certain mothers: If
your daughter wishes, or is obliged, to tread this path, do not stand in
her way armed with views which reflect credit neither on you nor on
your daughter, and which take the form of a newspaper advertisement:
"Position required for my daughter's compulsory year's service.
Requirements: central heating, hot running water, no children!"'[201]
Alas, mothers continued to seek out billets with central heating and
hot water, and many of them contrived to arrange things so that all
their daughters had to do was a little baby-sitting and washing-up. The
favourite trick was to swap daughters among friends. The real victims
were those who lacked the ingenuity or connections to engage in such
manoeuvres, e.g. daughters of the poor, overburdened or rural families
who were the intended beneficiaries of the scheme.

The whole operation, like all well-meant educational measures introduced by the National Socialist government, was a failure despite its
admixture of idealism. The domestic training of girls never went
beyond classes devoted to oven-cloth crocheting and plain needlework.
Opportunities for intellectual advancement dwindled and academic
standards dropped. Neither integral calculus nor household budgeting
was considered important to a girl, for what did a German male expect
from a German female? Richard Walther Darré, the expert on human
livestock, made that clear in the SS Calendar: 'A young man of good
stock, whose mind is uncontaminated by vulgar music-hall ideas,
possesses an innate understanding of what the opposite sex of his species
is there for, and can take disinterested pleasure in a well-developed and
racially pure girl, mindful of her value as a future mother of children
with well-formed minds and limbs . . .'[202]

The more strictly a woman's function in the National Socialist State
was ideologically limited to her biological contribution, the more
loudly Hitler extolled her vast store of political intuition. 'When I
returned from gaol after thirteen months' imprisonment to find the
Party in ruins,' he flatteringly informed a Women's Association audience at the 1935 Nuremberg Rally, 'it was mainly the Party's women
members who sustained the Movement. Instead of weighing the odds
in a prudent and rational manner, they followed the dictates of their
hearts and have stood by me, emotionally speaking, to this day.' This
heart-warming tribute also formed the motto on the official Women's
Association programme for 1937, where it helped to conceal that the
political influence wielded by this body of women was precisely nil.

Its sole purpose was to school members in specifically feminine tasks, from baby care to the use of substitute foodstuffs.

It had not always been so. The first local women's groups were highly welcome to the Party, not only as welfare workers but also as effective propaganda teams. Elsbeth Zander had established the Order of German Women for 'women and girls of German blood' aged eighteen and over. Younger girls from fourteen upwards were commanded by older 'sisters of the Order' and nurtured in German mores and patriotism. On the occasion of the first Party Congress at Weimar in 1926, Hitler gave the Order of German Women his blessing as an auxiliary service of the NSDAP. Its terms of reference were: 'The Order undertakes to withdraw women from the turmoil of party politics so as to employ their energies in the social domain; it must nevertheless acquaint itself with major political questions and, above all, be familiar with the laws which radically affect the family.'[203] In addition, there were the 'joint associations of folkish-minded women' and the local women's groups attached to the Party. These were dissolved in July 1931, to be followed into limbo three months later by the Order of German Women itself. It was a significant development, and one which clearly showed that independent women's associations were no longer tolerated in a man's world. The newly founded National Socialist Women's Association was subordinated to Party Headquarters.

The Movement's growing success boosted masculine self-confidence to such an extent that a firmer line was gradually adopted. The social energies of woman were less in demand now; her role as guardian of the race was considerably more important, so the great process of political orientation had become superfluous. *Nationalsozialistische Monatshefte* declared as early as 1930 that feminine involvement of this kind was 'an unedifying manifestation of the liberalistic age . . . In our belief, it is the very masculinity of National Socialism which will most intimately appeal to every genuine woman, for only this will enable her to become a complete woman once more'.[204] The words were hot air but their intention was plain. In March 1935, the law securing the unity of Party and State provided a chance to make the Women's Association a limb of the Party once and for all, and also to neutralize the last faint aspirations to an autonomous women's movement inside the National Socialist system. Speaking at the Party ('Freedom') Rally in 1935, Hitler gave a clearer picture of the benefits accruing to women from the masculinity of National Socialism: 'The reward which

National Socialism bestows on women in return for her labour is that it once more rears men, real men, decent men who stand erect, who are courageous, who love honour. I believe that, having watched the marching columns of the last few days, these stalwart and splendid youngsters from the Labour Service, our healthy and unspoiled women-folk must say to themselves: What a robust and glorious generation is growing up here!'[205] This ill-disguised commendation of human stallions to fecund females was hailed by the assembled women with orgasmic jubilation.

The functions of the Women's Association were nonetheless restric-ted to welfare work of a trivial nature. Members could not even bring up their own offspring because girls were drafted into the BdM and thus controlled by the Hitler Youth. The Women's Association held maternity courses for 1.7 million women in 1937–38. Over the same period, courses in domestic science acquainted 472,000 women with ideologically correct and economically permissible recipes and cleaning methods. The Women's Association also introduced classes for future brides, derisively nicknamed 'erotic handicraft lessons'. The Women's Auxiliary Service, Neighbourhood Assistance and Women's Voluntary Aid Service – all these welfare organizations helped to develop and strengthen what was peculiar to womanhood. The Führer paid his zealous Reich Women's Leader the following tribute in a speech at the Party Rally of 1937, whose theme was 'Labour': 'The start you have made – and this I can say to you, Party Comrade Scholtz-Klink – is the right one. So far from creating a counterpart to man by the organiza-tion of woman, you have ensured with truly remarkable success that organized German womanhood has become a complement to the male fighting organization.'[206]

Even this modest assignment of role embodied a latent exaggeration. The Women's Association was not complementary to the male fighting organization. Rather, it was a gigantically distended ladies' sewing-circle calculated to exclude women completely from the political struggle and banish them to the realm of bed and board. It was living institutional proof of the condescension – or rather, disdain – with which National Socialism regarded the creatures it dismissed as house-keepers and bearers of children. The programme of the Women's Association contained no reference to female education, a staple demand of the former women's organizations which had been 'incor-porated' in it. Even ideological guidance was unusually lax in this mammoth organization, less than one-third of whose members belonged to the Party. In a country where ideological permeation of the entire national community was writ large on the régime's runic banner, this figure was highly informative. The term 'master race' was to be taken literally: women served only to procreate and wait upon their masters.

Compliant and credulous though they were, the leaders of the Women's Association inevitably lost some of their enthusiasm. In vain they waited for their Führer to entrust them with a political mission, a major executive function. Instead, he spun them his yarn about the great joint assignment which was, 'in the last analysis, nothing less than the perpetuation of the human community'[207] – in other words, biological reproduction. They had no choice but to be good wives and diligent mothers.

The Women's Association was only a loose framework designed to contain outbursts of excessive zeal – a paddock for pedigree cows. Since grown women could not be re-educated, it sufficed to circumscribe their activities. What was far more essential was to gain control of the younger generation and imprint it with the required behaviour patterns. School was one means to that end; the second and more important was the Hitler Youth.

Youth is always right

Baldur von Schirach declared war on 'mothers' darlings' in the name of the 'German Young Folk'. It was clear that any right-minded Pimpf already regarded such boys as pretty poor specimens, but the Reich Youth Leader's spirited call to arms was a major advance on this natural boyish attitude. Schirach proclaimed the Young Folk's contempt for 'what are commonly called children'. His members were boys, not children. ' "Children" is the term we apply to those non-uniformed creatures of junior age-group who have yet to attend an evening assembly or a parade.'[208] For a fluent speaker who was distinguishing himself as the poet of the new era, albeit more by verve than talent, this was a significant choice of words. It meant that these non-uniformed creatures, alias children, were at an almost pre-human stage of development which had to be surmounted as swiftly as possible.

In fact, the Party planned to 'incorporate' all boys and girls by the age of six, at latest, in children's groups affiliated to the Women's Association. Here, even before their intellects had properly awakened, togetherness and regimentation were to squeeze them into the strait-jacket of the national community: 'Children will wear uniform play-clothing of regional character.'[209] However, the peaceful phase of the Thousand-Year Reich proved too brief to allow the plan for a 'German Children's Troop' to be put into effect. The Women's Association lacked sufficient leaders, so children at primary school had to wait impatiently until their tenth birthday entitled them to the coveted uniform and fluttering pennant, the glamorous excursions and solemn evening assemblies. Nevertheless, the future pattern was set: childhood was sanctioned only until the age of literacy. After that, uniform transformed the indeterminate being into a German. Hitler had taught that young people could not be trained too early in a proper sense of nationhood.

The organization of this venture was entrusted to Baldur von Schirach and the Hitler Youth. Like his Führer and his colleague Reichsleiter Ley, the Reich Youth Leader made it quite clear that no one had any further claim to a private life: 'The rearing of young people is an inalienable sovereign right of the State. The aim of State youth education is the systematic development of the unmindful youngster into a mindful citizen of the State and upholder of its principles.'[210] Pursued to its logical conclusion, this system entailed a direct transition from the infant's nursery to the State youth organizations. The role of parents was thus reduced to their unavoidable biological function and that of schools to providing equally unavoidable courses of instruction in the alphabet and twice-times table.

The new masters implemented their plans without delay. When the Party assumed power in 1933, its Hitler Youth organization was already under the command of Schirach, a twenty-five-year-old student who belonged to the Party's general staff in his capacity as Reich Youth Leader of the NSDAP. He was the originator of the hard-hitting slogan 'Youth must be led by youth'. In October 1932, when the Movement badly needed a fillip after some stinging reverses, Schirach took advantage of the 'Reich Day of Youth' to gratify his Führer with an ovation from 100,000 rapturous youngsters who had been transported to Potsdam from all over the country. 'You are the nation-to-be,' Hitler emphasized yet again. 'On you depends the consummation of what we are now fighting for.'[211]

He meant it. As leader of the Party he was having to carry through his revolution with the aid of mass-sufferers from a variety of liberal and individualistic notions, but as leader of the Reich he planned to erect his Greater German national community on the shoulders and self-sacrifice of a blindly credulous younger generation – *his* younger generation.

After the seizure of power, rival youth organizations were methodically disbanded, smashed, taken over or absorbed. Schirach, who was appointed Youth Leader of the Reich on 17 June 1933, set to work with all the vigour and ruthlessness of a man who believed implicitly in Hitler. His faith was further rewarded when, on 1 December 1936, he was given the status of a Supreme Reich Authority and commissioned to incorporate all young Germans on Reich territory in the Hitler Youth. Paragraph 2 of the 'Law Relating to the Hitler Youth' stipulated that 'All young Germans in the Reich area are, except in the parental home and at school, to be physically, mentally and morally reared in the spirit of National Socialism for service to the nation and the national community in the Hitler Youth.'[212] 5.4 million young people had already joined the Hitler Youth by that time, though it is hard to say what decided them in favour of entry – the romantic appeal inherent in any youth movement or the pressure exerted on those who remained unorganized.

The theatrical upgrading of the younger generation continued. 'You are Greater Germany!' Hitler assured a youthful audience in Berlin's Olympic Stadium on 1 May 1939. 'In you, the German national community is taking shape!'[213] In March 1939, all young Germans between the ages of 10 and 18 were finally conscripted for service in the Hitler Youth, which was declared a form of 'honorary service to the German nation'. This did not sound like pre-military training – it smacked of war and was meant to.

As a State youth organization, the Hitler Youth clashed with parents and schools from the outset and did so even more as time wore on. There was something different, and not merely bigger, involved here than the old generation gap which was a legacy of the early twentieth-century German Youth Movement. Although this conflict was certainly aggravated by the 'youth leads youth' principle, it derived quite another emphasis from the authority which the State – a totalitarian State – delegated to youthful HJ leaders.

Boys and girls were compelled to join the Hitler Youth. Their keenness and enthusiasm for a youth-oriented way of life which was apparently free and progressive enabled them, with equal alacrity, to swallow the precepts and slogans that were fed them between sing-songs and sessions round the camp fire. Back home, they proceeded to retail these doctrines to their parents, many of whom were uncommitted, non-committal or secretly opposed. The trust between parents and children was severely disrupted. For many fathers and mothers, caution and silence replaced candour and guidance as the twin commandments of family life.

The Third Reich's theory of political education was ultimately crowned with success. Parents no longer ventured to speak openly in front of their children. The war years brought a growing incidence of cases in which sons or daughters reported their own parents to the authorities for making defeatist remarks, and denunciation by children became one of Nazism's most shocking by-products.

Even greater difficulties beset the educational function of schools. Their adjustment to National Socialism was inevitably hampered by the attitude of older teachers, whose predominantly conservative outlook was such that they withstood re-educational pressure from the National Socialist Teachers' Association and were regarded with due suspicion. Secondary schools, in particular, remained noticeably unresponsive to the wind of change.

However, recalcitrant teachers found themselves confronted by class-rooms full of boys and girls who were exposed to the true ideological gospel during their service in the Hitler Youth. Boys assessed themselves by the part they played in their HJ units, where industry and academic achievement counted for nothing beside dash, daring and obedience, where intelligence was unimportant compared with what it took to be a 'stout fellow'. Stout fellows were put in charge of sections, platoons or companies.

All HJ and BdM leaders claimed authority. How could a teacher deal with such pupils when they performed badly in school, often because they were overburdened with official duties? Baldur von Schirach recommended that they be treated with particular 'tact'. They were pupils like the rest, true, but they were also leaders whose authority should not be 'needlessly' diminished in front of their classmates: 'Should a remark against the HJ be actually uttered in the heat of the moment, the trust between pupils and teaching staff will be impaired and not easily restored. But the more a teacher himself tries to enter into the spirit and code of the HJ, the greater his success.'[214]

In other words, teachers had to subordinate themselves to the Hitler Youth. Many did so, among them Lisl Schmid, who thought it dangerous to give young people a completely free hand during their spare time: 'My approach to the subject of schoolmistress and Hitler-girls would be incomplete if I did not additionally bear in mind the leader-teacher. I myself am one, having built up the Young Folk organization in Munich's Central District from a nucleus of ten girls. So I think I am entitled to tell you something about the schoolmistress as a leader, especially when I add that, apart from my job, I am active as a leader every spare hour I have, every afternoon and Sunday off – indeed, almost throughout my holidays. The private individual has ceased to exist – he is dead and buried. Thank God, I feel healthy into the bargain.'[215] Healthy enough, certainly, to play cops and robbers, sleep in dormitories, draw rations from a field kitchen and march 'to attention' with her girls for as far as an ageing pair of legs would carry her.

But too many teachers had yet to grasp the beauties of their educational mission. Too many pedants, as Schirach called them, stood aloof from the new era and failed to recognize that youth 'is, in a higher sense, always right'.[216] Effusions of this kind received support from the highest quarter. Hitler, who had never got over his poor showing at school, grabbed the opportunity to revenge himself for personal failure on the teaching profession as a whole. This not only constituted a threat to teachers who resisted ideological adjustment but helped the Hitler Youth to establish an ascendancy over schools.

In June 1934 the Reich Department of Youth Leadership scored what was, on the face of it, a signal success. By arrangement with the Reich Ministry of Education, it established a 'State Day of Youth'. On Saturdays, HJ members were excused school so that they could serve the nation in their brown-and-black uniforms. Other pupils devoted these hours to 'national-political instruction'. At the same time, Wednesday was officially declared the day for HJ evening assembly.

The scheme was a sorry failure. The Hitler Youth did not have enough leaders to cope with the Saturday rush. As a result, many boys and girls remained at a loose end, marring the neat week-end spectacle of marching columns. In December 1936 the ruling was lifted and the HJ simultaneously declared the national youth movement. Two free afternoons were now set aside for HJ service, but the semi-free Saturday had exercised a considerable effect. 60 per cent of all young people were already in the Hitler Youth. Many schoolchildren had joined because they preferred the prospect of outdoor fun and games in the HJ to national-political instruction in school. Besides, they were treated as 'chaps' instead of children.

The temptation was strong. The Reich Youth Leader confirmed to ten-year-olds when they joined the German Young Folk (DJ) that their childhood was over and that they now belonged to the country's youth. Henceforward, they were to labour for Germany's future and the beloved Führer to whom 'we belong, today, tomorrow, and for ever'.[217]

Children spent four years in the Young Folk and were 'transferred' to the HJ proper at fourteen. Their career began with the Pimpfen-probe, or test in which candidates for compulsory service had to satisfy certain minimum requirements in the sphere of athletics and ideology. These included running 60 metres in 12 seconds, long-jumping 2.75 metres, throwing the soft-ball 25 metres, taking part in a 36-hour hike, and knowing the words of the *Horst Wessel* and *Hitler Youth Flag* songs. Pithy slogans were also declaimed, e.g. 'Young Folk boys are tough, silent and loyal. Young Folk boys are comrades. To Young Folk boys, honour is supreme.' Whatever these sentiments may or may not have meant to a ten-year-old, service in the Young Folk endowed form with content.

Training in the Hitler Youth included athletics, para-military physical training, and indoctrination. Evening assemblies, excursions and camping supplied an emotional façade which the régime fostered by all available means. This was one of its motives for gaining prompt control of the radio. Every Wednesday at 8.15 p.m. Schirach's department broadcast a programme entitled *Hour of the Young Nation* to coincide with HJ evening assembly. It consisted mainly of radio plays based on incidents from the nation's great historic past, their aim being to instil love of heroism and contempt for weakness. The Department of Youth Leadership also employed visual training aids. There were 2,500 projectors in Hitler Youth hostels by the end of 1938, and 5,000 film-strips were distributed monthly. Explanatory texts were supplied so that even HJ leaders of limited intelligence could deliver stirringly patriotic lectures at their evening meetings. Titles included *The Healthy Family*, *The Healthy Nation*, *Hereditarily Diseased Offspring*, *5,000 Years of Germanic Civilization*, *The Vanquishing of Versailles*, and *From the Old Army to the New*.

Schirach could stoop to almost any absurdity when singing the praises of his system: 'Through the hostel, young people render themselves independent of the public house and, thus, free from alcohol and nicotine.'[218] But hostel activities could be irksome to growing boys and girls. All too soon, the monotonous proceedings began to smack of duty alone. The official evening assembly programme prescribed that communal songs should be sung, the training theme of the day discoursed on, and *Hour of the Young Nation* listened to. Young Folk boys of the ten-to-fourteen age-group were still susceptible to such ritual, but signs of boredom soon manifested themselves among older members of the Hitler Youth. There was a shortage of leaders able enough to command the respect of their peers. Devotion to duty crumbled under the onset of teen-age problems and outside interests. Adolescents found it unappealing to play at being 'stout fellows' in the Hitler Youth at the age of seventeen or eighteen. They disguised themselves – Schirach's word – as adults and felt more manly in the smoke-filled tavern than they did in the aseptic atmosphere of the HJ hostel. The teen-age gangs of the period were a symptom of this revulsion.

Camp life, proclaimed the Reich Youth Leader, was the ideal form of youthful existence. Why? Because boys and girls could be more closely supervised than they were during brief week-end excursions or walking tours which inevitably suffered from improvisation and a relaxation of the requisite soldierly discipline. Young people were attracted by the romantic façade of tents and open-air cooking, field sports and camp fires, which camouflaged the military nature of life under canvas. There was a daily programme of gymnastics, athletics and sport, ideological instruction, and sing-songs and chants designed to promote esprit de corps. A typical day looked like this:

> 5.45 a.m. – Reveille
> 7.00 a.m. – Hoisting the Colours
> 7.30–8.30 a.m. – Ideological Instruction
> 8.30–9.30 a.m. – Sport
> 9.30–10.30 a.m. – Medical Training
> 10.30–11.45 a.m. – Camp Administration
> 12 noon – Lunch, Rest Period
> 2–3.30 p.m. – Evening Assembly Activities
> 3.30–5.30 p.m. – Field Work
> 5.30–6.30 p.m. – Free Time
> 6.30 p.m. – Evening Parade, Lowering the Colours
> 7.00 p.m. – Supper
> 7.30–9 p.m. – Camp Fire
> 9.30 p.m. – Lights Out

Scenic beauties and crackling camp fires notwithstanding, this was no life for happy wanderers, vagabonds and romantics. Roughly twelve hours on duty, eight hours' sleep and four hours off: such was Hitler's avowed method of eradicating weakness in the young – a process of attrition to which Schirach, who called it 'youth's loveliest dream' and 'the unforgettable experience of a lifetime',[219] subjected every member of the Hitler Youth for three long weeks.

The concentrated courses held at the thirty Hitler Youth leadership schools also lasted three weeks. Ideological instruction (38 hours) was confined to ethnology and population policy, to the older Germanic and more recent National Socialist history of Germany ('Two thousand years of German vigilance against Asia'), and to current political themes such as 'Nations fight for Lebensraum'.[220] HJ leaders were expected to communicate such gems of knowledge to their boys and girls at evening assemblies, ceremonies and celebrations organized on appropriate lines. They had also to be in peak physical condition, so 48 hours were devoted to physical training and field sports.

In addition to classes in writing and 'Pronunciation', the heading 'Miscellaneous' in the training schedule concealed an item entitled 'Small-bore Shooting'. This was not to be construed as military training, Schirach emphasized, because National Socialism was rearing its young people to help in the pursuit of Adolf Hitler's peace policy. Rather, it was a logical component of the soldierly attitude which manifested the Führer's desire for peace.

In 1938, which the HJ officially christened the 'Year of Understanding', the organization possessed over 15,000 rifles and as many instructors whose job it was to train 1.25 million young people to become peacefully proficient in the use of fire-arms. Next year the HJ added a marksman's badge to its awards for shooting. Specialized branches such as the Motor Transport, Air, Naval and Signals Hitler Youth had been established earlier on. These élite formations, whose members could acquire qualifications as useful as a driver's licence and study subjects as interesting as radio engineering, were naturally more attractive to older boys than monotonous service in the 'General' Hitler Youth. Their courses were also of interest to the armed forces and Waffen-SS, who gladly supported the training of potential recruits and aided 'their' HJ units by supplying equipment and instructors.

'He who swears on the Führer's flag has nothing more to call his own!'[221] Any youngster whose ears had been assailed throughout his eight years in the Young Folk and HJ by ritual chants of this kind, by catchwords such as Führer and allegiance, courage and obedience, honour and blood, national loyalty and racial superiority, was deemed to have undergone sufficient preparation to hazard his life for the Führer and future of his nation, armed in mind and body. The aim of

National Socialist education was neither more nor less than this. The confusions, contradictions and inhumanities of such an ideology could not, and were not meant to, penetrate young minds which had been systematically warped. Its very irrationality helped to commend it to impressionable youngsters because any misgivings were neutralized by their obligatory devotion to Fatherland and Führer.

The more the regimentation of youth progressed, the surer its prospects of success seemed to become. The Hitler Youth, a coercive organization, was acclaimed as a preliminary consummation of the true national community. Speaking at Marienburg castle, that tradition-steeped symbol of Teutonic sallies into the East, Baldur von Schirach joyfully declared in April 1938: 'All are equal under the banner of the Hitler Youth. All boys and girls are clad in our uniform so that no amount of money can embellish or enhance it. It is due in no small measure to these uniforms that Germany has acquired a new social order.'[222] The naïvety of this distortion is staggering. The compulsory uniform of the State youth organization was stylized into evidence of a National 'Socialist' uniformity of outlook transcending all class barriers.

Short black trousers, grey stockings, Bundschuhe (stout shoes with leather ankle-straps) and military hair-cuts for boys, dark-blue pleated skirts, white blouses and socks, chaplet hair-style and plaits for girls – this not inexpensive HJ order of dress became the everyday garb of many children. Parents of slender means had no choice but to obey the official call for 'practical and durable clothing'[223] in this way. Far from being evidence of a new social order, however, it merely exemplified the totalitarian trend towards complete regimentation of all citizens – children, schoolchildren and adolescents included.

Your body belongs to the nation

Like boys, girl-members of the Hitler Youth were intended to be reared in a folkish sense of duty and National Socialist self-sacrifice. When the new era dawned in 1933, Paula Siber of the Women's Section at Frick's Ministry of the Interior painted this goal in glowing colours: 'A generation of young women must grow up with joy in its heart, so that from this joy it may derive the strength to make lifelong sacrifices from a natural sense of duty.'[224] The emphasis on joy almost concealed the fact that a lifetime of self-sacrifice can be a rather lugubrious business.

Self-sacrifice began when the girls had to subordinate the development of their own personalities to other objectives. Trude Bürkner, who was responsible for educational work in the BdM at the Reich Department of Youth Leadership, revealed with merciless candour the distinction which 'total education' drew between boys and girls.[225] The principles of service, regimentation, discipline and obedience applied to both sexes. In the case of boys, however, a personality was moulded – the warrior personality – whereas the education of girls merely shaped 'the face of the family of tomorrow'. Addressing the Berlin youth rally of 1 May 1936, the Führer reduced this to the following formula: 'And you of the BdM, train me girls so that they become strong and courageous women!'

The man in the street had nicknames for the functions of the girls' organization which compensated in clarity and relevance for what they lacked in reverence. *Bald deutsche Mütter* (German mothers-to-be), *Bubi drück mich* (Squeeze me, Sonny), *Bedarfsartikel deutscher Männer* (Requisites for German males), *Brauch deutsche Mädchen* (Make use of German girls), and *Bund deutscher Milchkühe* (League of German milch-cows) – such were a few popular interpretations of the initials BdM. They were also turned to good use in family squabbles because they enabled the diminutive Pimpf to assert his male superiority over elder sisters.

By 1937, the largest girls' organization in the world numbered almost three million. Its task was to rear representatives of the National Socialist ideology in the Reich Youth Leader's preferred mould – in other words, one which excluded parliamentary orators and intellectual bluestockings. At first glance, its educational curriculum resembled that of the male species of Hitler Youth: German history, global politics from the National Socialist viewpoint, the Party programme, ethnology and the law of heredity. The co-ordination of BdM with HJ extended from its mode of organization to its activities, which included regular evening meetings, excursions and spells in camp. Some fanatical BdM leaders also tried to match the boys at route-marching and field sports. The curious toughening-up system was a spur to such ambitions. A ten-year-old girl had to sprint 60 metres in 14 seconds, long-jump 2 metres and throw the soft-ball 12 metres, also perform two somersaults forwards and two backwards. She had then passed the Jungmädel test and was entitled to wear the neckerchief and 'woggle'. The strong and courageous woman of future years had to demonstrate her courage, agility and alertness in a physical manner, by throwing the soft-ball at a target and performing a flying forward roll,

marching cross-country armed with ordnance survey map and jumping
into cold water from a height of 3 metres. This qualified a German
'Mädel' for the BdM's bronze proficiency badge.

There was no drill – officially, though this too depended on the
'leader personality' in charge. Melitta Maschmann describes her own
subdistrict leader, Johanna, as an exception to the general run of BdM
leaders, with their distressingly uncouth manners. But even Johanna
knew how to apply ideological instruction in practice. 'She sometimes
marched us down the Kurfürstendamm in threes and doubled us part
of the way. We had to stamp our feet as loudly as we could. "The
rich Jews live here," she used to say. "No harm in disturbing their
afternoon nap a little." '226 This early, militant, conception of BdM
service became less common in later years but was no rarity. The
BdM suffered from a shortage of suitable leaders, like the whole of
the Hitler Youth. Just as the ban on drill was half-hearted, so the
words of command and whistle-signals in the BdM were muted but
strident enough to irritate that connoisseur of feminine charm, Goebbels,
in his more reflective moments. 'I certainly don't object to girls taking
part in gymnastics or sport within reasonable limits,' he confided to
Wilfred von Oven, one of his departmental chiefs. 'But why should a
future mother go route-marching with a pack on her back? She should
be healthy and vigorous, graceful and easy on the eye. Sensible physical
exercise can help her to become so, but she shouldn't have knots of
muscle on her arms and legs and a step like a grenadier. Anyway, I
won't let them turn our Berlin girls into he-men. If the Hitler Youth
fails to make louts out of the girls, the Women's Labour Service can
be relied on to finish the job.'227

Among the more sensible aids to health and vigour were ten commandments published by the Reich Physician to the Hitler Youth in
1939, the 'Year of Hygienic Duty':

1. Your body belongs to your nation, to which you owe your
existence and are responsible for your body.

2. Always keep yourself clean, tend and exercise your body.
Light, air and water can help you in this.

3. Look after your teeth. Strong and healthy teeth are a source
of pride.

4. Eat plenty of raw fruit, uncooked greens and vegetables, first
washing them thoroughly in clean water. Fruit contains valuable
nutrients which cooking eliminates.

5. Drink fruit juice. Leave coffee to the coffee addicts. You do not need it.

6. Shun alcohol and nicotine. They are poisons which impair your development and capacity for work.

7. Take physical exercise. It will make you healthy and hardy.

8. Sleep at least nine hours every night.

9. Practise first aid for use in accidents. It can help you to save your comrades' lives.

10. All your activities are governed by the slogan: Your duty is to be healthy![228]

These injunctions doubtless applied with special force to girls, whose State-owned bodies were vessels of the national future. At the same time, they pointed the way to a sphere of activity which was admirably suited to the natural feminine disposition. As well as 40,000 budding field-surgeons, the Hitler Youth trained 35,000 girl medical orderlies aged fourteen or over. Seventeen-year-old BdM girls had to do twelve two-hour classes in nursing and hygiene, after which the best of them joined the Health Service Troop and were entitled to wear, in addition to their uniforms, a white kerchief and a white apron adorned with the Rune of Life.

Once girls had attained this age, the continuous organization of the female sex was interrupted by an undesirable hiatus. BdM service ended at eighteen, but twenty-one was the prescribed age for admission to the Women's Association. In January 1938 a new Party organization was summoned into being to combat this evil: 'The 17-year-old girl will be transferred, pursuant to her voluntary decision and on a set date (the Führer's birthday), to the BdM service "Faith and Beauty". Also admitted on this date will be girls aged 17–21 who have not hitherto belonged to the Hitler Youth.'[229] The outbreak of war cut short the development of this organization, which did not sound particularly voluntary.

The Faith and Beauty scheme, whose high-flown name might have been borrowed from the outlawed world of the pre-Nazi flapper, was not unskilfully conceived. Girls who had completed their BdM service, with its focus on discipline and good order, were suddenly offered 'means to personal development'[230] which made allowances for the individuality of adolescent girls and young women but kept it under control. 'Pursuant to their wishes and inclinations', girls were intended to collaborate in smallish syndicates – 15–20 strong – affiliated to the

BdM service. They were free to choose their own sphere of interest, always provided that – for versatility's sake – they did a spell in each syndicate during their four years of membership. There was nothing very novel about the three main subjects: sport ('thorough training of the body'), gymnastics ('beauty of free and natural movement'), and hygiene and care of the body ('knowledge of the human body, healthy habits, baby-care').

Apart from ideological indoctrination and occupational training, a new note was struck. These senior members of the BdM were distinguished from their juniors by something more than the badge they wore on their uniforms: a blue ground set with two stars emblematic of faith and beauty, one gold and one white. They were also expected to develop their social graces, and not only by becoming proficient in the group dances which they performed at special functions like Party rallies, clad in flowing white robes designed specially for the purpose. No, they must be equally at home on a ballroom floor, learn to ride and play tennis, sunbathe in leisurely tribute to their own physical charms. Privileged activities of this kind were surely aimed at something different and less limited than the faith- and beauty-inspired training of future mothers.

There was a second way of maintaining Party tutelage over girls who had outgrown the BdM, if only temporarily. From 1934 onwards, Gertrud Scholtz-Klink had numbered a 'German Women's Labour Service' among her numerous organizations. In 1936 it was swallowed up by the energetic Reich Labour Leader, Konstantin Hierl, and his Reich Labour Service (RAD), and renamed 'Reich Labour Service for Young Women' (RADwJ) – yet another indication that no Party agency of any importance could be left in the hands of a woman, and that even the Reich Mother-in-Chief, with her seven children and (second) model marriage to SS-Obergruppenführer August Heissmeyer, was a mere figurehead. Meanwhile, in 1935, labour service was statutorily declared an obligation 'for all young Germans of both sexes'.[231] It goes without saying that this, too, was construed as a form of 'honorary service' to the national community, its object being to train young people in a 'true approach to work'.

Although a woman's work had to accord with her feminine disposition, she was naturally expected to work efficiently. In a significant analogy, Hierl declared that to restrict obligatory labour service to young men would be as unjustifiable as restricting compulsory school attendance to boys.

The scheme progressed slowly until 1939, when a growing man-power shortage brought it into practical operation. 100,000 senior BdM members aged between 18 and 25 were quartered for six months each in the RADwJ's 2,000 camps, in semi-requisitioned buildings and hastily erected hutments – for their own benefit, as Guida Diehl per-suaded herself: 'Helping the maternal soul means helping the State!'[232] 90 per cent of Labour Service girls were employed for seven hours a day as auxiliary farm-workers. Life in these strictly supervised camps – uniform bed-making, locker inspections, kit inspections, camp disci-pline, indoctrination classes – was just about as grim and unfeminine as the charwoman's outfit the young women wore at their merry work, for merry it had to be.

Work, the ideology of the Labour Service proclaimed, was the focal point of life, but it had to be done joyfully. That was why propaganda literature showed nothing but smiling faces and radiant expressions, 'freshness of spirit, youthfully joyous vigour in girlish bodies of harmonious proportions'.[233] Their owners were depicted skipping and playing ball, doing callisthenics and – just occasionally – riding 'high on the yellow hay-wain', though here they exchanged their trim little gym-slips for a hair shirt.

The Reich Labour Service for Young Women was born simply of economic necessity, hence the eventual recourse to conscription when the number of volunteers (40,000 in 1938) failed to meet the level of demand. Agricultural forced labour was naturally represented as an educational blessing and, just as naturally, exploited in the interests of further National Socialist indoctrination. It also produced a welcome side-effect which surprised the prophets of Germany's male-dominated society.

The original belief at Labour Service headquarters had been that camp administration would be too exacting a job for the female temperament and disposition. However, experience showed that women camp leaders were quite capable of instilling discipline into their squads and swift to grasp how the fair sex could be toughened for National Socialist purposes. The authorities abruptly changed tack. 'Outside the family, there is no feminine occupation which so epito-mizes a self-contained environment and a demand for the utilization of all feminine energies as that of the woman camp commander.'[234] Camp schools, district schools and a Reich School of the RADwJ were built. Their task was not only to groom hand-picked RADwJ members for positions of responsibility but also to train professional women – doctors, lawyers and teachers – for specialized jobs in the Reich Labour Service. The inference was plain: along this prescribed line, women could legitimately carve out a career for themselves in the National Socialist State and Labour Service.

Women in prominent positions did, however, pose another problem of far more immediate concern to Party chieftains and senior administrators than any ideological principle. 'Dear Pancke,' Himmler wrote uneasily to an Obergruppenführer (SS lieutenant-general), 'I cannot escape the impression that your wife's behaviour in Gau Hanover is not invariably fortunate. Kindly ensure that she lives as unostentatiously as possible and also that, being a young woman, she does not – even allowing for her four children – maintain an unduly large number of maidservants and domestic staff. I would also ask you to instruct your wife not to voice her opinions on this or that political development in the Gau or on the Gauleiter himself, loudly and in a wide variety of places.'[235]

Similar complaints about the pomp and ostentation of senior officials' wives came from Party headquarters. In the view of the Führer's secretary, Martin Bormann, they were too prone to speak out of turn. By order of the Führer, he reminded district officials that 'The wives of senior Party members must refrain from all interference in their husbands' official business. It is positively obnoxious that wives should seek in any way to influence their husbands' decisions or the personal reports which the latter have to submit.'[236]

Censure from the highest quarter was not confined solely to political activity, garrulity or extravagance on the part of blameworthy wives. Marital conduct in the upper reaches of the régime only too often fell short of what was expected of an exemplary National Socialist marriage. Party veterans were quick to produce an explanation which was not only convenient but in keeping with the Nazi tenet of male dominance: wives had failed to keep pace with their husbands' growing responsibilities. Whatsoever their undoubted merits as dutiful housewives and willing helpmates in the 'time of struggle', their veteran spouses had since scaled political heights where simple housewifely talents were no longer enough – where wives had to entertain and make an elegant showing.

It did not matter that this was often a transparent excuse, nor that many husbands were quite as unequal to social requirements as their wives. What mattered was that their wives no longer satisfied them, and that they had the power and opportunity to seek their pleasures elsewhere. And seek them they did, from the top of the SS and Party hierarchy to the bottom. Divorce was officially sanctioned and encouraged: a man had only to list his wife's failings and add that he wanted more children. Significantly enough, the new wives were not ardent supporters of the régime so much as blonde and innocuous young creatures whose domestic interests were centred on Carinhall pomp à la Göring or countrified splendour à la Berchtesgaden. This was equally troublesome to the régime. Whether old wives genuinely became rather dowdy, or new wives wallowed in luxury, or petty potentates ran amok in quest of sexual gratification, the Party's prestige suffered. Malicious gossip and rumours spread like wildfire, as witness these 'Mottoes of a true German':

> Be prolific like Hitler,
> simple and unostentatious like Göring,
> loyal like Hess,
> silent like Goebbels,
> sober like Ley,
> and beautiful like Scholtz-Klink![237]

Official directives were to no avail. The Gauleiter of Hessen-Nassau decreed that drastic measures were to be taken to deal with 'strong rumours' concerning prominent figures in the Party, and that anyone who disseminated them must be tracked down, handed over to the police, and publicly stigmatized. It was a vain hope.

No, the question of women and womanizing in exalted circles demanded a more radical solution. Provision had, after all, to be made for the next thousand years. Heinrich Himmler, ever receptive to sweeping schemes for reform and improvement, was the man for the job. Recalling the Vestal Virgins of Rome and the Wise Women of Germanic antiquity, he devised – in order to remedy 'a crying need in our ranks' – his ideal vision of the Hohe Frau, or Exalted Woman.

The Reichsführer-SS advised his Führer to establish 'Women's Academies of Wisdom and Culture'.[238] These would be open to a select circle of females who, apart from their staunch devotion to the National Socialist world of ideas, were blessed with 'superior intellectual gifts and grace of mind and body'. Their minds would be moulded by 'a good grounding in history', a knowledge of several languages, and thorough instruction in the arts of diplomacy. Himmler considered chess and fencing to be activities particularly suited to the development of intellectual scope and swift reactions, but the Exalted

Woman's syllabus would also include riding, swimming, car-driving, pistol-shooting and – needless to say – 'special courses in cookery and housekeeping'. Waiting for those who completed this exacting course was the title Exalted Woman – 'the supreme distinction attainable by a woman in the Greater Germanic Reich'. It would rank on a par with the Mother's Cross in silver and gold, and what could be a greater incentive to the German spinster than that?

Examining Himmler's plans for this élite institution, one has no difficulty in rediscovering the tendency which was timidly manifest in the BdM's 'Faith and Beauty' venture. Here at the Academy, the flower of young womanhood would be carefully cultivated to a pitch of perfection. This was essential, because only thus could the requisite successes in human breeding be guaranteed. Behind this plan, whose execution Hitler entrusted to the Reichsführer-SS, lurked Himmler's racial concept. The Exalted Women with their Mata Hari training could doubtless be employed by the Foreign Office and Intelligence services at some later stage. For the moment, their job would be – quite literally – to meet the demand for wives among the praetorian guard of the National Socialist régime.

Only blonde and blue-eyed Germanic girls would qualify for admission to a Women's Academy of Wisdom and Culture – naturally, since they and their offspring were to provide the Greater Germanic Reich with its racial criterion. The Exalted Woman was expected to choose a racially worthy spouse from the leadership corps of the Party and government. If she took too long, the Reichsführer-SS hinted, the right of choice would pass to the male sex. Existing wives must not be allowed to obstruct this process of racial ennoblement: they would be honourably divorced and awarded a respectable government pension. The child-products of this exemplary breeding syndicate were to be educated at State expense and regarded as natural candidates for future leadership, members of the nation's new nobility.

The surprising aspect of this far from Utopian scheme is neither its crude principle of racial breeding nor its plan to nurture thoroughbred mates for the élite, for both ideas were consistent with the Nazi ideal of a national community. What really strikes one is its banal but crucial contravention of official ideology. The masters of the system did not yearn for the Exalted Mother or the industrious Hausfrau whom their doctrine commended to the nation as embodiments of true German femininity. For their own use and delectation, they hankered after women of wit and charm whom a man could parade in public to the envy and admiration of his peers. They even conceded that such women might ultimately talk their way into male concerns. In short, a woman's worth was suddenly held to repose in her feminine attractions, not her maternal mien. She was not only accorded intrinsic value but required to have a personality as well.

So two different standards applied, even to the German ideal of womanhood. The dividing line lay somewhere between the ordinary citizen and the Party potentate. The romantic in Himmler waxed rapturous when he extolled the superior feminine qualities of flirtatious Queen Elizabeth, scheming Madame Pompadour or the prolific Empress Maria Teresa. Flown with bourgeois emotionalism, he pictured the charms of his Exalted Women: 'Athletic grace and cultured intelligence, delicacy of feeling and subtlety of expression – these women will have all that.'[239]

The programme of national education was hardly designed and certainly ill-equipped to develop feminine virtues such as these.

Hermann Esser: Divorce, Nazi style

One of Hitler's earliest comrades-in-arms, Esser belonged to the small band of tough and intellectually unendowed bruisers who formed themselves into a devoted bodyguard round the ambitious and approbation-seeking demagogue. Its other members included Hitler's rugged ex-sergeant-major, Max Amann, the one-time butcher's apprentice Ulrich Graf, and the ex-bouncer Christian Weber. Esser, born in 1900, differed from his fellow-bruisers in that he could speak at rallies as well as clear them of troublemakers. Even his chief called him a scoundrel. He was notorious for his incessant affairs with women and openly boasted of being kept by his various girl-friends. The political theorists of the aspiring young Movement, from Anton Drexler to Gregor Strasser, regarded him as an intolerable liability. Hitler found him useful, and that clinched it.

When the Party leader was sent to Landsberg Gaol after his unsuccessful putsch of November 1923, he quickly scribbled a note entrusting the leadership to Rosenberg. Esser and Julius Streicher, who outdid one another in their vile persecution of the Jews, were deliberately obstructive. Their boss, only too happy for the Movement to lie fallow in his absence, raised no objection. Rosenberg, Gregor Strasser, Ludendorff and Pöhner called for the two men's expulsion from the Party, but Hitler took their part just as they, in their turn, backed Hitler when he advocated that the Party should not contest the parliamentary elections of 1924. The Party leader *in absentia* rewarded them for their loyalty after his release from prison. In February, Drexler demanded Esser's expulsion. Hitler shouted back: 'Go to hell!' Esser stayed. A loyal scoundrel was better, any day, than a man with a mind of his own.

On 9 March 1933, after the Nazis came to power, Bavaria acquired a National Socialist cabinet of its own. Hermann Esser became its first Minister of Economics. He made his first contribution to Bavaria's renaissance the same night, when he summoned Dr Stützl, formerly Minister of the Interior in the Held cabinet, to the Brown House and poured boiling water over his feet. Stützl was eventually trampled to death by SS men on 30 June 1934.[240] Meanwhile, the President of the

Bavarian Chamber of Deputies had appointed Esser Second Vice-President of the German Reichstag, under Göring and Kerrl. Although not a fit candidate for offices of the highest rank, he could cope with posts such as that of President of the Reich Tourist Association and Deputy-President of the Reich Committee on Tourism. In 1935, Rosenberg expressed the joyful hope that his former 'associate' of 1924, 'quite as immoderate today as he was then', would soon be dismissed by the Führer.[241] On 27 January 1939 Hitler appointed Esser State Secretary at the Reich Ministry of Public Enlightenment and Propaganda.

At this juncture Esser was already involved in a civil suit whose subject, course and background shed light on something rather less savoury than the worthy life-style expected of a distinguished veteran of the Movement.[242]

On 5 July 1923, Party Member Hermann Esser had conducted a blameless young woman named Therese Deininger to München IV Register Office and there married her. A first son was born in January 1924, a second in June 1926. After three years, Esser seemed to have exhausted his monogamous repertoire. In 1926 he formed a liaison with one Frau Strassmeir. It was not his only liaison, because one day he turned up at his mistress's establishment with gonorrhoea – a circumstance which Frau Strassmeir confidentially relayed to Frau Esser by telephone. This intimate disclosure cast a blight on the Party member's hearth and home. In summer 1933, by now a government minister, he deserted his wife and brace of German sons. In spring 1934 he returned to them, but not in a spirit of remorse. He did not relinquish his long-standing relationship with Frau Strassmeir until May of that year, by which time he had provided for a successor and forged intimate links with a woman named Anna Bacherl. Their sexual relationship must have begun during the summer months at latest, and in September 1934 Esser was once more able to dispense with his wife and sons. Reinforcements were already on the way, because the first of his three children with Anna Bacherl was born early in 1935.

Presumably from a wish to clothe his official status in respectability, Esser had filed a petition for divorce as early as 1933, the seventh year of his affair with Frau Strassmeir. It was refused, and the Herr President returned to his conjugal abode. In 1935 he filed another petition, also without success. Four years later he tried again, and on 23 December 1938 a Berlin court granted his divorce decree as a sort of Christmas present. Unfortunately, Esser's harassed wife lodged an appeal, so on

17 March 1939 the whole case was reviewed by the Berlin Court of Appeal. Esser renewed his petition and the learned judges, wholly uninfluenced – one presumes – by the fact that he held a senior post in Goebbels's Ministry, upheld the lower court's decision.

The Court of Appeal described Therese Esser as 'an honest and well-meaning woman of the highest character' who had been her husband's faithful comrade and companion during the Movement's time of struggle. It then dismissed her appeal.

The grounds for this bewildering legal contortion were provided by Paragraph 55 of the new marriage law. The Esser marriage was deemed broken and its restoration unlikely because the petitioner declined to be reconciled with his wife. His wish to marry Anna Bacherl, the mother of his illegitimate children, rendered divorce not only morally justified but consistent with the interests of the national community.

The judgement was so absurd and its reasons so contradictory, even as stated in the court records, that one is immediately tempted to suspect legal chicanery. Justice had indeed miscarried, and the abortionist was the entire judicail system.

But difficulties still dogged Esser's attempts to obtain a divorce. After sundry manoeuvres behind the scenes, Hans Heinrich Lammers, who headed the Reich Chancellery, sought Hitler's reaction to the case. 'The Führer seemed unpleasantly surprised that the dissolution of the Esser marriage might yet be refused, even after the new marriage law.' On 23 November Lammers acquainted the Reich Minister of Justice, Franz Gürtner, with Hitler's views. Were the courts alive to the possible repercussions if they failed to dissolve irreparably broken marriages? They should proceed with care because there was a risk of 'overestimating the value of a formal continuance of the married state'. This veiled warning was followed by a message in clear: 'Should the courts, in applying Paragraph 55, not concur with this interpretation, on which the Führer based his original consent to the law, there would be no alternative but to consider a change in the wording of the ordinance.'

In fact, there was no need for any redrafting. Reich Legal Director Hans Frank had already issued the following directive as far back as 1936: 'Judges have no right of review over decisions by the Führer which take the form of a law or ordinance. Judges are also bound by other decisions of the Führer in so far as they express an unequivocal determination to make legal rulings.'[243]

5 Bundles of Joy

'IN Hitler's conception of the folkish State, female education had but one invariable goal: the future mother.'[244] With equal dexterity, he reduced the programme of the National Socialist women's movement to a single item: the child. The institution of marriage likewise served a single purpose: the production of offspring. From the National Socialist angle, sexual development and sexual relations became a straightforwardly biological matter. Their object was the earliest possible mating of vigorous males with healthy females, their ultimate aim the maximal propagation of the species.

There are two elements in every breeding programme of this type: quantity and quality. The demand for a specific quality was really no more than a concomitant, just as ideological fixation was secondary. Even the boy who keeps guinea-pigs will soon steer their reproductive activities in a particular direction and eliminate cross-breeds. Every biological reproduction scheme carries within it the seeds of breeding and selection. The National Socialists called their production target the Aryan race and their ideal type Germanic Man. Élitist fanatics like Himmler and Blood and Soil mystics like Darré might actually see in it the manifestation of a new man, a zoological consummation of the German species. A brutal realist like Hitler, for all his detestation of the alien countertype, did not yield to the notion that this new pedigree breed could bring him to his goal unaided. To attain it he needed the countertype as an embodiment of evil which would hold the nation together, provide it with an outlet for aggression and make it feel 'superior'. Tactically speaking, the conception of an ideal type was obstructive because it impaired the requisite sense of community and togetherness. What Hitler wanted was unlimited power. What he needed for its procurement was a human mass dedicated to faith, obedience and service.

Seen in this light, the population policy of pure number took precedence over the racial policy of pure Aryanism, both from the

...ope revives in the German Breast: 'Before me, a white swan. And so we advance gently, from out the ...rk waters, through the dawn light – advance to where, far off, ripples rise to meet the new-born day.' (Richard Dehmel.) From *Kladderadatsch* 1933.

Eva Braun at the wedding reception of her sister Gretl (1942).

Hitler's birthday at the Berghof, Obersalzberg. Eva Braun shows the Führer his presents.

Dr Goebbels and his wife Magda at a picnic.

Reich Minister Dr Goebbels gets married. The bridegroom on his way to church with stepson Harald Quandt and witness Adolf Hitler.

'On 14 February, all Germans will be sitting down to their stew like one big family, both in restaura
and at home. To give joyfully and enlist in the patriotic front – that is the purpose of this day.'
(Drawing Rudolf Lipsius.) From *Das Schwarze Korps*, 4 February 1937.

The Festival of the Amazons in the grounds at Nymphenburg, Munich, 30 July 1938.

A group from the big parade in celebration of German Art Day, Munich 1933.

'And at the frontier many days I bide,
seeking the Germans' country with my soul . . .
(Freely adapted from Goethe's *Iphigenie*, I, 1.)
From *Kladderadatsch* 1935.

The German Games at
Berlin in 1934.
Gymnastics on the 'Rhön
wheel', a piece of
apparatus much favoured
by the German Girls'
League.

'Community Day.' Members of the German Girls' League going through their paces in the Party Rally grounds.

Dr Robert Ley enjoying a taste of his own medicine. He joins other Strength through Joy passengers in the 'Kilometre March', a daily ritual performed after concerts on the promenade deck.

Troops marching through the Old City during the Party Rally at Nuremberg in 1936.

The Party Rally at Nuremberg, 1938. Anti-aircraft searchlights project
a 'Dome of Lights' into the sky.

German Solstice Festival in the Berlin Stadium, 21 June 1938.

Harvest Thanksgiving Day on the Bückeberg, 6 October 1935.

Goebbels with his wife
and Winifred Wagner
at Bayreuth.

Below
Hitler inspecting the
House of German Art.

Ernst Röhm, SA Chief of Staff, with his closest associates.

Martin Bormann marries the daughter of Party Judge Buch at München-Pullach. Left to right: Buch, Gerda Buch-Bormann, Martin Bormann, Hitler (witness) and Driver Steinbinder.

The Birth of Venus (Max Ehlert) from the 'Night of the Nymphs', one of the glittering galas held to mark German Art Day in Munich. The Goddess of Beauty arises from a shining couch. The Peters-Pawlinin Romantic Ballet modelled this scene on the celebrated painting by Botticelli. From the *Berliner Illustrirte*, 20 July 1939.

Mother and Child (drawing by Wolfgang Wilbrich). From *Das Schwarze Korps*, 15 May 1935.

Mother's Day, Nazi style. Prolific mothers are inve with the Mother's Cross at a Berlin ceremony

The Führer's birthday. Hitler with a group of 'Berghof children' belonging to Bormann, Speer and his manservant Linge.

Above
Village school in the
Warthegau. Children
being lectured on the laws
of heredity.

Below
Reich President Göring
and SS-Oberführer
Heinrich Himmler on
their way to the
Reichstag in Berlin,
19 September 1932.

'The road to renewed artistic creation is clear!'
From the *Völkischer Beobachter*, 15 September 1933.

Führer's point of view and, consequently, from that of the Third Reich. The same consideration was uppermost in directives on population policy propaganda issued by the 'Reich German Family Association'.[245] Designed to combat the 'loss of national stock' caused primarily by a declining birth-rate, this propaganda coupled an appeal to German hearts and German self-sacrifice with a demand for public enlightenment on 'widespread misconceptions'. The false prophet whom it singled out for special attack was the English political economist Thomas Malthus, whose largely outmoded doctrine stated that a rising birth-rate was bound to cause impoverishment because the output of goods could not be increased *pari passu*. Nazi ideologists retorted that national success depended on national growth. Although no less questionable, their argument became binding on individual behaviour: 'The teachings of the "birth-controller" merit equal opposition.' The 'league for the promotion of large families among the hereditarily fit' devoted only secondary attention to racial quality, demanding selection and improvement of good stock and a resolute campaign against the breeding of undesirable offspring. Finally, the directives reverted to the commandment of number. The National Socialist norm was at least four children; moreover, 'Propagation and the establishment of a family are no private matter in the folkish State, but a supreme duty to the community'.[246]

Principles of racial ideology were manipulable, as witness the Aryanization of certain useful 'aliens'. The only immutable principle was that of power, and power meant power over the masses as a means to still more power. When Hitler 'brought home' Austria and the Sudeten territories he was not prompted by any such lofty aims as the restoration of the national community or the integration of Greater Germany. He was concerned with human material – one division of troops to every million inhabitants. Austria plus the Sudetenland equalled another twelve divisions with which to push Greater Germany's frontiers to the Urals.

Thus Nazi clichés such as 'on the birth front' or 'the major decisions in national life are taken at the cradle' should be construed quite literally. A rising birth-rate gave promise of more divisions which could be hurled into the international fray. Where the function of marriage was concerned, Hitler assigned priority to the 'propagation and preservation' of the race, not selective breeding. His prime emphasis was always on martial values, not racial: 'If for that reason alone, early marriage is right because it gives youthful wedlock the vigour

which is indispensable to the production of healthy and hardy offspring.'[247] Speaking at the Harvest Festival Rally on the Bückeberg in
1935, Hitler ecstatically gave thanks to Providence for the year's
abundant harvest. The army – the nation's strength – had arisen once
more; the air force and navy would soon follow. And then: 'Far above
and beyond that, however, we wish to render thanks for a special
harvest. We want at this hour to thank the hundreds upon hundreds of
thousands of women who have again presented us with the finest gift
they could bestow: many hundreds of thousands of little children!'[248]

One child = 250 marks

These gifts to the Führer – the children belonged just as much 'to their
mothers as they do, at the same time, to me',[249] he generously conceded
to a female audience at the 1936 Party Rally – did not go unrequited.
Once in power, the régime systematically proceeded to combat the
falling birth-rate and foster population growth by dint of financial
incentives and material reliefs, honorary awards and ideological
pressure.

Matrimonial credits were introduced by law as early as June 1933.
The granting of these interest-free loans of RM 1,000 was at first condi-
tional on whether the bride gave up work after her marriage and so
made room for someone else. However, the conditions of repayment
were themselves indicative that this statutory measure was designed to
do more than combat rampant unemployment. For every birth that
resulted from such a marriage, 25 per cent – RM 250 – of the outstanding debt was remitted. Four children, the target figure set by
National Socialist family planners, cancelled the debt altogether. Not
unsurprisingly, the employment proviso was dropped in due course.
Instead, the authorities demanded a health certificate attesting the
hopeful couple's Aryan descent and hereditary fitness. One million
matrimonial loans worth a total of RM 650 million were granted up to
1938. Demand was so heavy that the sum had to be cut to 500 marks,
but even 125 marks per child was a respectable premium on procreation.

Hitler's words of encouragement to courting couples had little to do
with his fussy concern for more robust offspring. Early marriages not
only meant earlier children but might also, thanks to the carefree
irresponsibility of youth, mean more children. Gentle pressure was
applied wherever possible. Budding civil servants were expected to
start a family young, thereby setting a good National Socialist example

in a traditional Prussian way. Exemplary conduct merited its due
reward: as soon as he married, a civil servant drew the top salary for
his grade irrespective of length of service. Reich Forester-in-Chief
Hermann Göring swiftly co-operated in his own sphere of responsibility and acknowledged that the promotion of early marriage was a
major aspect of population policy. He procured maintenance grants
for the young married men in his forestry service and raised the
salaries of married forestry officials.

Each could contribute to the grand design in his own humble
domain. The mayor of Wattenscheid in Westphalia devised a special
award for high performance and earned an expert tribute from the
SS weekly, *Das Schwarze Korps*, which commended his example to
other civic leaders. For each addition to her family after the first two
children, a Wattenscheid mother was awarded RM100. The birth of
a fourth, fifth or sixth child guaranteed the parents enough capital to
acquire a house or four-roomed apartment of their own.

Three children = one nursemaid

The authorities also sought to popularize motherhood by alleviating
family burdens. Welfare benefits for the 'German family which is
worthy of support, hereditarily fit and in need of assistance'[250] were
administered by the National Socialist Public Welfare Organization's
(NSV) 'Mother and Child' auxiliary service – a scheme in the grand
manner, and one which aimed at the customary blend of administrative,
ideological and social perfection.

Local Party 'wardens' and the directors and administrators of the
NSV, the Women's Association and other Party agencies were
instructed to register expectant mothers with the Mother and Child
service, whose first duty was to attend to their 'spiritual welfare'. A
directive issued by the Party Chancellery in 1944 shows where this
essay in direct influence on the family circle was to lead. In it, Bormann
urged local headquarters to institute 'National Socialist family evenings'.[251] Every four to six weeks, family groups of manageable size
were to be convened for an informal political discussion. The lines on
which to conduct these cosy soirées would be worked out and laid
down by NSDAP authorities such as the Central Training Bureau of
the Reich Department of Organization, the Head Cultural Office at
Reich Party Headquarters, and the Party Chancellery itself.

The Mother and Child auxiliary service rendered more practical forms of assistance as well. Food subsidies were provided for the needy, hostels for solitary mothers and domestic help for large families. The burdens of the latter were further alleviated by the NSV's day-nurseries, defined in keeping with the usual nexus of social and ideological functions as 'centres of National Socialist human guidance'.

However, practical difficulties stood in the way of practical assistance. There were simply not enough helpers to put this ambitious welfare scheme into effect. The 'Domestic Service Year' and the compulsory year's service for girls proved a wash-out, the neighbourhood aid scheme barely got off the ground, and maidservants were in short supply.

The position was serious enough for Himmler to entertain grave misgivings about the nation's biological future: 'I see a great danger that very many women's undoubted desire to have children – numerous children – will founder on the hard fact that they cannot get maids and have to do all the housework by themselves.'[252] In 1941, having brooded on various remedies, the Reichsführer-SS communicated his far-seeing solution to the head of his Race and Resettlement Bureau (RuSHA) and the Reich Commissionership for the Strengthening of German Nationhood (RKF).

In Poland and the Ukraine, girls of first- or second-class racial status (by SS standards) were to be selected for employment as maidservants, cooks or nursemaids in German households with three or more children. By way of recompense, they were treated to the prospect of acquiring German citizenship in a few years' time and the attendant privilege of taking a German husband. The Reich's breeder-in-chief promised himself a triple return from this investment: '1. Part of the shortage of maidservants in large families – particularly the best families – would be eliminated. 2. These girls would provide the German nation with valuable potential mothers of good stock. 3. Valuable mothers of good stock would be taken from the foreign nation for which they bear the best children.'[253]

Not even this crude directive could ease the situation. Girls conscripted from the occupied territories were indeed placed with the 'best' families, to wit, those with the best SS connections. Here they created new problems, either by arousing the envy of less fortunate neighbours or by prompting the German housewife to 'unworthy', i.e. friendly, behaviour towards menials of alien blood. Quite apart from that, the young women were also employed irrespective of racial merit in agriculture and heavy industry, where the need for them was even more pressing.

Medal-winning mothers

Himmler announced that the most important decoration bestowable on citizens of the future Greater German Reich would be the 'German Mother's Cross'. Hitler had instituted the Mutterkreuz in December 1938 for outstanding services in the fight against a falling birth-rate and the danger of national extinction. It symbolized that the new State paid tribute to a prolific mother's expenditure of effort just as it honoured the courage of her soldier husband. Like every reputable order, it had more than one class: bronze for four children, silver for six, gold for eight. Recipients were invested on 12 August, the birthday of Hitler's mother, whose five confinements would only have earned her the bronze version. In design, the Mutterkreuz was a significant combination of Party badge, Pour le mérite and Iron Cross. Its inscription – *The child ennobles the mother* – was expressive of national gratitude.

More important than maternal ennoblement was a mother's readiness to give birth often and nobly in the national interest. *Das Schwarze Korps*[254] trotted out the usual arguments in favour of a large family— 'Only when the number of cradles constantly exceeds the number of coffins can we look forward with good cheer to a better future!'—but combined them with a novel conjecture. What human assets the nation might have lost by applying the liberalistic-materialistic two-child principle! Bach, Mozart and Richard Wagner (author of *Judaism in Music*), Kant, Lessing and Emanuel von Geibel, Frederick the Great, Bismarck and General Ludendorff (author of *The Secret of Jesuitical Power and its End*), the Luftwaffe ace Boelcke and the U-boat hero Weddigen – none of these later-born offspring would have seen the light or been able to help mould the national character. The SS weekly proceeded to expound a fanciful theory of probabilities. To call for a large family was precisely the opposite of worshipping numbers for their own sake; a large family was the parents' sole guarantee that they had done everything in their power to produce the finest fruit of which their union was capable – that they had not deprived the nation of a single great man in the making. Maxim: 'Only out of many good ones comes a selection of the best!'[255]

Reporting on public attitudes to the Mutterkreuz after its first four years of existence, the Security Service submitted that it was regarded as a distinction of the highest order, a major contributory factor being the ceremony of investiture itself.

This exultant claim was a trifle exaggerated. Mothers whose throats were adorned with the coveted award on its blue ribbon certainly felt honoured. On the other hand, the sight of this warlike emblem adorning the bosoms of heavy-hipped matrons not only brought grave protests from the Church but was a positive invitation to scorn and ridicule. Near Oppeln, two boys stopped to stare at a trio of 'gold' mothers. 'Look at them,' said one, half-awed and half-facetious, ' – they've been good she-hares!'[256]

The Reichsführer-SS had hit on the idea of signalizing maternal services to the nation at an even earlier stage, in 1936, when he commissioned a special brooch for presentation by SS men to their wives – as long as they were mothers. Small wonder that he attached such high social prestige to the Mutterkreuz in gold. Its wearers would be saluted by sentries, enjoy unrestricted access to the Führer and occupy a supreme place of honour in the State. In face of such appeals to human vanity, mothers would compete on a piece-work basis for the privileges which 'golden mummy' status brought with it. 'There'll come a day,' Himmler assured his sceptical confidant, Felix Kersten, 'when a delegation wearing the Mutterkreuz in gold will inspect the Führer's bodyguard, the premier unit of the Greater Germanic Reich – and then you'll see some results!'[257]

The problem of unmarried mothers and illegitimate children was a favourite stamping-ground for preachers of National Socialist morality, who emulated their Führer in feeling and acting like champions of a freer and more sensible ethos. They were loud in their condemnation of the hypocrisy of the bourgeois outlook which sanctioned pre- and extra-marital intercourse by men – just as they did – but spurned and disparaged the results where mother and child were concerned.

How healthy, Hitler argued on the subject of family policy, was the peasant custom of the 'trial'! (It was, and still is, customary in many rural districts of Germany for a bride to prove her fertility before marriage by becoming pregnant.) How many great men, he said, stressing the spiritual aspect of the matter, had emerged from foundlings' homes! How ignoble it was, he lamented, demonstrating his human understanding, to pour scorn on an unmarried mother and her child when their status was the product of authentic passion!

An illegitimate child was no disgrace. On the contrary, the State and national community had a duty to tend the mother and child – provided, of course, that they were hereditarily fit and of good stock. The auxiliary service 'Mother and Child' was made expressly responsible for this task. Unmarried mothers in the civil service enjoyed protection against dismissal. Contrary to a judgement of the Prussian Administrative Court, adultery ceased to be valid grounds for disciplinary proceedings. The Deputy Führer, Rudolf Hess, who sought reassurance on this point, received the following reply from Hans Lammers, State Secretary at the Reich Chancellery: 'The Führer considers a universal ruling by the Reich Government impracticable in this matter, which affects the private life of the civil servant concerned.'[258] The Führer's attitude was quite unconnected with respect for a person's private life. He always considered universal rulings impracticable or failed to adhere to them.

It was Hess who came closest to an unambiguous statement of policy on this subject in his open *Letter to an Unmarried Mother*,[259] published at the beginning of the war. Its sensational message: the unmarried mother whose 'betrothed' was killed in the war would be treated from the aspect of maintenance (widow's pension) exactly as if the marriage had taken place. When her child's birth was recorded at the registry office, the designation 'Kriegsvater' (war-father) would either replace or supplement the father's name. The mother would retain her maiden name but be addressed as 'Frau', and the Party would, if so required, provide the child with a guardian.

Grandiose examples were quoted in support of this offer. Charlemagne, who was the son of a bastard, Leonardo da Vinci, Wilhelm Busch, Graf Yorck – none of them would have seen the light if illegitimate children had not been tolerated by contemporary society. Besides, it was war-time: 'What would it avail if a nation emerged victorious but succumbed to national extinction because of losses sustained for victory's sake?'[260] Therefore, the highest respect was due to any woman who, in these precarious circumstances, took it upon herself to become an unmarried mother – provided, of course, that her age was right, her hereditary disposition sound and her chosen partner of high racial quality. Hess turned a visionary eye on the years ahead: 'I am convinced that my attitude will shortly be shared by the entire German nation, and that the entire German nation will in future support all those mothers who, by transgressing the bounds of civic usages and conventions which may possibly be needful at other times, help to offset the losses inflicted by war – just as the rural population has from time immemorial displayed a more liberal attitude to the problem.'[261]

The Deputy Führer's epistle unquestionably did more than pledge protection to the soldier's careless girl-friend. It could also be construed as *carte blanche* for warriors home on leave from the front. Moreover, it discreetly gave notice that other rules would obtain in future: 'Higher than all principles devised by man, higher than all conventions, which are expressive of accepted usage but not expressive of morality itself, and higher by far than prejudice, stands the welfare of the totality and the life of the nation.'[262]

In face of such announcements and of massive exhortations to boost the birth-rate, it gradually dawned on people that, in the Party's view, a woman's main function was to produce children, whether in or out of wedlock, and that only childbirth qualified her for full membership of the national community.

This impression, however well-founded, was temporarily inconvenient to the Nazi rulers because it mobilized old prejudices and bred fresh opposition. The national community was not yet ripe for consistent measures in the field of population policy. Accordingly, the ideologist Georg Usadel issued a disclaimer entitled *Discipline and Order*, which outlined the foundations of National Socialist ethics. Although no disgrace, he emphasized, an illegitimate child was undesirable from the aspect of disciplined breeding and selection. It was fundamentally incorrect to assert that the begetting of illegitimate children was being encouraged and that women must give birth at all costs: 'Where prominent figures have said this, it was always meant as an ideal requirement of the purest hue, never as an invitation to unbridled behaviour.'[263]

This was true, of course. The moral tenets of National Socialism were far from aimed at propagating an uninhibited life-style. That no inhibitions should trammel the begetting and rearing of children was another matter. Facilities for unmarried mothers, no childless woman capable of bearing children, unhampered dissemination of healthy genes – all these problems were tackled in a wholly practical manner. The final solution of population policy was a favourite preserve of the Reichsführer-SS, with his grand design for a Greater Germanic future.

Recipes for male children

One of Heinrich Himmler's major concerns was how to neutralize the war-time wastage of able-bodied men by inducing a further increase in the birth-rate. Wasn't it always the most valiant young men who fought and died in the forefront of battle? The Reichsführer-SS applied himself to this problem with characteristic precision, ever mindful of the most remote complications and devious solutions.

On the strength of an alarming report from Leonardo Conti, the Reich Director of Health, Himmler requested his Statistico-Scientific Institute for its comments on the post-war surplus of women. Richard Korherr, who headed the institute, established that one million dead would produce a post-war ratio of women to men of 100:94, or 100:86 in the event of two million fatal casualties. The situation would be grave enough, declared the statistician, but even more important than such absolute ratios was the problem of regional balance. In this respect, a temporary surplus of men prevailed in lowland areas, where there were only four females to every five males.

Himmler's anxieties persisted. His ultimate concern was not with sexual equilibrium but with biological output and, more particularly, the volume of male offspring. In 1942 he had commissioned his Inspector of Statistics to study possible methods of sex-determination. Korherr discovered that the male-to-female ratio of offspring from marriages of SS men (109:100) was higher than the national average (106:100), but he warned his chief against attributing this result to the youthfulness of parents and the high proportion of first-born. The figures did not seem reliable enough, especially as past experience had taught him to be chary of statistical data supplied by the SS. Dr Gregor Ebner, director of the Lebensborn (Fount of Life) organization, had once claimed a personal victory on the birth front: at 4 per cent, infant mortality in SS maternity homes was two points better than the norm. Korherr checked. Ebner's glad tidings proved to be 'a pack of lies from start to finish'.[264] At 8 per cent, the Lebensborn figure was actually two points worse than the national average.

When statistics got him no further, Himmler delved into the healthy subsoil of popular tradition. In 1944 he instructed Lebensborn to open a file on 'The Question of Producing Boys or Girls'. The Reichsführer himself supplied the first entry. His Central Office chief, Gottlob Berger, had told him of a custom from his native Swabian Alps which he, Himmler, deemed worthy of putting on record. 'Having, like his wife, consumed no alcohol the week before, the husband sets out on foot at 12 noon and tramps the 20 kilometres to Ulm and back. He must not stop at any inn on the way. The wife does no work for a full week prior to the day in question, eats well, sleeps a great deal and refrains from exerting herself in any way. Copulation takes place when the man returns from his march. This is said to result invariably in the birth of male children.'[265] SS Reich Medical Officer-in-Chief Ernst Grawitz was requested in all seriousness to comment on this weird technique. He declined.

Frustrated in his efforts to predetermine the sex of children, the all-powerful Reichsführer devoted himself with added zeal to ensuring that they were at least begotten. The *Berliner Börsenzeitung* of 17 May 1941 reported that a registrar had refused to marry a thirty-four-year-old man and a woman thirteen years his senior because their difference in age offended wholesome popular sentiment, violated the National Socialist conception of the nature of marriage, and precluded any expectation of issue. The would-be bridegroom took legal action, however, and Munich's Court of Appeal ruled that current law did not recognize differences in age as an impediment to marriage.

Outraged, Himmler scribbled 'Incredible!' on the press report and passed it to his Race and Resettlement Bureau. The really incredible feature was the courage of the judges concerned. Although statute law did not recognize age differences as a bar to matrimony, the contemporary administration of justice most certainly did. In the Austrian city of Graz, for example, an eighteen-year-old spinster sought leave to marry a sixty-two year-old man. The competent court granted permission but hastily back-tracked when objections were lodged by a relative and the Gau legal office. At Salzwedel, north of Magdeburg, the registrar refused to marry a forty-three-year-old man and a fifty-year-old woman because the latter's age made it unlikely that they would have children. An appeal court confirmed the ruling: in the National Socialist State, the private interests of the parties concerned must conform to those of the State and nation.

Himmler took care at every level that the potency of his black knights became fully operative and benefited the national interest. Shocked by a report from Sepp Dietrich in France that there were two hundred cases of gonorrhoea in the Adolf Hitler SS Guards, the Reichsführer evinced sympathy for the needs of his sex-starved élite and decreed a general amelioration. He ordered medically supervised brothels to be established for all units of the Waffen-SS. Meetings were to be contrived between SS husbands and their wives so that their union would produce the requisite number of children. The supreme lord of the concentration camps was touchingly eager that his élite Germans should enjoy a full sex-life. He also bent a sympathetic ear to the pleas of staff officers when visiting the War Academy and arranged reunions between married couples, commenting that one must pay due regard to the emotional life of the fair sex and bear in mind that time spent together might some day prove a great source of national strength.

It was with the aim of contributing to national strength that one SS wife wrote to SS headquarters requesting compassionate leave for her husband. Himmler's personal secretary, Rudolf Brandt, passed the applicant's request to Operational Headquarters and sent her a heartening note: 'I would, however, advise you at this stage to have yourself examined in advance by a gynaecologist so that it can be ascertained when the most favourable time for conception would be, because only leave taken at the right time will, as far as it is humanly possible to judge, afford some guarantee that your and your husband's desire for a child will be fulfilled.'[266]

As Chief of the German Police, Himmler wrote personally to Benno Martin, the police chief of Nuremberg, instructing him to procure sufficient hotel accommodation near the Grafenwöhr military training area so that he, Himmler, could invite the wives of the officers and men of the Germanic Corps and the Netherlands Division to join their husbands there. 'I want to deliberately encourage the association of married men with their wives because we cannot otherwise expect their marriages to produce the children that are so desirable and necessary.'[267]

Himmler's concern for personal hardship and the folkish duty to beget children did not desert him even in more precarious times. In June 1944 he was respectfully informed by Karl Theodor Weigel, head of the Teaching and Research Centre for Runology and Emblematology administered by the Ancestral Heritage organization, that he had decided to cohabit with a certain Frau M. Frau M. had been divorced by her husband after refusing to present him with more children 'because he neglected her and was always having extra-marital affairs, some of which assumed a form wounding and degrading to his wife'.[268] Obersturmführer Weigel was also anxious to divorce his wife because she suffered from a nervous ailment. After a three-month inquiry, Weigel's supreme boss sanctioned the union provided that it was blessed with offspring. Weigel already had three children and Frau M. two.

At the same time, Obergruppenführer Fritz Schlessmann, deputy Gauleiter of Essen, complained to Himmler of matrimonial unhappiness. The Reichsführer's consoling response was to inquire whether the tormented husband had a loving woman who was ready to collaborate with him in presenting the nation with children. Schlessmann had. On 30 January 1945 he reported success: his twenty-four-year-old secretary, Isolde G., was three months pregnant. He now asked whether the Reichsführer could – in the strictest confidence, because his Gauleiter must know nothing about it – find room for her at a Lebensborn maternity home. Himmler replied promptly, assigning Fräulein Isolde to the Hochland home in Bavaria: 'Your letter did not annoy me in the least – on the contrary, I was delighted to receive it.'[269] The date was 12 February 1945 and the Russians were already overrunning Silesia, but the newly appointed C.-in-C. Army Group Weichsel found time to rejoice in the forthcoming arrival of another little German. He was building for the future.

Himmler had already made general provision for that future on 28 October 1939, when he issued an order to the entire SS and police service. Worse than the sad but inevitable wastage of good men in war, he lamented, was the number of unbegotten children. Only the man who knew how to preserve his kind could die at peace with himself. To the fallen soldier's widow, her husband's posthumous child was a supreme boon. Himmler vied with Hess's *Letter to an Unmarried Mother*: 'Beyond the bounds of civil laws and constraints which may at other times be needful, it may prove to be a noble duty – even outside marriage – for German women and girls of good blood to become, not irresponsibly but in a spirit of profound moral solemnity, the mothers of children fathered by departing soldiers of whom fate alone knows whether they will return home or die for Germany.'[270] The victory of the sword was futile unless followed by the victory of childbirth. To guarantee this, the SS undertook to provide for all legitimate and illegitimate children of SS men lost in the war (*a*) guardianship and education until they came of age, and (*b*) financial support and economic assistance, both during the war and thereafter.

This blunt injunction to procreate caused a storm of protest. On 30 January 1940 Himmler followed it up with a second order designed to dispel 'misunderstandings'.[271] Its main points were that: (*a*) illegitimate children were no novelty, as witness the Deputy Führer's open letter to unmarried mothers; and (*b*) SS men were not encouraged to make overtures to the wives of soldiers absent on active service. Not only would this be 'uncomradely', but most SS men were married and on active service themselves – also, the women of Germany knew how to defend their honour. 'This should dispose of any misunderstandings. It is nonetheless your duty, men of the SS, as at all periods when ideological truths are being defended, to secure the understanding of German men and German women for this present matter of national survival, which transcends all frivolity and mockery.'[272]

Misunderstandings had indeed been dispelled. It had quite clearly been reiterated that the SS and police had a sacred duty to their nation and Führer to beget children in defiance of outworn conventions – though preferably not on the wives of their comrades in the armed forces. The Black Order would assume responsibility for the fruits of their devotion to duty. Where this subject was concerned, ideology had long ago quelled any misgivings about legitimacy or its opposite.

The sacred fount of life

Fantastic rumours surrounded the Lebensborn or 'Fount of Life' association, not only during the Third Reich but even more so after its downfall. SS brothel or stud-farm, or a cross between the two – such were the sensational constructions placed upon it by each according to his particular flight of fancy. The truth, at least initially, was far simpler and less lurid. Lebensborn was in fact a rather bourgeois institution founded in conformity with a conservative sexual code, serving to keep up an appearance of middle-class respectability and run in accordance with an almost monastic set of regulations.

Gunter d'Alquen, the experienced journalist who edited *Das Schwarze Korps*, described the venture as follows in a prize essay addressed to the SS: 'The Lebensborn association consists primarily of members of the SS. It provides mothers of large families with the finest possible obstetrical treatment in excellent maternity homes, also facilities for rest both before and after confinement. It also affords an opportunity for pre- and extra-conjugal mothers of good stock to give birth under relaxing conditions.'[273] What could be more exemplarily respectable and philanthropic? Himmler, too, saw his institution in a predominantly philanthropic light. Lebensborn, he once averred, could teach the churches a lesson in practical charity.

First registered in September 1936, the Lebensborn association was founded under the auspices of the SS Race and Resettlement Bureau. The inaugural announcement from Himmler's headquarters was highly informative.[274] It reminded the officer corps of the SS of its duty to set an example to other ranks and the nation at large by producing a healthy family of at least four children. Anyone unable to do so should sponsor 'racially and hereditarily worthwhile children' instead; Lebensborn was available for the 'selection and allocation of suitable children'. In other words, the adoption of illegitimate children from Lebensborn maternity homes would help to make up for any deficiency of offspring in SS families, which were especially 'worthwhile' by definition.

This child-reservoir idea did, of course, exceed the functions of a normal maternity home. Lebensborn's ultimate objectives were clarified by the association's second set of articles in 1938: 'Its functions fall within the scope of *population policy*. Lebensborn's task is to promote large families in the SS, protect and care for mothers of good blood and tend mothers *in need of help* and children of good blood.'[275]

Himmler had good reason to be concerned about his Order's attitude towards population policy. Statistical analysis showed that, as of 31 December 1939, his 115,650 married SS men had produced only 1.1 children per head. Even the officer corps set a poor example with 1.41.

SS heads of department were automatically required to join and subscribe to the Lebensborn association. The Reichsführer, who continued to take a lively interest in his hobby-horse during the war years, personally conducted an involved correspondence on the subject of whether the annual contribution could be reduced to RM 1 in a particular instance. The venture could hardly thrive on sums of this order. In 1938, 13,000 members – of whom only 8,000 belonged to the SS – paid RM 27,000 into the kitty. This was barely enough to provide financial support for large SS families, let alone maintain half-a-dozen maternity homes.

The premises themselves were 'acquired' on favourable terms. The municipality of Pölzin had in 1937 presented Heim Pommern to the Führer, who passed it on to the Reichsführer-SS for his Lebensborn project. Klosterheide in Brandenburg was leased by Berlin's health insurance fund. Heim Wienerwald had been expropriated from Jewish owners by Himmler's Gestapo. Schloss Oberweiss – not yet in operation – had likewise been 'made over' to the association. By the beginning of 1939, the list also included the maternity homes Hochland in

Bavaria, Friesland at Hohehorst near Bremen, Wernigerode in the Harz Mountains, and Neulengbach in the Wienerwald, which was planned as a crèche. Expansion continued under the association's new chairman, Blood Order-wearer Max Sollmann of the Reichsführer's personal staff. In 1944 Lebensborn submitted a list of nursing staff which provides some idea of the thirteen homes' capacity: Heim Taunus 22 nurses, Hochland 18, Sonnenwiese 18, Wienerwald 15, Pommern 14, Kurmark 12, Harz 10, Schwarzwald 9, Ardennen 9, Westwald 4, Moselland 3, Friesland 3, Alpenland 1.

The main aim of this non-profit-making and charitable concern was stated in Clause 2 of the articles: 'To care for racially and genetically valuable mothers of whom it may be assumed, after careful investigation of their own family and that of the father, that they will give birth to equally valuable children'.[276] First in line came the wives and girl-friends of SS men and members of the police, followed by unmarried mothers-to-be who satisfied the racial requirements of the SS and were compelled to swear an oath of secrecy. Standartenführer Ebner not only commended the principle of strict selection – only forty out of a hundred applications were considered – but praised the protective function of Lebensborn on the grounds that it shielded valuable but illegitimate children and their mothers from malicious gossip. The homes had their own facilities for registering births in a way which satisfied legal requirements but precluded public scrutiny. Lebensborn also acted as guardian and kept infants in its homes for up to a year, if need be, before they were allocated to childless or unprolific SS families. Accommodation was extremely cheap. Mothers received an allowance of 400 marks, and the daily fee was only RM 2, later RM 2.50. Single women moved in during the early months of pregnancy. SS men's girl-friends attended courses in mothercraft and could thus acquire the certificates of suitability on which the Reichsführer insisted before issuing a marriage permit.

The matrons were specially selected, as befitted those who had to administer the lives of genetically valuable mothers and babies in an atmosphere of National Socialist harmony and ideological orthodoxy. Their task was no easy one, because although all inmates were meant to be treated equally and squabbles over legitimacy obviated by the universal use of Christian name plus full married title – Frau Maria, Frau Elisabeth, and so on – some inmates were more equal than others. The wives of senior SS officers were quick to complain to the Reichsführer when they thought the matron or one of the nursing staff had neglected them or, worse, given preferential treatment to an unmarried fellow-patient – for an inmate's true status seldom remained secret for long.

Himmler took a personal interest in all such minutiae because 'Under our laws, the fiancée or wife belongs as much to this community, this Order of the SS, as the husband'.[277] He was as capable of telling a ruffled senior officer's wife to simmer down and fit in as he was of investigating embezzlement charges against a Lebensborn caterer. He always looked with special pleasure and favour on confidential requests for admission addressed to him personally. Another subject close to his heart was natural and wholesome nutrition. The prescribed breakfast consisted of fruit and porridge, and Himmler conscientiously requested statistical data about its effect on blood pressure. When some inmates complained that they were gaining too much weight, Himmler drew their attention in schoolmasterly fashion to the slimness of the English aristocracy, which was attributable to just such a diet. 'For this reason the mothers in our homes must get used to porridge and be instructed to feed their children on it. Heil Hitler!'[278] Later, when Sollmann dropped this elixir of life from the menu after skimmed milk was rationed, Himmler sent him a word of admonition through his secretary: 'The cooking of oatmeal porridge with full-cream or skimmed milk does not accord with the wishes of the Reichsführer-SS. Porridge is to be cooked with water only. He assumes that the cooking and serving of porridge will now be resumed.'[279]

In view of such asceticism, one is not surprised to learn that men were strictly forbidden to visit the homes except on special occasions. Male guests might then be invited to sip a cup of coffee, but any more intimate form of hospitality was taboo. The Lebensborn motto – 'Every mother of good blood is our sacred trust' – was puritanically followed to the letter.

Mothers of good blood who owed their hallowed condition to activities unhallowed by matrimony were relatively hard to find despite the Reichsführer's ample encouragement. On 27 October 1939, the day before his procreation order to the SS and police, Himmler took the precaution of decreeing that Lebensborn must legally appoint itself the sponsor of legitimate and guardian of illegitimate children fathered by SS men killed on active service. This provided his black-uniformed élite with a moral and material incentive to look upon the Lebensborn institution as a major asset. But the effect, in terms of population policy, was meagre. Of the 12,081 children sired by married

SS officers, only 135 – or little more than 1 per cent – were illegitimate. Other ranks were equally slow to avail themselves of the facilities provided. The ratio of wives to unmarried mothers in Lebensborn homes was 60:40. Considering the small number of vacancies and a total strength of 250,000 potential fathers, this hardly suggests a boom in pre- or extra-conjugal sex – or certainly not one which materially affected the birth-rate.

Thanks to the failure of its intended beneficiaries to meet their quota, Lebensborn was able to extend its services to a wider circle of racially meritorious mothers. They consisted primarily of women in the Party administration, who were bluntly reminded of their duty to bear children and of the facilities for doing so in a discreet manner.

One such reminder was issued at a meeting of the 'Syndicate of Leaders of the German Women's Groups' at Minsk. A memorandum filed at Rosenberg's operational headquarters for the occupied Eastern territories in April 1943 recorded that the ladies' attention was drawn to the Lebensborn SS maternity home 'to which is attached a separate registry office where births can be recorded without any need to notify the home authorities. Party Member Wurster . . . stressed how important every genetically sound child is to our future, and that everything must therefore be done to support the mother and child and guarantee their health and survival'.[280]

Offers of this kind were made with the sanction of Himmler, who also devoted exhaustive consideration to the complete 'skimming off of healthy blood' in the occupied territories. In August 1943 he restated his findings in a circular addressed to his principal departments and nine Senior SS and Police Commanders (HSSPF) in these areas. Reliable German gynaecologists must be posted to the occupied territories, there to lend discreet assistance to pregnant German women and girls. There was no need to establish maternity homes abroad for those who wished to give birth in secret: 'They will be enabled to bring their children into the world on Reich territory, peacefully, safely and under the requisite and desirable conditions of secrecy, through the facilities of the Women's Association, the National Socialist Public Welfare Organization, and Lebensborn.'[281] Finally, the most stringent measures must be taken to combat abortion.

Abortion among foreign women, on the other hand, was to be encouraged unless they were pregnant by a German male. The child's importance was paramount. Should it be racially valuable, care must be taken at the appropriate time that it 'comes into the Reich, either alone or with its mother in her capacity as a repository of German blood or mother of a German child'.[282] This was where Lebensborn re-entered the picture. It was instructed to set up hostels where Himmler could accommodate children of Germanic type. These he 'procured' from Poland and Russia, Czechoslovakia and Yugoslavia – even from Greece. 'It is obvious that there will always be some racially good types in such a mixture of peoples. In these cases I consider it our duty to take the children and remove them from their environment, if necessary by abduction. Either we acquire any good blood we can use for ourselves and give it a place in our nation, or we destroy it.'[283] Lebensborn was required to take over these children for preliminary Germanization and test them for racial aptitude. Those whose ancestry was suspect could be returned to their parents. The rest would be given a German forename and lodged with German foster-parents – another contribution to the Lebensborn reservoir from which childless couples were kept supplied. The sole purpose of this inhuman and predatory scheme was national aggrandisement and the triumph of pure number. Himmler's aim was to 'bring home' 30 million human beings 'of our blood' so as to make the Reich, with a population of 120 million Germanic souls, the dominant power in Europe. The project never became fully operational. Its scope is unknown and its barbarous traces were obliterated by the abduction and renaming of its youthful victims.

Himmler affected to be highly delighted with the success of his Lebensborn venture. Despite all the mud that had once been flung at its irreproachably respectable maternity homes, he smugly declared in 1944, opposition had now waned.

The Reichsführer's confidence probably related more to his future plans than to what he had achieved with the dozen-odd homes which he fondly thought of as the succour and sanctuary of all who conceived out of wedlock. The heyday of Lebensborn, he assured Kersten, was still to come. He had already allowed it to become known that any unmarried woman desirous of a child could turn to the organization with complete assurance. It would then recommend racially flawless males as 'reproduction assistants'. Himmler's post-war dream was that all women of thirty who were still childless should be statutorily enabled – if not compelled – to contribute to the racial assets of the Greater German Reich in this manner.

Motherhood for all

On 6 April 1942, Himmler issued his men with a somewhat bizarre order of the day: 'It is unworthy of a decent man to seduce an under-age girl, plunge her into unhappiness and then, in most cases, deprive our nation of a future wife and mother. Always bear in mind how outraged you would be if a young daughter or sister of yours were ruined. You would quite rightly insist that the culprit be brought to book without mercy.'[284] The founder of Lebensborn evidently assumed that no girl who had lost her innocence would ever find a husband. What makes this pronouncement even more grotesque, however, is that the Reichsführer-SS, while categorically encouraging his men to have sexual intercourse outside marriage, should simultaneously have posed as the guardian of maidenly innocence. One finds the same perverted petty bourgeois morality reflected in his address to SS generals at Posen on 4 October 1943, when he expounded the inherent moral inviolability of the Black Order: 'Most of you must know what it means when 100 dead bodies are lying side by side, or 500, or 1,000. To have endured this and at the same time, discounting exceptions attributable to human frailty, to have preserved one's decency – that is what has made us hard. This is a glorious page in our history which has never been written nor ever will be.'[285]

Decently committed atrocities . . . Only the logic of a fanatic could have reconciled such a contradiction in terms. Himmler's SS men had to exterminate subhuman elements without compunction, yet their hands remained clean. The precious racial nucleus of the German people had to be enlarged in defiance of bourgeois conventions, whether by wholesale copulation or kidnapping raids on occupied territory, but the innocence of German virgins must be cherished and protected as a point of honour. Himmler called this 'having an absolutely natural attitude to the laws and circumstances of life'.

This did not, of course, imply that under-age girls were taboo from the aspect of national propagation. Although their inexperience must not be unscrupulously taken advantage of, it was another matter if they themselves were sensible of their duty to Fatherland and Führer and desirous of performing the same. Being the aim of National Socialist education for girls, this attitude merited full support.

The woman superintendent of one training camp wrote gleefully to the mother of an inmate that her daughter and five other girls were shortly to 'present the Führer with a child'. Parents could do little about such matters because, as one Labour Service girl wrote to her family: 'You better not beat me if I come home with a baby, or I'll denounce you!'[286]

The mayor of a Palatinate town drew public attention to the relevant civic duty by announcing the establishment of a fund to support girls who wished to present the Führer with a baby, though they and their prospective mates had to observe bureaucratic niceties by notifying their intention in advance. The mayor of Wattenscheid endeavoured to mobilize spinsters of less tender age. In the case of women born before 1910 but still unmarried, the municipality undertook to sponsor their first or, should the happy occasion arise, second child until it reached the age of majority. The solicitous city fathers additionally offered a bonus of RM 500 for each announcement of birth.

'Wheels must turn for victory!' proclaimed the posters calling for greater industrial effort. 'And pram-wheels for the next war!' added those who viewed the dictates of population policy with ironical amusement. In fact, the outbreak of war lent momentum to measures in this field, which at first tended to be random. The authorities avoided issuing precise official directives which might close the door to innocent disclaimers at a later stage. After all, there were plenty of zealous and well-placed Party members who knew where their duty lay without being told.

But the public caught on. At meetings in the Lower Taunus, the local Party leader was bombarded with awkward questions. Was it true that girls in the youth organizations were encouraged to have babies and accommodated for that purpose in SS-run institutions? Were girls likewise released from the Labour Service if prepared to have children by SS men?[287] Complaints and rumours were far too widespread and specific for Party officials to dismiss them simply as enemy propaganda.

Ruth H., a Labour Service girl posted to a small village near Dillenberg, sent her fiancé, Karl L., who was on active service, this naïvely candid account of her enrolment in the Labour Service: 'The first question they ask a Labour Service girl is, who's going to have a baby for the Führer? Then the girls go into a camp and have to stay there for a year. First be used by SS men, then stay for a year and have a child. If you do all right they slip you RM 1,000 and let you go . . . The second thing is, they put something in the girls' food so they don't have a period . . .'[288]

It was useless to deny such things. In a report to the Party Chancellery, regional headquarters at Magdeburg-Anhalt referred in passing to a current rumour that Labour Service girls of exceptionally fine physique were asked if they would like to present the Führer with a child. Something else had percolated the public consciousness, too: 'It is said that, after the war, every man will have two wives because Germany needs children and people.'[289]

The German Girls' League was second only to the Labour Service as a means of alerting inexperienced young females to their responsibilities. As one senior Party official explained to an audience of under-age BdM girls: 'You can't all get a husband, but you can all be mothers!'[290]

Measures aimed at the full exploitation of German motherhood gave rise to conjectures of the direst hue. The Bingen headquarters of the Women's Association reported a rumour which it classified as dangerous enemy propaganda: 'Soldiers on leave from the front are alleged to have been told that the wives of men rendered impotent by war-wounds will be forced to associate with other men in premises established for the purpose, in order to produce children.'[291] This was untrue, of course, but the Party authorities certainly ensured that bachelors on leave were provided with female company. 'The creation of a good social environment for the soldier on leave from the front,' Bormann decreed in Circular 83/44, 'is essential for reasons of population policy.'[292] So that they could strike up 'well-founded acquaintanceships with girls', the Party Chancellery recommended in April 1944 that the various regional Party headquarters should arrange special socials and dances. The Women's Association and BdM were to select suitable girls to attend these functions, not in uniform but in attractive afternoon dresses or regional costume. Joint excursions, sightseeing trips and factory tours were also regarded as likely aids to matchmaking. 'By arranging social functions, the Party will not only give the soldier on leave a chance to enjoy himself and meet girls with a view to choosing a companion in life, but also steer him back to the Party and its organizations.'[293] Though dry and decorous, this formula did not rule out the possibility of 'minor accidents'. It was as characteristic of Bormann's power-hungry pose of respectability as it was of his concentration, even when playing the matchmaker, on methods of reinforcing Party influence.

No rumour, however wild, surpassed the future imaginings of National Socialist population experts. Even the most apparently ludicrous exaggeration contained a germ of truth. The grounds for speculation were quite concrete in many cases, although conjecture often outweighed definite knowledge. The Bingen rumour, for example, had a very obvious cause.

Leonardo Conti, the Reich Director of Health, had in 1942 equipped every Gau with a medical advisory service for infertile married couples entitled 'Aid to Childlessness in Marriage'. The responsible public health department soon reported widespread public interest and a good flow of visitors to the advisory centres. However, the new service aroused exaggerated hopes which could not be fulfilled: medical assistance bore fruit in only 20 per cent of cases, partly because war-time conditions made it difficult to administer thorough clinical and therapeutic treatment. The department also reluctantly conceded that many husbands fought shy of entrusting themselves to the service and that religious objections had been encountered.

Aid to Childlessness in Marriage was a sensible enough institution and quite compatible with the functions of any government health service. It nonetheless played a subordinate role in Conti's all-embracing plan for population growth and was only meant as a preliminary step towards future measures so radical that they would abolish childlessness altogether.

In June 1942 the Reich Director of Health tried to interest senior Party authorities in a paper entitled 'Raising the Birth-Rate by Marital Introduction, Marriage Guidance and Fostering'. This neglected no means to the attainment of its lofty objectives.[294]

Conjugal productivity, Conti declared in support of the steps he had already taken, must be further augmented by encouraging early marriage. Nevertheless, his findings showed that too many worthwhile women remained unmarried. In order to pair them off, the Party should collaborate with medical bodies in arranging planned introductions. The accent was on the word 'planned'. Conti's proposal assigned the principal role to genetically expert physicians who would, as it were, bring suitable mates together on the basis of their genetic horoscope. He adduced another argument in favour of controlled matrimony which must have impressed the proponents of a Greater Germanic Reich: his scheme was particularly suited to the requirements of future colonies and the Eastern territories, where women would be scarce.

The complete system of marriage guidance envisaged by Conti went far beyond the modest welfare service which he was at first able to establish. He contemplated an artificial insemination scheme which would not only use a husband's semen but exploit the valuable genetic characteristics of married friends. Being himself a physician versed in genetics, Conti was evidently attracted by the thought of experiments in group-interbreeding designed to Mendelize the pure Germanic homunculus into existence. Technical difficulties prevented him from considering the related idea of a semen bank for the élite.

Latent in the innocuous term 'fostering' was the idea that every woman should be compelled by the State to make her biological contribution to the national community. Conti left it to single women to choose whether they had children by their lovers, by genetically tested strangers, or by artificial insemination. In each case, Lebensborn would assume financial responsibility for the 'foster-child'. The Reich Director of Health further recognized the importance of safeguarding the social status of such women, but that was outside his sphere.

Himmler, who was no stranger to bold solutions, read Conti's paper with outraged surprise. Somebody was poaching on his preserves, and he said as much to Martin Bormann. Let Conti look to his own position. His doctors should confine themselves to curing sterility. Anything beyond this was (a) a hot potato, (b) a thing of the future and (c) better left to the Party's initiative.[295]

It was certainly a hot potato, but Himmler had long ago grabbed it and, with the Führer's knowledge, evolved precise ideas of what must be done later on, after final victory. Lebensborn was only a beginning. The 'honourable houses of love' where Germany's finest and most lovely women would in future perform the sex-act with the finest and most valiant of German males – a Hitlerian flight of fancy – were only a random by-product of the Führer's verbal diarrhoea. No one who assessed the prospects realistically could have expected such establishments to produce 'millions of human beings . . . who would otherwise never be born'. The Reichsführer-SS, with his more methodical turn of mind, was preparing a fundamental reform of the marriage laws in consultation with Heydrich and Bormann.

The childless marriage, he pontificated as early as 1941, should be assessed as a relationship undeserving of State support and encouragement. The personal happiness of Herr and Frau Müller was unimportant – all that mattered was whether they had children. For that reason, the new marriage law would embody provisions under which a union must be dissolved if it remained childless for longer than five years. Himmler felt confident that such a law, being based on the Germanic sense of clanship, would herald a fresh 'intellectual and spiritual advancement of the German nation'.[296]

As the war progressed and casualties mounted, Himmler's Germanic sense of clanship entered another evolutionary phase. 'The present form of marriage is a satanic achievement on the part of the Catholic Church; the marriage laws are themselves immoral.'[297] His moral grounds for this assertion reflected the bad conscience and specious old arguments of the inveterate bourgeois. A woman, he pleaded, simply took no trouble with her husband under this immoral marriage law because her claims on him were legally certified; a husband, who could not make do with one woman throughout his life, was driven to unfaithfulness and hypocrisy. The Reichsführer hastened to garnish this transparent argument with a motive based on population policy: men failed to produce more children with their wives for reasons of personal distaste and did not dare to do so with their mistresses for fear of social ostracism.

In May 1943, Himmler radiantly confided to his masseur that the Führer had decided to legalize bigamy as soon as the war was over.[298] Not universally, but as a mark of distinction reserved for war heroes, namely, holders of the German Cross in Gold, the Knight's Cross and, later on, those who had been awarded the Iron Cross First Class and close-combat clasp. 'This would encompass the majority of those with proven fighting qualities, it being of vital importance to the Reich that they should transmit these to their children.' Experience of the new system would show whether it was feasible to abolish monogamy altogether.

To the Reichsführer, this was a foregone conclusion. He could see nothing but advantages in store. Two wives would produce far more children, compete for their husband's favour and satisfy his polygamous disposition. Rivalry would be impossible, of course, because the first wife would receive special privileges and the title 'Domina'. No heed must be paid to tender emotions and sensibilities because the welfare of future generations was at stake. After all, 'Who will inquire in 300 or 500 years' time if a certain Fräulein Müller or Schulze was unhappy?'[299] Himmler had some equally straightforward solutions for the economic problems involved. War-heroes would in any case be given farms in the East, where living was cheap; permission to contract a second marriage must be accompanied by the bestowal of a remunerative government post; and, finally, the Minister of Finance would have to exempt legal bigamists from income tax. All in all, there were high times ahead for the more privileged members of the master race.

These long-term aspirations were not unknown to the senior members of the Nazi hierarchy. The Reich Department of Youth Leadership also devoted sporadic consideration to the subject of 'legalized bigamy', or the sanctioning of temporary or morganatic marriages. According to the former BdM leader Melitta Maschmann, male heads of department were all in favour of these SS schemes for the improvement of racial stock.[300] Senior women officials in the BdM firmly opposed them. Similarly, far from deeming it a mark of exemplary conduct if one of their number conceived a child out of wedlock, they expected her to resign her post.

Something of these plans filtered through to the general public, too. This was not surprising, since they were only the logical consequence of thunderous Party pronouncements and demands in the sphere of population policy. Everyone could draw his own inferences with ease. However, rumour hurried on ahead of actual developments and tinged them with a vulgarity which, though near the mark, offended the bizarrely puritanical outlook of Nazi experts on planned breeding. Controlled reproduction on a massive scale, as envisaged by Himmler, Conti and associates, simply could not permit this. The breeding of human livestock must be conducted in a decent and disciplined fashion. Lebensborn maternity homes were not houses of ill fame, Labour Service camps for women were not al fresco brothels, and the BdM was not a recruiting office for amateur prostitutes. Yet these same Party institutions were also, and in particular, subject to the régime's commandments on the subject of population growth. The call to girls of all ages to present the Führer with illegitimate children was common knowledge and a frequent topic of conversation. The response was poor. In Munich, for example, the illegitimate birth-rate remained almost constant and tended to fall rather than climb. Records kept by the municipal juvenile welfare department show that the numbers of children born to unmarried women ranged from 2,727 (1930) to 2,374 (1940). The rise in subsequent years was probably attributable to wartime conditions rather than ideological influence.

Given a totalitarian educational and administrative system, time alone could tell whether this 'more liberal attitude toward the child' would prevail. Plenty of government authorities and youth leaders made strenuous efforts to see that it did. Scant opposition was voiced by high-ranking functionaries or BdM leaders. One senior BdM official declared her readiness to speak out at a public demonstration and reject SS endeavours in population policy on behalf of all women youth leaders. She inserted such a reference in the text of her speech, but it never passed her lips.

Martin Bormann: The model husband

THE couple whom Hitler's Mercedes wafted to the registry office on 2 September 1929 were destined more perfectly than any other husband-and-wife team to meet the ideal requirements of National Socialist family planning and population policy. In a certain sense, the occupants of the car personified the human basis and success of the entire Nazi movement.

The three men wore SA uniform. Ensconced in his customary place beside the driver sat Adolf Hitler, who had just taken a major step on the road to power by concluding an unholy alliance with the German National Party, the Stahlhelm and the Pan-Germans. The Party leader was taking time off to act as a witness. The bride's father sat behind him with the happy couple. Major Walter Buch (ret.), the son of a Baden judge, had emerged from the war a battalion commander, been active in veterans' associations and joined the NSDAP at an early stage. Commander of the Franconian SA under Streicher's Gauleitership in 1923, he soon obtained a transfer to Munich. In 1927 the compliant and socially acceptable ex-major was appointed by Hitler to head the Party's Investigation and Arbitration Committee (USCHLA). Here, in company with Ulrich Graf and Hans Frank, Buch was supposed to watch over the morals of the Party but spent most of his time checking infractions of the Führer's will. On 30 June 1934, both these functions coincided. Buch assembled a band of veteran toughs for the Röhm operation in Munich and put them at Hitler's disposal when he flew in from Bonn. He was subsequently appointed senior Party judge.

The bride, twenty-year-old Gerda Buch, had only been a Party member for six months but was proving an exceptionally faithful devotee of National Socialist ideology. There was no exercise or abuse of power in which she failed to discern the obscure but noble outlines of the Führer's grand design. Somehow, Gerda managed to weave everything she read, saw and experienced into her homespun version of the National Socialist gospel. She was a sure candidate for the Party's gold badge.

The bridegroom was Martin Bormann. Born into a lower-middle-class family from Halberstadt, he ended the First World War as an ordinary gunner and then became an estate overseer. Bormann belonged to the 'League against Jewish Arrogance' and was a section commander in the old Rossbach Free Corps organization. He first won folkish renown for his complicity in a political murder. On 31 May 1923, some Free Corps men butchered the schoolmaster Walter Kadow in a wood near Parchim because he had allegedly betrayed Leo Schlageter, a German saboteur and subsequent Nazi martyr, to the French. The ring-leader, Rudolf Höss, was given ten years' penal servitude, the man in the background twelve months' imprisonment. Höss was later rewarded for his noble deed with the commandantship of Auschwitz concentration camp. Bormann's term of imprisonment earned him the Blood Order in 1938. On his release, Bormann drew closer to the NSDAP and in February 1927 joined the Party as member No. 60508. Starting off as a Party official and regional secretary in Thuringia, the immensely hard-working executive assistant beavered his way on to the staff of the Supreme Command of the SA in Munich, where he established himself in 1928. Steadily and unobtrusively, he climbed from the lowest to one of the highest rungs on the Third Reich's political ladder. In 1933 he became a Reichsleiter and chief of staff to the Deputy Führer, Rudolf Hess. He gradually relieved his chief of day-to-day business and took a grip on the reins of Party administration. In 1938 he joined the Führer's personal staff and never thereafter left his side, noting, checking, reporting, implementing. Bormann knew how to make himself indispensable. He polished off the chores that Hitler deferred for reasons of convenience, laziness or indecision. One word from the Führer, his mentor, and Bormann amplified it into a directive for insertion in his files and memoranda. After the Deputy Führer's flight in 1941, he formally assumed Hess's duties as head of the Party Chancellery and became a Reichsminister into the bargain, and a year later his title was 'Secretary to the Führer'. Bormann was the chief clerk *par excellence*. Always in the background but always on tap, always one step ahead of his rivals, superior to them in brutality and arrogance, cunning and flattery, usually better informed and certainly closer to the Führer's ear. Nobody by-passed Bormann, neither Himmler nor Goebbels nor – least of all, now – Göring. Bormann became the régime's best hated and most influential man – its brown eminence.

He made an equally thorough job of his marriage. His choice of wife proved ideal. A bare nine months after their marriage Gerda bore a son, Adolf Martin. Hitler naturally stood sponsor. Nine more children followed in quick succession, among them a godson – Heinrich Ingo – for Uncle Himmler. Nothing could deter the indefatigable Gerda from presenting her beloved Führer with more children. On 24 September 1944 she wrote to her 'best and dearest Daddy' at headquarters – the Allies had already crossed the German frontier in the Aachen-Trèves area – that as soon as the situation in the West improved she wanted another child. Since Bormann had, she fondly believed, touched no alcohol in recent months – he was renowned among the Führer's boisterous aides as a hard drinker – and had also given up smoking, it was bound to turn out an intelligent youngster in spite of his over-work.

Using the resources of the Adolf Hitler German Industry Fund, which was administered by the Deputy Führer, Bormann built up a vast acreage round Hitler's Berghof residence on the Obersalzberg. Farmers were bought out and their land registered in Bormann's name. In the course of these large-scale development schemes he naturally acquired a sizeable property for himself and his family in the Führer's immediate neighbourhood. This not only cordoned off the area from the general public but ensured that other Nazi notables could not dispute his position by settling there too. They were only visitors to the Obersalzberg; he was on home ground.

Apart from anything else, the Alpine panorama of the Berchtesgaden retreat provided an excellent scenic backcloth for Bormann's model family, which none of Hitler's other vassals could rival. And what a spectacle it made! The laughing German mother with her youngest on her arm, and, ranged beside her like a set of organ-pipes, the rest of the happy band in leather shorts and peasant dresses. There was nothing farcical about this wholesome idyll. Bormann's marriage was exem-plary in the genuine sense. Hitler visited the Berghof often enough to enable his shadow to devote time to his family. True, the afternoons and evenings were reserved for the Führer's circle, of which Bormann was an indispensable member, and true, he occasionally vanished into a young secretary's bedroom for an afternoon nap when disinclined to make the short trip home – but who was Gerda to complain of pecca-dilloes when her Führer magnanimously overlooked them?

The couple's correspondence during the closing years of the war, most of which the trusty secretary spent far from the Obersalzberg saving the Reich (Gerda's conception of his duties) at the Führer's side, bears witness to their unclouded conjugal bliss. 'Daddy' wrote faithfully to his 'beloved Mummy-girl' about the tribulations of his job. His own

account of it often seemed to reduce the international stage to the
dimensions of a puppet-theatre in which he pulled the strings – but
perhaps that was not so wide of the mark. Bormann evidently had
plenty of fun as well, because the final New Year's party at Hitler's
headquarters lasted from 30 December 1944 until 2 January 1945, with
much dancing and drinking on the part of exuberant aides and secretaries. Succumbing to a brief fit of the blues on New Year's night,
Bormann wrote to his 'dearest heart' not to be annoyed with him if
fifteen years of arduous work had aged him. He would never stop
loving her.

He proved this during his rare twinges of uncertainty about final
victory by directing Gerda to dry enough apples because it was better
to eat dried apple than nothing at all. She must also lay in a large and
bomb-proof stock of honey. Tunnels driven into the Obersalzberg
provided suitable storage space. Bormann pressed ahead feverishly with
these shelters and would have liked to store all his household effects
there. As early as 1943 he urged Gerda to drive the car inside at the first
hint of an air-raid, before the gates were shut.

In October of the same year Bormann renewed his acquaintanceship
with the youthful actress M. He was enchanted beyond measure – so
much so that, having discovered during his last visit home that he was
ten pounds overweight, he yielded to her promptings and cut out
breakfast in favour of apple-juice and a teaspoonful of magnesia. Gerda
marvelled at this news and opined that M. – who also knew the family
well – must be an 'incredible' girl. On 21 January 1944 Bormann put
his 'dear Mummy-girl' straight: he was the incredible one, not M.
'You can't imagine how overjoyed I was. She attracted me immensely,
and in spite of her resistance I kissed her without more ado and set her
afire with my burning delight. I fell madly in love with her. I arranged
it so that I saw her again many times, and then I took her in spite of all
her refusals. You know how determined I can be, and M. naturally
couldn't hold out for long. Now she is mine, and I – lucky fellow! – am
doubly and unbelievably happily married. At least, I feel I am.'[301] He
added that M., the good girl, was smitten with pangs of conscience,
which was – of course – sheer nonsense. What did Gerda think of her
crazy boy? The question didn't need answering because he knew her
too well and was always raving about her to M. But M. thought Gerda
would be angry with her. 'Oh, my sweet, you can't imagine how
happy I am with the two of you! Really, Heaven has been good to me.
All the happiness you have given me through yourself and the children,

and now I have M. as well! I shall have to be doubly and trebly careful now, and see that I keep well and fit.'[302]

Bormann had not miscalculated. Gerda had long sensed that there was something between him and M. She liked M. so much, and so did the children, that she couldn't be angry with him. 'It is a thousand pities that fine girls . . . should be denied children. In M.'s case you will be able to alter this, but then you will have to see to it that one year M. has a child and the next year I, so that you always have a wife who is mobile. (WHAT A CRAZY IDEA!) Then we'll put all the children together in the house by the lake, and live together, and the wife who is not having a child will always be able to come and stay with you in Obersalzberg or Berlin. (THAT WOULD NEVER DO! EVEN IF THE TWO WOMEN WERE THE BEST OF FRIENDS. BETTER EACH ON HER OWN. VISITS, ALL RIGHT, BUT EVEN THAT WITHIN LIMITS.)[303] The comments in capitals were added by Bormann, who returned Gerda's letters for filing. But Gerda had thought still further ahead. M. was bound to have a baby – 'you being you!'[304] – in which case it would be best if M. and the child moved in with her.

The matter evidently preyed on Gerda's mind, because three days later, on 27 January 1944, she communicated some more suggestions. 'I'm only worried that you may have given the poor girl a frightful shock with your impetuous ways. (I EXPECT I DID, AT FIRST.) Does she really love you, then? (I BELIEVE SHE LOVES ME VERY MUCH. OF COURSE, IT DOESN'T GO AS DEEP AS OUR LOVE; FIFTEEN YEARS OF ONE'S YOUTH, RICH IN SHARED EXPERIENCE, AND TEN CHILDREN WEIGH HEAVILY IN THE SCALES.) You say in your letter that you are now doubly and both times exceedingly happily married. Beloved, does she love you as a wedded wife should, and will she remain yours for good even if she cannot bear your name! (TIME ALONE WILL TELL.) It would be a good thing if a law were to be made at the end of this war, like the one at the end of the Thirty Years War, which would entitle healthy, valuable men to have two wives. (THE FÜHRER IS THINKING ALONG SIMILAR LINES!) So frighteningly few valuable men survive this fateful struggle, so many valuable women are doomed to be barren because their destined mate was killed in battle – should that be? We need the children of these women too! (ABSOLUTELY, FOR THE STRUGGLES TO COME, WHICH WILL DECIDE THE NATIONAL DESTINY.)'[305]

Bormann's general comment on this letter: 'MY DARLING MUMMY! YOU ARE WONDERFUL AND I LOVE YOU MADLY!'[306] He sent her some literature on the subject under discussion and she studied it with

characteristic zeal. A fortnight later she informed him of her conclu-
sions. The measures to be instituted must on no account give *carte
blanche* to sexual adventurers who claimed to want children. On the
contrary, every man who was sound in mind and body and a valuable
member of the national community must be given an opportunity to
contract one or two additional liaisons. These ties would have to be
protected by the State and possess the same legal validity as marriage.
The required protection might be afforded by declarations made to the
civil authorities, as follows:

'I, Martin Bormann, born 17 June 1900, declare that, with the
knowledge and consent of my wife Gerda, born 23 October 1909,
I wish to contract a National Emergency Marriage (*Volksnotehe*) with
M. This union shall have the same validity before the law as my first
marriage.'
'I, Gerda Bormann, *née* Buch, consent to the decision of my husband,
Martin Bormann, to contract a National Emergency Marriage with
M., and I agree that this union should have the same validity as the ties
which unite us.'[307]

Apart from lavishing his love and solicitude on her, Martin Bormann
paid his wife the highest tribute she could have hoped to earn by her
wifely understanding: 'You come of National Socialist stock; as a
Nazi child you are dyed in the wool, so to speak. Your colour doesn't
fade in the sun or wash, nor does it run, and no one knows better than
I do what that means.'[308]
To this brace of turtle-doves, with years of married life behind them,
Bormann's behaviour was perfectly compatible with the joys of petty
bourgeois existence. On 7 October 1944 he wrote home: 'You know,
I've become only too familiar with every kind of meanness, distortion,
slander, nauseating and false flattery, toadying, ineptitude, folly, idiocy,
ambition, vanity, greed for money, etc., etc., in short, all unpleasant
aspects of human nature . . . I've had enough!'[309] He dreamed of with-
drawing into private life, of retirement to some pleasant manor-house
which the Führer would bestow on him in recognition of his services,
and of joining his wife and children there in a splendid existence remote
from political activity of any kind. Whether his No. 2 wife would have
a share in this idyll, he did not say.

6 The New Man

THE GERMAN SPECIES OF THE GERMANIC GENUS

ADOLF HITLER seldom neglected an opportunity to demonstrate his artistic sense. If Providence and national necessity had not decreed otherwise and called him to become a statesman, he often lamented to his private circle, he would have been a great painter or architect. The frustrated artistic genius took dictatorial revenge by distorting architecture, sculpture and painting to match his own ideas and aims.

Ever to hand on the Führer's desk lay a pile of drawing-paper on which, during the leisure hours he gladly spared for the purpose, he scribbled designs for gargantuan edifices to be built in his own honour. His taste in architecture may be deduced from his megalomaniac plans for the Nuremberg Rally complex or his new urban lay-out for Berlin, for the 1,000-foot-high Hall of the Nation and gigantic triumphal arch – projects which he commissioned his personal architect, Albert Speer, to design and then amended with his own hand. They were bizarre records of one man's boundless claim to authority – they transcended all human scales of measurement and conceptions of time. Even at the planning stage, it was borne in mind that their vast granite remains must still bear witness to the Führer's unique greatness thousands of years after his death.

Hitler's talent for draughtsmanship and predilections in painting formed a homely counterpart to this cold gigantomania. The views of old house-fronts and picturesque corners which he drew and painted in water-colours and got a crony to hawk for him during his days as a casual labourer display a photographic attention to detail so destitute of any life and originality that it stamps them as the amateurish efforts of an uninspired copyist. Hitler's value-judgments in art history followed the same pattern. He favoured the German painters of the late nineteenth century – Waldmüller, Grützner, Makart, Leibl, Thoma – for whom sculptural accuracy, often accompanied by false ostentation or suspect romanticism, took the place of artistic expression. Being the pets of Hitler's private collection, these artists were accepted as grand masters of neo-German art.

Hitler laid as much claim to artistic judgement as he did to the art of statesmanship. He also took it just as seriously. In his speech on the Enabling Act of 23 March 1933, which effectively armed his 'thousand-year' régime with full dictatorial powers, the Führer also expounded his new art policy: 'Art will always be the expression and reflection of the yearning and reality of an age. Cosmopolitan contemplation is in the throes of rapid decline. Heroism is passionately emerging as the future fashioner and leader of political destinies. It is the function of art to be an expression of this determinative spirit of the age. Blood and race will again become the source of artistic intuition. It is the government's task to ensure that, especially in a period of limited political power, the nation's intrinsic worth and will to exist should find even mightier cultural expression.'[310] In other words, Hitler commanded the spirit of the age, and his orders were that art should heroically testify to blood and race. As in all spheres of public life, the catchword was co-ordination. This entailed the elimination of dissent by burning books and raiding art galleries, purging universities and academies of Jewish and other subversive elements, imposing professional disabilities, censorship and the combing of museums and galleries for un-German works of arts. Those artists who did conform were absorbed by the system, organized into Reich Chambers of Culture, supervised by Party officials and – when they stepped out of line – denounced by Party zealots.

A world of fair illusion

'The road to renewed artistic creation is clear!' announced the *Völkischer Beobachter* on 15 October 1933. On that date, having already devoted a day each to the German worker (1 May) and the German farmer (Harvest Festival), the régime of national renaissance celebrated a 'Day of German Art'. In Munich, the newly designated capital of the German art world, Reich Chancellor Hitler laid the foundation-stone of a 'House of German Art' where the mind and spirit of Germany could make their permanent abode. 'To the artist, there accrues the exalted task of being, not merely a painter or sculptor, architect or draughts-man, author or actor, but also the custodian of all that is great and noble in the German. May he take his place in the great revolutionary front of workers and peasants, and may he, as a soldier of Adolf Hitler, become a proclaimer of all that is essentially German.'[311] The hammer broke as Hitler ceremonially tapped the foundation-stone of his Muses' grove dedicated to German realism.

Four years later, the public were given a taste of what German realism could not and might not be by a Munich exhibition entitled *Degenerate Art*. This assailed such monuments to cultural decay as masterpieces of the 'Brücke' and 'Blauer Reiter' schools, abstract paintings by Kandinsky and Klee, and social satires by Käthe Kollwitz and George Grosz. Placards made it easier for the crowds to arrive at a proper appreciation of degenerate art: 'This was how sick minds regarded Nature – German peasants seen through Yiddish eyes – German heroes of the World War being abused – The German woman ridiculed.' The works were so arranged as to illustrate the un-German nature of this artistic bolshevism: 'Group 6: Extinction of the last vestiges of racial awareness; Group 7: Idiots, cretins, paralytics; Group 8: Jews; Group 9: Utter lunacy.' A stylish crescendo, but one for which people had been well prepared by a campaign against the 'fraudulence of false fashion design'. Visitors flocked to the exhibition at the rate of 20,000 a day and eventually topped the 2 million mark. They cannot all have been clandestine admirers of modern art, or the organizers would hardly have been so gratified. Happily, they cabled spontaneous public reactions to Berlin: 'The artists ought to be tied up next to their pictures so that every German can spit in their faces, but not only the artists – also the museum people who tossed hundreds of thousands of marks into the jaws of these manufacturers of botched-up works at a time when millions were starving in the streets.'[312]

Concurrently, on 19 July 1937, Hitler opened a contrasting exhibition at his new home of 'true and eternal German art' in near-by Prinz-regentenstrasse. His inaugural address was larded with virulent attacks on the unnatural scrawlings and daubings of so-called modernity, which had, he said, been praised to the skies by spineless and unscrupulous literary hacks. For his part, he was irrevocably determined 'as in the sphere of political disorder, so, here too, to eliminate the claptrap from German artistic life'. Hitler replaced it with some of his own. The Vienna Academy reject propounded yet another truism – 'art stems from ability' – and the vilest demagogue in German history went on to inform his rapt opening-day audience that 'To be German means to be lucid! But that would signify that to be German also means, logically and above all, to be true.' On Hitler's submission, this 'sublime law' provided a criterion for the essence of art – of the new German art.[313]

This first Great German Art Exhibition cleared the way, as Hitler himself said later, 'initially for the decent, honest mediocrity'.[314] The show was organized by Adolf Ziegler, a brush-wielding veteran Nazi whom the Führer appointed professor and President of the Reich Chamber of Fine Arts. Of the 15,000 works submitted, 900 were selected. The main criteria, declared the art critic of the *Kölnische Volkszeitung* with prudent admiration, were lucidity, realism and expertise. Hitler, who was appalled by the preliminary selection, intervened in person to amend it, having previously commanded his court photographer, Heinrich Hoffmann, to cast an expert eye over the entries. Being 'a symbol of pure and invigorated German character', the exhibition at the House of German Art was intended to reflect the 'recovered Germany of today'[315] – the image of reality as National Socialism wished to see it.

The 750 paintings were dominated by landscapes (40 per cent) – German landscapes, of course. Almost swamped by this partly pastoral, partly heroic (i.e. stormy) lyricism were a handful of urban views depicting historical or National Socialist scenes. To judge by this exhibition, the workers of Germany were largely peasants (7 per cent of all themes) who busied themselves with plough and ox-cart while their dutiful wives plied the distaff. Germans were also shown exerting muscle and sinew in occupations of a more up-to-date nature (motorway construction), but machinery, factories and urban life – the whole modern labour process with all its attendant problems – found no place in these pictorial clichés of a secure and orderly world. Instead, much was to be seen of home, hearth and the simple life – a series of sham idylls ranging from the ironclad warrior mounted on his noble steed to the happy family circle having its elevenses.

Although these arts-and-crafty products may have accorded with the Führer's wretched personal taste, their themes were far less an expression of new realism than a reflection of what the new era yearned for. They served to distract the gaze from reality and titillate the public with visions of a lovelier and more delectable existence. The Minister of Public Enlightenment stated this quite openly at the annual meeting of the Strength through Joy association in 1937: 'A world of wonder and of fair illusion is meant to unfold here before our marvelling gaze. With simple and unclouded delight, people approach the illusions of art and dream themselves into an enchanted ideal world which life permits us all to sense but seldom to comprehend and never to attain.'[316]

Antiquated ideals and a wondrously mediocre and medieval world went to make up this fair illusion that hovered so dimly in the dreams of petty bourgeois and reactionaries. Not even the heroic, muscle-flaunting pose of many such pictures could obscure that impression. Attendance figures at Nazi exhibitions were as satisfactory as the controlled public response to them, and sales were unusually heavy. Pictures were always in demand for front parlours where, for all the heroism of the new era, plush and pleureuses still reigned in musty state.

Ideological nudity

Probably the most conspicuous but ideologically camouflaged element in the kaleidoscope of National Socialist imagery was the nude. Full-bosomed and voluptuous female forms of unambivalently ambivalent character were vividly committed to canvas on the most specious of artistic pretexts. President of the Chamber Adolf Ziegler, whose skill at capturing detail earned him the nickname 'Master of the Pubic Hair', concentrated on allegory. *The Four Elements* was his title for a painting in which a quartet of stalwart-thighed, firm-breasted beauties, symbolically garnished with torch, wheat-sheaf, water-pot and un-dulating hair, provided an ideologically orthodox demonstration of 'delight in a healthy body'. Ziegler's *Terpsichore* is notable for its wholly unballetic distortions above and below the waist: crooked in her demurely flexed left arm – the right is coquettishly raised, the better to tauten her breast – the Muse of Dancing holds a baton with all the grace of a drum-majorette. Paul Padua, an even defter exponent of the human form than Professor Ziegler and esteemed in later years as a society portraitist, was still more direct in his approach. His *Leda and the Swan* is as vapidly obscene as the unimaginative arbiters of contemporary taste allowed. Sepp Hilz of Upper Bavaria dressed carnal lust in rustic guise. His plump prostitutes with their prominent belly-rolls and sculptured nipples were identified as village damsels at their evening toilette by a peasant bed or baroque cupboard in the background.

The subjects chosen were variously insipid and the modes of artistic expression invariably feeble, but that was not the point. Writing in the prestige magazine *Das Reich*, Karl Korn very gingerly complained that Karl Truppe had perhaps shown a trace of 'outworn artistic technique' in his painting *Sein und Vergehen* (roughly: Present and Past).[317] This allegory depicted a seated crone in rusty black, and lying beside her a sun-drenched naked girl whose silken charms were calculated to exert a potent effect on those who viewed them. They could not have been lost on Adolf Wagner, the woman-fancying Gauleiter of Munich, because he craved the work as a gift from the Führer. Korn's gentle rebuke, penned without regard to this fact, earned him extreme disfavour in high places. The moral: beauty was whatever pleased the Führer, his paladins and cultural administrators; furthermore, the paying public needed a little something to stimulate the eye and senses apart from heroics and family bliss. During the war, one of the Führer's secretaries was bold enough to complain about the abundance of nudes which he tolerated at his German Art Exhibition. The greatest military commander of all time justified this bias with a reference to his trusty soldiers: 'Coming home from the front, he said, they had a physical need to forget all the filth by admiring beauty of form.'[318]

For once in a way, this was true, though it did not go far towards explaining the lewd hypocrisy of the nudes in question. It was this pin-up aspect of nudity which, uncurbed by genuine artistic appreciation of any kind, lent spice to the tasteless hotchpotch of sterile National Socialist hero- and warrior-figures by Thorak or Mölnir, Willrich or Breker. Racially conscious lust was as much a part of the muscular tumidity of this mediocre visual art as it was of the sentimental slush that abounded in native literature, where folkish high-mindedness was interspersed with passages such as this: 'It was the marvellous, godlike purity of her skin. Her slender little neck, her bare shoulders, the beginnings of her apple-sized breast. The urge to slide Thild's dress down, far down, all the way, so as to revel in the beauty of this superb girlish body just like someone viewing a work of art, arose unbidden and was hard to suppress.'[319]

The primacy of national biology

It must at the same time be conceded that displays of nakedness served another purpose, which was to exemplify the ideal racial type. Just as landscape painting could be German only if its theme was the German landscape, so portraiture and nude studies could call themselves German only if they depicted the German body. And German it was – Aryan, Germanic and Nordic from hair-line to instep. Indeed, so ultra-Nordic did it become in Arno Breker's colossal statues that the sculptor could no longer work from live models and was driven to consult anatomists instead. The racial perfection extolled by National Socialism could be far better demonstrated with the aid of ideal effigies than by reference to the physique of the National Socialist leaders themselves. This being so, the licensed artists of the Third Reich conscientiously helped these dream-figures to materialize, if only in galleries and museums.

One of the most effective champions of this new artist-created human being was the architect Paul Schultze-Naumburg. Schultze-Naumburg was a classic example of how the well-meaning petty bourgeois cultural romantic could turn into a zealous apostle of racism. In Wilhelmine times, he had made a name for himself as a costume and landscape reformer, as the founder of an arts and crafts centre housed in a fortress-like building of his own design, and as an architect of country mansions. In the mid-1920s he came under the influence of Hans F. K. Günther and Walther Darré, who were fellow-contributors to the folkish magazine *Kunstwart* (Art Guardian). To their racial theories and mystic love of the soil he added his own theory of 'physiognomic racial fitness'. Thuringia's first Nazi Minister of the Interior, Wilhelm Frick, appointed Schultze-Naumburg Director of the State Academy of Art at Weimar (birthplace of the Bauhaus movement!). Becoming a lecturer for Alfred Rosenberg's League of Struggle for German Culture, Schultze-Naumburg now took the field against 'degenerate art'. With diabolical skill and an unerring instinct for maximum audience-effect, he pilloried the artistic avante-garde. His lectures contrasted works by Nolde, Barlach, Heckel or Hofer with photographic reproductions of the clinically diseased – cretins, idiots and congenital cripples. It was obvious to any right-minded philistine that such works of art were sick, depraved and degenerate. 'To us, the name Schultze-Naumburg is a programme in itself!' rejoiced the folkish and National Socialist press.[320]

The art-agitator's programme took its physiognomical criteria from the cathedral statuary at Naumburg and Bamberg. 'There are enough of us, even today, whose faces are as well suited by the steel helmet as the Rider of Bamberg is by his crown.'[321] On this exalted plane of fashion reform, it was culture's task to participate in the struggle for racial selection and the eradication of inferior elements. 'It must undoubtedly be accepted that a substantial scattering of good things will also perish in this cruel test of survival. Viewed as a whole, however, this is no loss to mankind.'[322] That which was so expressly claimed for the Darwinian law of natural selection and heredity now applied,

by transference, to art. The professor and doctor (*honoris causa*) allotted
to art the task of lending visual expression to the new physical
ideal.

Buttressed by the anthropological findings of his friend and racial
adviser Hans Günther, Schultze-Naumburg defined the salient features
of Nordic beauty – 'vivacity, strength, cleanliness' – with such precision
and in such detail that his pupils had no excuse for straying from the
path of righteousness. Nordic dolichocephalism was associated with a
lofty brow and narrow temples; the overhanging occiput resulted in a
'backwards-sloping frontal bone inaptly called a "receding" fore-
head'.[323] The strongly protrusive nose with its pronounced bridge and
root might properly be termed aquiline. The lips must be as thin as the
nostrils, the jutting chin – a symbol of will-power – angular and devoid
of curves. Beneath strong supraorbital ridges and horizontal eyebrows
(which must never merge!), the large and mobile German eye (well
separated from its fellow-orb!) bent a pale-grey, pale- or dark-blue –
at all events, lustrous – gaze on the German world. Nordic beauty was
luminous and radiant, its fine-pored skin pale or rosy, its undulant
hair fair and fine.

This colourless thoroughbred's head, a combination of soft pastel
and rugged woodcut, sat atop a long neck flanked by broad shoulders.
The tall, long-legged body was further characterized by the 'mobile
contour' of the arms, which terminated in long slender hands with
curved finger-nails. The rib-cage was broad and strongly arched, the
pelvis clearly discernible, the waist or belt-line unaccentuated in either
sex. The spinal column supported this superb body nobly and with
ease. 'It must rise vertically like a jet of water, and may, at most,
emulate the same by swaying gently in the wind.'[324]

Already in his sixties, Schultze-Naumburg devoted particular
attention to the ideal female form. Familiarity with the dimensions
of four successive wives must have aided him in his exhaustive comparative research. His findings more or less corresponded with traditional predilections. Breasts nice and rounded, middle regions not too
bulky, legs long, calves slim and thighs full – such were the characteristics of the female German thoroughbred. Schultze-Naumburg
also stipulated broad shoulders and a narrow pelvis, which, while not
obstetrically desirable, was visually more attractive. The abdominal
wall had to be flat and firm – another feature which demanded considerable gymnastic exertion from a mother of four. Schultze-Naumburg
made comparative pictorial studies of the Nordic bosom. The nipple

had to be inverted and its areola flat, and the breasts themselves, pale-pink with weak pigmentation, must sit full and well-rounded on the thorax. The whole body, Schultze-Naumburg declared in Pygmalion-like ecstasy, impressed one by its 'wonderfully harmonious proportions and balance between grace and strength'.[325] That might have applied to his ideal woman, who had been devised in a mood of blithe sexuality, but his description of male beauty in the Nordic mould reminds one of a bloodless wooden soldier.

The painter Wolfgang Willrich chose an entirely different approach to the task of portraying 'the healthy human being of Nordic stock as an artistically worthwhile object of artistic creation in general'.[326] Willrich's star rose when that of Schultze-Naumburg had already begun to wane. Born in 1897, Willrich was an authentic product of the Nazi system and a discovery of Darré, the Reich Farmers' Leader. The Nazi art expert Walter Hansen, a careerist and denunciator of the first order, was unusually accurate in describing the abilities of his like-minded colleague. Willrich, he said, so arranged his studies at Dresden Academy 'that they enabled him to portray the healthy human being with good craftsmanlike technique'.[327] Willrich compensated for any deficiencies in craftsmanship by engaging in literary agitation. His writings purged race and art along the lines preached by his patron, Darré: 'The concept of race aspires to recreate the German aristocracy from sound national stock through the selection of the hereditarily first-rate by a voluntary process of eugenics, which aristocracy shall lead the nation, exemplary in manner and conduct, by dint of superior determination and valid example. To kindle the German nation's yearning for such an aristocracy, to define and cogently instil beauty and sublimity, not merely as the prerogative of incredible gods but as a human feasibility and visual objective of racial improvement – what a noble mission for art to perform!'[328]

In quest of Nordic form and Nordic expression, Willrich toured the country, crayon in hand. His aim was to capture the German countenance from Frisia in the north to Upper Bavaria in the south. The tangible result of his endeavours was a series of bovinely resolute-looking male and female visages with a faintly pensive undertone – heroism plus contemplation. Nude studies were not in Willrich's line, but he did manage to produce *Guardian of the Species*, a pregnant woman staring into space with lack-lustre eyes and hands folded on her pro-tuberant belly. He himself supplied the interpretation: 'Audacity and pride, circumspection and reserve, earnestness, resolution, integrity, loyalty – these are the qualities which can be perceived in the face of a typical Nordic German such as this.'[329] A noble mission indeed! Much in demand at Strength through Joy exhibitions and with the SS weekly *Das Schwarze Korps*, Willrich was the type of art-manufacturer whom the Security Service commissioned when it wanted 'artistically worthwhile reproductions' as opposed to trashy field postcards.[330]

Looking at these sexless girls and women, one finds it easy to understand why 'the racially inferior girl used to get asked to dance because she was, shall we say, more attractive, whereas the racially superior girl used to be the wall-flower because our national ideal of beauty had changed so utterly. It is quite clear that racially inferior elements in our nation always mature earlier than the genuine kind. They are always sexually more attractive and compliant than our own kind.'[331]

Sentiments like these, with which Himmler once warmed the hearts of a Hitler Youth audience, illustrate the complex-laden relationship that existed between folkish romantics and racial fanatics. One recalls Thild of the apple-sized breasts – not racially unobjectionable, maybe, but sexually more appealing than the German ideal of womanhood. Carried to its logical conclusion, this hinted at a rather joyless state of affairs. The authentic German woman was a magnificent breeder but no great shakes as a purveyor of carnal delight, a frigid late-developer incapable of arousing a man with blood in his veins. Himmler, who spoke from personal experience, treated himself to a 'more compliant' mistress. Bormann was the only Nazi grandee to possess an ideological dream-wife, and she was well enough schooled to share him with a concubine.

Officially, there were no such conflicts. Willrich's female types accorded perfectly with Himmler's conception of the Nordic maiden. Their faces, he confided in a foreword, seemed more and more familiar to him the longer he studied them. There was also an imperial affinity whose consequences Willrich deemed highly auspicious. Just as Himmler stole blond Germanic children from the Eastern territories and recruited Germanic warriors for his Waffen-SS in the West, so the egregious Willrich planned to collect 'fine examples of European yeomanry' from Brittany and Normandy in preparation for a Greater Germanic Empire. 'Once I have established a base of operations in one or two places there,' he perceptively announced, 'I shall have no further doubts about the success of the venture.'[332]

Whether winsomely naked or animate of countenance, the human form demanded neither realism nor ability, clarity nor veracity from the Third Reich artists who depicted it. It was their bounden and remunerative duty to turn out convincing portrayals of the ideal racial type. In the expert jargon of *Das Schwarze Korps*: 'What really matters in the portrayal of the naked human form and Nordic racial type is the manifestation – the exposure, in the true sense – of an animate beauty, the discovery and artistic fashioning of an elemental, godlike humanity. Only then does it become an effective means of educating our nation in moral strength, folkish greatness and, last but not least, resurrected racial beauty.'[333]

So here was yet another supporting plank in the great racial programme: like German lessons or physical training, art appreciation was to demonstrate the incontestable superiority of German blood. The National Socialists were the last people to rely on the remote long-term effects of their educational measures. Being in power, they had not only the pedagogic but also the legal means to speed up the creation of the new man. It was unanimously emphasized by their most disputatious supporters that this, though only a means to an end, was the first commandment of folkish rejuvenation.

The Nazis' crude Social Darwinism was reduced to a brief and seemingly innocuous formula in the first issue of *Nationalsozialistische Monatshefte*. In April 1930, it presented a schematic summary of the Party's organization and functions, mentioning *inter alia* the National Socialist German Medical Association. Succinctly, it proclaimed the 'primacy of national biology over national economics'. The more unthinking and credulous disciples of Hippocrates must indeed have felt flattered to be entrusted with so high a responsibility for the health of the nation, while chauvinistic conservatives felt confirmed by this simple formula in their abhorrence of Marxism and Bolshevism.

A glance at Alfred Rosenberg's pseudo-philosophical concoction *The Myth of the 20th Century* is enough to clarify the underlying aim. History, preached the Nazis' overrated but little-read chief ideologist from the Baltic, was a series of racial struggles in which the better blood always prevailed. According to Rosenberg, the best blood of all flowed in the veins of Nordic man, whom he credited with every major cultural achievement in the ancient, medieval and modern world. The inference to be drawn from this blood-myth: 'Either we ascend through the rejuvenation and selective breeding of age-old blood, coupled with intensified fighting spirit, to an act of purification, or the last Germanic-Occidental values of civilization and political discipline will sink into the filthy mire of the great cities.'[334] As elsewhere, discipline was a key-word in this 'ideological belch' – to quote Goebbels's description of Rosenberg's masterpiece.

Walther Darré, the soil-mystic from Argentina, was likewise convinced of the historical superiority of the Nordic race and postulated a *New Aristocracy of Blood and Soil* as *The Breeding Objective of the German Nation* – thus the titles of two of his written works. The future Minister of Agriculture and head of the SS Race and Resettlement Bureau (RuSHA) defined biological primacy in categorical terms: breeding should be construed as applied knowledge of the laws of heredity. One of Darré's contributions to breeding practice was the idea of 'farm reservations' where superior human livestock would be 'biologically' encouraged to reproduce under conditions which – monogamy apart – resembled those of a battery farm. Impure and inferior human material had, in Darré's terminology, to be 'rooted out'.[335] All this was down in black and white, even before 1933, and no one in the Party raised any objection.

Only a few months after their seizure of power, the members of the Nordic master race set to work to justify the eradication of inferior human material. The law for the prevention of hereditarily diseased offspring (14 July 1933) provided for the sterilization of persons suffering from incurable hereditary disabilities such as manic-depressive psychosis or epilepsy. This prophylactic measure took the form of a discretionary ordinance. In reality, it had a compulsory flavour because the attendant physician was obliged to notify the authorities if one of his patients displayed a clinical picture of the relevant type. The medical officer of health, in his turn, had to apply for a sterilization order in cases where he deemed it necessary, and a 'hereditary health tribunal' considered such applications as they were submitted. In other words, the system was such that sterilization could be carried out on persons who had not requested it.

This in itself constituted a dangerous infraction of the basic right of physical inviolability. The State reserved the right to suspend individual and existential rights in the higher interests of the community. Even in a constitutional State, considerable dangers attach to any such provision for the avoidance of irreversible hereditary damage. In the Third Reich, with its fanatical allegiance to national health and purity of blood, wholesome popular sentiment and racial laws, the door to despotism was flung wide. The inexorable consequence of such ideas was that the very existence of the congenitally sick seemed a threat, and that mentally ill and incurable people in need of care were seen as an unnecessary charge on the nation as a whole. Hitler's address to the Reichstag on 30 January 1934 made this quite clear, and on 1 September 1939, the day Poland was invaded, he signed the following decree: 'Reichsleiter Bouhler and Dr(med.) Brandt are hereby instructed to extend the authority of physicians designated by name in such manner that those who are, as far as it is humanly possible to judge, incurably sick may, after the most scrupulous assessment of their state of health, be granted a merciful death.'[336] The euthanasia programme was in direct line of succession from the law for the prevention of hereditarily diseased offspring enacted in the early months of the totalitarian régime.

The Problem of Sex in Popular Education (1936), outwardly a no-nonsense book on sex education, shows how abruptly and in what respectable guise this form of inhumanity can become manifest. Its author, Reinhard Gerhard Ritter, indignantly complained that the evil bourgeois individualists of the nineteenth century had infected society with their modern sex propaganda and sacrificed the interests of a wholesome and normal majority to the frailties and failings of a minority. However, the pernicious effects of this process could now be countered by racial hygiene. Ritter's concern must have seemed quite natural to the healthy 'normal-minded' citizen of the Third Reich. He went on to justify the law for the prevention of hereditarily diseased offspring by citing two arguments whose bare-faced brutality would be hard to surpass,[337] but which were so often paraded in a variety of disguises that they seldom raised an eyebrow.

Argument No. 1: Anyone who sabotaged these measures out of 'false sentimentality' (a dig at the Roman Catholic Church, which opposed the law), 'considering that a congenital invalid who attains the age of 60 has cost the Reich 60,000 marks', could have no conception of his ultimate duty to the nation.

Argument No. 2: Driven to utter desperation, a mother hanged her 13-year-old epileptic son after one of his seizures. 'Inside, she fully realized the dreadful nature of what she had done – indeed, she was tormented by the most frightful pangs of conscience.'[338] That was why she atoned for her terrible deed by hanging herself as well.

The reader's inference: a healthy Reich could not afford sick people because they were too expensive. Also, there was a moral obligation to relieve parental distress – or eliminate it. On closer inspection, these specious examples justify the killing of sick people rather than the avoidance of hereditarily diseased offspring. The same method was developed in the euthanasia film *Ich klage an* (I accuse), which linked the problem of death on demand with the elimination of unwanted human beings, a policy which was already being secretly implemented. SD reports described the public response as 'sympathetic'.[339]

Two years after statutory measures had been taken to cleanse Nordic blood of morbid excrescences, the Nuremberg Laws took steps to preserve it from contamination with alien blood and so 'secure the German nation for all time'.[340] The Law for the Protection of German Blood and German Honour (15 September 1935) prohibited, with immediate effect, marriage and extra-marital intercourse between Jews and nationals of German or related blood. The penalty for violations of this law was penal servitude. Such was the stringency of legal commentaries on the new statute that sentences became heavier as a matter of course. Jews found guilty of 'racial desecration' were more and more often condemned to death. Their 'Aryan' partners got off with terms of imprisonment, but they too became subject to increasing discrimination. In November 1942, a memorandum from the Party Chancellery announced: 'The Führer has decided that permission for a soldier to marry a woman formerly married to a Jew must be rejected in every case. A German woman who has lived in matrimony with a Jew has thereby displayed such a lack of racial instinct that her subsequent union with a soldier can no longer be countenanced.'[341]

Writers on sex education were quick to seize on the subject of racial purity and its protection. The new edition of Max von Gruber's celebrated book on sexual hygiene (1939: 334th–343rd thousand) referred first and foremost to the law of heredity and the 'systematic elimination of inferior strains'. The editor, a Berlin dermatologist named Wilhelm Heyn, prefaced sexual instruction with some tips on choosing the right partner, a choice to which he ascribed a 'Nordicizing' purpose. 'Alien cross-breeds' were condemned in popular biological parlance as 'mongrels'.[342]

These pronouncements could, of course, be couched in different and quasi-respectable terms, just as they were by Viktor Lutze for the benefit of foreign diplomats and press correspondents in Berlin. With orotund self-righteousness, the SA Chief of Staff proudly professed himself (in 1936!) an adherent of positive Christianity and prophet of a new German ideology. He also exhumed the socio-revolutionary claptrap which used to be popular with the brown-shirted Storm Detachments but had lain buried since the ousting of Strasser and the murder of Röhm. The SA, he said, was a living example of the aristocracy of German socialism, and one of its noble tasks was the racial improvement of the German people. 'For us, the crux of this problem reposes in preserving our own race, not fighting another. Our recognition of race is the basis of our national consciousness and has, on principle, nothing to do with racial hatred.'[343] Dulcet words such as these helped also to allay minor pangs of doubt or scruple among the citizens of the Third Reich. They were admirable prophylactic and soporific arguments in support of the official policy on race.

The Nazi ethicist Georg Usadel adopted precisely the same stealthy line of approach. Where Lutze aspired to purify the national bloodstream but disclaimed racial hatred, Usadel protested against trivial biological ideas. If parents adjusted their conduct to the National Socialist values of race, heredity and nationhood, he moralized, they would breed and rear National Socialist children of ever higher quality. Better leaders, better followers and a racially superior nation could then go striding into the German world of tomorrow. 'The idea of breeding, all too readily confined to the natural plane until now, is elevated by a responsible attitude to the plane of morality.'[344] So intensified racialism had been promoted to the moral plane. On the subordinate, 'natural', plane, there was sterilization for the hereditarily unfit, euthanasia for those in need of care, and the death penalty for racial desecration. However, these measures had nothing 'on principle' to do with racial hatred.

To foster a responsible attitude towards selective breeding among Germany's human livestock, the NSDAP's Racial Policy Bureau published ten rules to be observed when choosing a partner in marriage:

'1. Remember that you are a German!
2. Remain pure in mind and spirit!
3. Keep your body pure!
4. If hereditarily fit, do not remain single!
5. Marry only for love!
6. Being a German, only choose a spouse of similar or related blood!
7. When choosing your spouse, inquire into his or her forebears!
8. Health is essential to outward beauty as well!
9. Seek a companion in marriage, not a playmate!
10. Hope for as many children as possible!'[345]

All this concentration on cleanliness and health was bound to persuade young people of the solicitous rectitude and sincerity of these maxims. If the advice seemed innocuous, however, the commentaries and interpretations that accompanied it carried a note of menace and compulsion. You owe what you are, the first commandment stressed, not to your own merits but to the nation, so the nation has first claim on your allegiance. Remain chaste, enjoined the third commandment, so as to preserve the purity of your racial heritage, which the 'pleasure of the moment' can destroy. All that matters is family continuity, clan and nation, the Introduction stated in amplification of the fourth commandment. Miscegenation precludes spiritual harmony, stated the sixth commandment. The rest of the catechism was devoted to guaranteeing offspring: in marrying someone, you marry his or her forefathers and entire clan; once human stock has become tainted, no offspring of value can be expected; make sure that you and your partner are medically examined for conjugal fitness; find yourself a companion for the breeding and rearing of children, not a partner in sexual dalliance; finally, only by producing four children can you secure the national stock to which, as a German, you owe your first duty.

Taken in conjunction with this forceful exegesis, the ten rules ceased to be a collection of friendly tips and suggestions which even non-Party parents might have been expected to welcome on behalf of their growing sons and daughters. They were, in fact, a skilfully presented breeding programme whose idealistic veneer was shrewdly trimmed to appeal to adolescent susceptibilities. Maxims, watchwords, slogans, speeches, calendar mottoes, health booklets, lessons in ethnology, biology and art appreciation, camp training, Reich legislation – young people were attuned, sometimes subliminally, sometimes overtly and by every medium of totalitarian guidance, to the task of selective breeding in the German manner.

What was a commandment for ordinary folk constituted a rigid law for the SS, that 'National Socialist military Order of men in the Nordic mould'. Its Grand Master, Heinrich Himmler, believed that only good blood could accomplish the greatest and most lasting things in the world. The men of an élite corps destined to endure for a thousand years had therefore to be at least 1.70 metres (5ft 7ins) tall '. . . because I know that men whose height exceeds a certain number of centimetres must somehow have the requisite blood'.[346] In accordance with this metric criterion, Himmler 'somehow' – to use his own word – introduced racial selection into a gang of roughnecks who fought their way up from the status of assembly-hall stewards to that of the Führer's bodyguard, eventually becoming an Order which united all the supervisory and executive organs of totalitarian rule under its Rune of Victory, from the regular police, Secret State Police and

Security Service to the Death's Head units that ran the concentration camps. 'I am aware,' said the Reichsführer in 1936, already assured of his men's reputation, 'that there are many people in Germany who feel queasy when they see this black uniform. We understand this, and do not expect to be loved by all and sundry.'[347]

The directives governing the SS assigned priority to the value of blood and selection. Third Reich historians acknowledged that Himmler had performed 'a supreme and vital service' because 'having courageously and consistently adapted the theoretical findings of National Socialist ideology in this particular field to his own organizational task of building up the SS, he clearly implemented them as well.'[348] The Reichsführer performed his first consistent test of courage by issuing SS Order A No. 65 on 31 December 1931:

'1. The SS is a formation of German men in the Nordic mould, selected from special points of view.

2. In keeping with National Socialist ideology and cognizant that our national future depends upon the selection and preservation of racially and hereditarily good stock, I am, with effect from 1 January 1932, introducing a "marriage permit" for all single members of the SS.

3. The intended aim is (to produce) a valuable clan of German stock in the Nordic mould.

4. The marriage permit will be granted or refused solely on grounds of race and hereditary health.

5. Every SS man who intends to marry must obtain a marriage permit from the Reichsführer-SS.

6. SS members who marry notwithstanding the refusal of a marriage permit will be expelled from the SS, the option of resigning being open to them.

7. The relevant processing of marriage applications will be the task of the "Racial Bureau" of the SS.

8. The Racial Bureau of the SS will keep the "Clan Book of the SS", in which the families of SS members will be entered after a marriage permit has been issued or a request for registration granted.

9. The Reichsführer-SS, the head of the Racial Bureau and its departmental chiefs are pledged to secrecy.

10. The SS recognizes that this order constitutes a step of major importance. We are unmoved by mockery, derision and misunderstanding. The future is ours!'[349]

Himmler laboured single-mindedly to perfect this pioneering measure. A further condition for the granting of a marriage permit was that both partners should have been awarded the Reich Sports Badge. An upward circle over the bar – a feat which the Reichsführer himself essayed with immense perseverance but no success* – was accepted as a guarantee of suitable reproductive capacity. SS officers were not permitted to marry until they had attained the age of twenty-four and served two years as an Untersturmführer (2nd lieutenant), presumably because a wife might have distracted them from their rigorous male duties. On the other hand, every SS man was expected to marry by the age of thirty at latest. For this purpose, Himmler devised a Germanic 'marriage vow ceremony' which was intended to replace the rites of the Church. The bride and groom exchanged rings to an accompaniment of pithy maxims and were given bread and salt. At the weddings of his senior officers, the Reichsführer happily recited passages from the *Edda*, delivered forceful addresses and presented thoughtful gifts from the SS-owned factory at Allach. On 27 July 1938, the oft-derided Marriage Order was made legally binding on SS members under the provisions of the new marriage law.

The whole thing was still further testimony to the obstinacy and persistence of that short-sighted, short-legged lover of physical perfection, the Reichsführer-SS. If women were to join his Order, which was how Himmler envisaged their union with SS men, they must naturally be subject to the same racial criteria as their menfolk. It was the only way of creating a pure Nordic strain and fulfilling his grand design for the future.

'I accept the runts'

To this end, the SS Race and Resettlement Bureau worked out some *Guides to Racial Determination*. Hauptsturmführer Professor Dr Bruno Schultz devised a test- or 'R'-card for use by members of the racial board before which every applicant for membership of the SS had to appear. 'R', needless to say, stood for race. The formula comprised (*a*) assessment of physique, (*b*) racial assessment and (*c*) general assessment of personality supplemented by a general assessment of the applicant's 'clan'.

* While Himmler was always a few centimetres short of the required standard for throwing the discus, the authorities successfully contrived to cheat so that he did get the coveted badge and remained unaware of the official deception.

There were nine grades of physique ranging from 'ideal' to 'deformed'. The first four ratings – ideal, excellent, very good and good – were acceptable; the last three automatically ruled a candidate out. The two intermediate grades left room for those whose smart bearing offset their physical inadequacies.

Racial classification was on five levels. Groups A (pure Nordic), B (pure Phalic or Nordic-Phalic) and C (harmonious cross-breeds with slight Alpine, Dinaric or Mediterranean infusions) were acceptable; Groups D (cross-breeds of predominantly Eastern or Alpine origin) and E (pure aliens and cross-breeds with an infusion of non-European blood) were not.

General assessment of personality was a fairly vague proceeding, and vagueness connoted unimportance. According to SS principles, members of the Order were expected to display love of liberty and martial spirit, loyalty, honour and obedience. Bearing in mind that the SS motto was 'Thine Honour is Loyalty', one can readily gather that strength of character was a hindrance and intellectual ability at a discount. More weight was attached to the 'Major Ancestral Certificate' which traced a man's forebears back to 1750, and Himmler's ultimate intention was to demand proof of Aryan blood going back to 1648, the year after 'the Great' or Thirty Years War.

The bureaucratic intricacy of the R-card typifies the wondrous superficiality of an aptitude test whose purpose was to define the new citizen of the Greater Germanic Empire. Little boxes were provided for the racial assessor to mark each candidate in respect of twenty-one physical characteristics, the latter being graphically correlated to produce a 'physical attribute diagram'. The following features had to be conscientiously and laboriously noted:

1. Height, standing and seated. 2. Physical development . . . 4. Relative length of legs. 5. Shape of head. 6. Occiput. 7. Shape of face. 8. Bridge of nose. 9. Length of nose. 10. Breadth of nose. 11. Cheekbones. 12. Position of eyes. 13. Eyelids. 14. Orbital creases. 15. Thickness of lips. 16. Outline of chin. 17. Hair-line. 18. Body-hair. 19. Colour of hair. 20. Colour of eyes. 21. Complexion. Should any doubts persist after this inventory, attention was further devoted to length of head, shape of brow, nasal root, distance between eyes, angle of lower jaw, length of arm, Mongolian spots, etc., etc.[350]

Order A No. 65 stipulated that, in order to obtain a marriage permit, the SS man and his prospective bride must fill in an RuSHA questionnaire, have their hereditary fitness certified by an SS physician, and submit – in addition to proof of Aryan ancestry – photographs of themselves in bathing costume. In the case of SS officers, the Reichsführer personally reserved the right of decision. He applied himself to the study of such documents with great care. 'I looked at the photographs of all of them and asked myself, can I see infusions of foreign blood? Why did I do this? Think back, if you will, to the soldiers' council types of 1918 and 1919, and you'll note that, in general, they were men who looked somehow comical to our German eye – who had a comical feature of some kind. They were the type of people who, at the moment when character and nerves are subjected to the last ounce of pressure, are somehow bound to crack because of their blood.'[351] 'Somehow' Himmler was perfectly convinced that no racial indiscretion on the part of a remote ancestor could escape his eagle eye. He found the notion that these physical criteria might be misleading quite incomprehensible. On one occasion, having encountered a blond and blue-eyed warrior in the street, he impulsively promoted him sergeant. Inquiries showed that this prize specimen of Germanic manhood had several convictions for pimping. Himmler was deeply shocked.

In regard to the Marriage Order, too, considerable discrepancies existed between the ideal and the actual. The regulation did not go undisputed in the ranks of the Black Corps, and not every SS man who disregarded it could be expelled. Inevitably, relaxation set in. In 1935 it was announced that only those who wilfully violated the edict would be dismissed. Two years later it was good enough if guilty couples observed the formalities after the event, and in November 1940 Himmler amnestied all those who had broken the regulation in question. As long as they were racially acceptable, they could rejoin the Order.

Marriage permit statistics for the years 1932–1940 illustrate the patchwork nature of the system. Only 7,518 applications out of 106,304 satisfied every requirement. Another 9,010 were approved without medical examinations or documents. Clearance was granted in 7,521 cases 'with slight reservations'. Only 958 requests were turned down. The majority – 40,388 – came under the heading 'provisional clearance in default of documentation'. Also on file were 19,439 cases in which the applicant had broken off his engagement, been dismissed the service, or died – though 'killed in action' might have been more accurate. According to the RuSHA's figures, 29,115 cases were still under consideration.[352]

At far below 10 per cent, the success rate was extremely meagre compared with the standard of racial purity to which the Marriage Order aspired. Most of the applications, or nearly 70,000, were effectively postponed or approved subject to later rulings. There was method in this. Himmler, who had meanwhile become the second man in the Nazi hierarchy, was a dutiful and obedient disciple of his master. For all his racial fanaticism, he bowed to superior political necessity. Political necessity meant power, and Himmler was planning for generations yet unborn.

Early in 1943, he received a complaint from Obergruppenführer Udo von Woyrsch, regional SS commander in Silesia, who reported that doctors were failing miserably in their duty to examine applicants for marriage permits. He quoted instances of epileptic wives, of wives with double uteri or other disabilities, of impotent SS men who had been granted leave to marry. Himmler's reply, dated 22 March 1943, was categorical. In time of war, he said, two choices were open to him: either to persevere with strict selection, or to enhance his men's matrimonial prospects. He had decided on the latter. 'The most important thing I am capable and desirous of achieving is that every SS man who can should have a child before he dies in battle. If this increases the total number of children, I accept the runts – in breeder's parlance – that will occur in the mass. Better a child than no child at all. Even the slightly inferior son of his father will be a German grenadier in twenty years' time, and his family will not have died out.'[353]

Social purity was a good thing, but mainly because Nazi ideology saw it as the surest guarantee of national strength. The preservation of one's own kind was of paramount importance, but its maintenance in times of stress could be achieved by temporarily confining oneself to the extermination of foreigners. The 'new man' was the supreme objective of racial policy, but occasional decelerations in the rate of progress were permissible.

Where power was at stake, even a perfectionist like Himmler could abandon quality for quantity.

Heinrich Himmler: The perverted bourgeois

The Reichsführer-SS was nothing if not consistent. He was a living example to his men of the conduct which he demanded of them. This he defined in broad terms to a meeting of SS generals at Posen in 1943: '*One principle must be absolutely binding on the SS man: we must be honest, decent, loyal and comradely to members of our own race, and to no one else.* How the Russians fare, how the Czechs fare, is a matter of complete indifference to me. Whatever other nations have to offer in the way of good blood of our own kind, we shall take, if necessary by stealing their children and raising them at home. Whether other nations prosper or starve to death interests me only in so far as we require them as slaves for our civilization. Whether or not ten thousand Russian women collapse from exhaustion while digging an anti-tank ditch interests me only in so far as the anti-tank ditch is completed for Germany. *We shall never be harsh and heartless where there is no need – that much is obvious. We Germans, who are the only people in the world with a proper attitude towards animals, will adopt a proper attitude towards these human animals too, but it is a crime against our own blood to worry about them and give them ideals so that our sons and grandsons have an even harder time with them.*'[354]

The moral principle was quite straightforward. On the one hand, there were the higher forms of human life, pure-blooded thoroughbreds to whom one behaved with due decency. On the other, there were the human animals, lower forms of life in human shape, either of poor stock or degenerate. One treated them decently too, on principle, except that a distinction had to be drawn between domestic animals, predators and vermin.

According to these standards – his own – Himmler was an exceptionally moral person. Had he not risen to become administrative head of the greatest murder-machine in history – fortuitously and strictly speaking against his better judgement, for he himself had once been in favour of 're-education' – no one would ever have doubted his moral integrity. At most, people would have wagged their heads at his racial obsessions or, as Hitler once did, ridiculed him as a mystical dabbler in the world hereafter.

Himmler's personal way of life was shaped by the moral severity of his modest background, a well-developed sense of responsibility, and his feeble constitution. Generally speaking, he kept a tight rein on himself.

Son of a schoolmaster, godson of a Wittelsbach prince, thwarted in his desire to serve as an officer at the front and recently recovered from a bout of paratyphoid fever, nineteen-year-old Heinrich Himmler enrolled as a student of agriculture at Munich's Polytechnic in autumn 1919. He joined a duelling association and acquired the coveted facial scar, but his weak stomach prevented him from matching the members of his fraternity at ritual beer-drinking. His approach to girls, too, was schoolboyish rather than impetuous. Almost as a matter of form, he fell in love with the daughter of his landlady, Maja Loritz: 'I am happy to be able to call this wonderful girl my friend.'[355] He conversed with her about religion and the relations between men and women, and finally convinced himself that he had found a sister in her. His favourite companion was a friend named Ludwig Zahler, with whom he attended discussion groups. He was also a conscientious diarist. Dancing did not appeal to him despite his love of parties, and sporting activities, for all his desire to excel, were not his *métier*. His girl-friend's sister accused him of detesting women, and he conceded the point. As he explained to his friend Zahler: 'A real man will love a woman in three ways. First, as a beloved child to be scolded and perhaps even punished when foolish, but also to be protected and cherished because of her frailty and weakness and because that is why she is loved. Secondly, he will love her as a wife, as the loyal and understanding comrade who assists him in life's struggle, always at his side but never cramping or shackling his spirit. Finally, he will love her as the wife whose feet he must kiss, and whose feminine tenderness and pure, childlike sanctity give him strength to persevere in the thick of battle and bring him something superlatively divine in the ideal hours of spiritual communion.'[356]

The first or Platonic relationship came easiest to Himmler as a young man. Once, while travelling by train, he met a child from Hamburg who was 'sweet and obviously innocent and very much interested in Bavaria and King Ludwig II'.[357] Had he been rich, he would gladly have bestowed enough money on a waitress, 'a pretty creature with a good figure and an appealing face', to preserve her from the pit of corruption into which she was bound to sink – or so he judged on the strength of a lunch-time's acquaintance. Feminine vanity he condemned, and the spectacle of a little three-year-old girl permitted by her parents to 'cavort around in the nude' shocked him: 'At that age, she ought to be taught a sense of modesty.'[358]

Here we can already glimpse the narrow-minded guardian of morality who itched to impose his prudish ideas on others. For the moment, young Himmler had little opportunity to practise his destructive solicitude except in the family circle. In 1923 his elder brother Gebhard became engaged to a girl whose innocence he mistrusted. He acquainted her with his misgivings in a manner which would have been downright impertinent in a prospective father-in-law, let alone a prospective brother-in-law of twenty-three: 'If your union is to be a happy one for the pair of you and beneficial to our nation, whose very basis must consist of healthy, morally pure families, you will have to be ridden on a tight rein and curbed with extreme severity. Since you do not impose harsh and rigid standards on yourself, your future husband being too kind-hearted for your own good, someone else must do so.'[359] The someone else was Heinrich himself. He not only engaged the Max Blüml detective agency to investigate Paula's past life but instituted some inquiries of his own: 'May I request you to inform me by return of all you know about Fräulein Stölzle and particularly about her relationship with your colleague, Daffner?'[360] Brother Gebhard was unequal to so much fraternal protection – he broke off his engagement.

Himmler was extremely strict with himself, but continence did not agree with him. While enhancing his self-righteousness, it reinforced his inhibitions and tendency to brood about sex. 'We discussed the danger of such things,' he confided to his diary after a conversation with Ludwig Zahler. 'Lying together side by side, hot and excited, body to body, one enters an inferno where one needs to muster all one's common sense. By then the girls are so far gone they don't know what they're doing. It's the fierce, concentrated yearning of the whole individual to satisfy a frightfully strong natural urge.'[361] But the feverish diarist fled from the torrid atmosphere of reprehensible lust to the limpid heights of moral conviction. 'That is why it's fraught with so much danger and responsibility for the man, too. You could weak-mindedly do what you like with girls, yet you have a hard enough time fighting yourself.'[362] This was a rather feeble vow of chastity, being indicative less of moral greatness than of timidity towards the opposite sex and a prudish self-righteousness typical of the Wilhelmine middle class. Heinrich Himmler resolved to preserve his innocence until the age of twenty-six. It was characteristic of him that he not only made such a resolution but stuck to it.

Meanwhile, he took his diploma in agriculture and carved himself a small niche in the militant nationalist movement, Munich version, by joining Röhm's paramilitary 'Reichskriegsflagge'. It was he who held its banner aloft in front of the barbed-wire entanglement protecting the War Ministry in Ludwigstrasse on the day of the November putsch. Impressed by the way the young man indefatigably toured the villages of Lower Bavaria on his motor-cycle, delivering National Socialist harangues, Gregor Strasser employed him as a maid of all work. Then Himmler met Hitler and made him his idol. He had at last found the man of supreme and infallible authority whom he needed to help him develop his remarkable talent for organization and lunatic or bewildering schemes for world reform. In 1925 he became Deputy Gauleiter of Lower Bavaria-Upper Palatinate, in the following year Deputy Gauleiter of Upper Bavaria-Swabia and the Party's Deputy Reich Director of Propaganda. Veteran members of Hitler's entourage poked fun at the pallid, patient bureaucrat, and Hitler's chauffeur, Julius Schreck, christened him 'pince-nez Heini', but the 'poor fish' – yet another nickname – continued to climb the Party ladder with a zeal and industry second to none. By 1927 Himmler was Deputy Reich Leader of the SS. Two years later he became its head and purposefully set to work to develop the small Schutzstaffel into a powerful Nazi élite Order pledged to the Führer and hostile to the brown-shirted SA.

In the meantime, with an impetuosity untypical of him, Himmler had plunged into matrimony just in time to enliven a rather dull period in his career. While staying at Bad Reichenhall in 1926, he took refuge in the hotel foyer to escape a sudden shower of rain and almost bumped into a blonde, blue-eyed Valkyrie. Margarete Boden, the daughter of a West Prussian landowner, was eight years his senior. She had served as a nurse during the First World War and had, after a short-lived marriage, acquired a private nursing home in Berlin. Himmler's initial reaction was to kiss her feet – wifely role No. 3 – but first Marga had to dispose of her nursing home for 10,000 marks so that the couple could purchase a plot of land at Waldtrudering, near Munich, and build a small wooden house there. On 3 July 1928 they were married at the Berlin-Schöneberg registry office. Himmler had wavered for a considerable time before taking the plunge in defiance of his parents' wishes. The plan was to raise poultry – 'dear Heini' erected the chicken-house for fifty brood-hens with his own hands – but a Party salary of

200 marks a month did not go far and the hens failed to come up to expectations. In May 1929 the 'naughty wife' wrote to her 'darling': 'The hens are laying terribly badly – two eggs a day. I worry so much about what we're going to live on and how we're going to save for Whitsun as well. We seem to be fated. I save so hard, but the money runs out just the same.'[363] It was barely enough to cover the cost of their shoe repairs.

Under these difficult circumstances, role No. 2 – 'the loyal comrade' – became operative. Heinrich was always away on Party business, and it gradually dawned on the gelid Marga that her marriage was over even before the birth of her only child, Gudrun, in 1929: 'Things aren't well with me. What's going to happen? I can't help wondering all the time. Oh my dear, what's to become of me?'[364]

Her destiny was to become the wife of the Reichsführer-SS, a figure who was politely banished to the background, seldom appeared at Himmler's Dahlem villa and rarely saw her husband at all. Himmler sold the property at Waldtrudering and bought his wife and daughter a house named Lindenfycht at Gmund on the Tegernsee. Here he occasionally played the solid family man, though more for his daughter's sake than to please Marga, in whom he took little further interest. She revenged herself on these occasions by tyrannizing him to the best of her ability. After visiting Himmler's home, Baldur von Schirach described it as a bourgeois idyll: the paterfamilias in leather shorts, peasant jacket and brogues, the gloomy fir-trees, the tawdry Bavarian décor with its embroidered cushions, the afternoon coffee-session a frosty affair. 'I never met a man so hen-pecked as Heinrich Himmler. He oozed amiability, but the more amiably he behaved the worse he was treated. At home, the head of the police and SS was a zero. He always had to defer.'[365]

Lina Heydrich ridiculed the boss's wife – 'Size 50 knickers. That's all there was to her'[366] – and blamed Marga for Himmler's insistence that Heydrich should divorce her: 'That narrow-minded, humourless blonde female, always worrying about protocol; she ruled her husband and could twist him round her little finger – at least until 1936.'[367]

The situation cannot have been quite as bad as all that. When Schirach returned the Himmlers' hospitality he was treated to the sight of a relaxed and forthcoming Frau Marga. It is understandable that she should have been embittered by her second marriage to a degree which made her cold and hard towards her husband. Himmler had secured a role which fulfilled and satisfied him, whereas she was compelled to play a bit part. Lina Heydrich had probably picked on the wrong person. It was far more likely that Himmler himself, and not his wife, took exception to Lina's outspoken remarks and extravagant way of life. Why, in the case of a right-hand man like Heydrich, should he have overlooked something to which he devoted such keen personal attention even in the most far-flung corners of his realm?

It seemed to Himmler's entourage that his private life was ruled by the wife he hardly ever saw. However, Himmler was not a man to be judged on the basis of outward appearances, least of all by his unprepossessing physiognomy. From the mid-1930s onwards, his personal staff included an attractive young secretary from Cologne, Hedwig Potthast. By 1937, if not earlier, Hedwig had made a favourable impression on her boss, and by 1940 at latest he was having an affair with her. He even planned to marry her, but dropped the idea and became a champion of legalized bigamy instead. On 15 February 1942, Himmler's mistress bore him a son, Helge, and two years later a daughter, Nanette Dorothea.

Himmler's only problem was how to support two families. All the men round him were blithely feathering their own nests. He, the head of a vast and ruthless organization with manifold sources of income, was not. Even when – by way of exception – he took his wife on a State visit to allied Italy, he paid her expenses himself. If he sent his parents for a drive in an official car, the cost of the petrol had to be deducted from his pay. Himmler lived strictly within his income, never accumulating capital, always mindful of his duty to set an example.

In order to set up a home for Hedwig, who occupied rented accommodation in Berlin, the Reichsführer-SS requested a loan from the head of the Party Chancellery. Bormann advanced him 80,000 marks. Himmler used it to build his mistress a house at Berchtesgaden-Schönau, not far from his Führer's residence on the Obersalzberg. Here at 'Schneewinkelchen' he relaxed in the happy family atmosphere of which he may have dreamt when planning his little house at Waldtrudering fifteen years before – but not with Marga. Hedwig was love No. 1: the beloved child-bride who needed to be cherished and protected. 'Heinrich told me yesterday,' reported Gerda Bormann, a near neighbour, 'that he had been hanging pictures, doing jobs about the house and playing with the children all day long. He wouldn't take any telephone calls either, but for once devoted himself at leisure to his family.'[368]

Heinrich Himmler was a weirdly average, weirdly contradictory character, also a man of weird consistency. One finds it incomprehensible, even now, that this perverted petty bourgeois should have succeeded in reducing his private life and public activities to a simple and, in his moral estimation, homogeneous common denominator. To quote another passage from his speech at Posen: 'Our concern, our duty, is our nation and our blood. It is for them that we have to care and take heed, toil and struggle, and for nothing else. The rest we can disregard . . .'[369]

7 'Degeneracy'

SEXUAL OFFENCES IN THE THIRD REICH

'LEGAL provisions enacted prior to the National Socialist revolution should not be applied if their application runs counter to the wholesome popular sentiment of today.'[370] This directive appeared in *Guiding Principles for the German Judge*, an aid to the 'independent' judiciary issued in 1936 by the Third Reich's supreme guardian of the law. Hans Frank, veteran Nazi and chief jurist of the Movement, was responsible for imposing National Socialist values upon the legislative and judicial processes in his capacity as 'Reich Commissioner for the Co-ordination of Justice in the Länder (territorial divisions) and for the Renovation of the Legal System'. Being a Reichsleiter (top-ranking Nazi official) at the Legal Office of the NSDAP, head of the Association of National Socialist Lawyers, president of the German Academy of Law and holder of ministerial rank, he was in a position to exert more than a little pressure.

The job of the Reich Legal Director – yet another title held by the future Governor-General of Poland – consisted primarily in enlightening judges, public prosecutors and attorneys-at-law on the inadequacy of current legal norms. Two things transcended the established legal code: the Führer's will and wholesome popular sentiment, that *fons et origo* of all racially flawless morality.

This was the spirit underlying the new penal code of 1935. *Nullum crimen sine lege* – the constitutional principle that only those acts may attract punishment whose liability to punishment has been previously laid down by law – was abolished. The new rule was *nullum crimen sine poena*, in other words, no act must go unpunished which contravened the sinister dictates of wholesome popular sentiment. And that, in turn, covered any infringement of National Socialist values, however vaguely construed. Government despotism had yet again been invested with the force of law. Legislation and jurisdiction were subordinated to political and pseudo-political considerations.

Hans Frank traced the correct National Socialist approach to criminal law in a speech delivered during October 1938.[371] He proceeded from the problem of guilt, which arose from four 'elementary sources': degeneracy, demoralization, temptation and opportunity. The first and paramount cause was an authentic figment of racial ideology. 'National Socialism regards degeneracy as an immensely important source of criminal activity. It is our belief that every superior nation is furnished with such an abundance of endowments for its journey through life that the word "degeneracy" most clearly defines the state of affairs that concerns us here. In a decent nation, the "genus" must be regarded as valuable *per se*; consequently, in an individual, degeneracy signifies exclusion from the normal "genus" of the decent nation. This state of being degenerate or egenerate, this different or alien quality, tends to be rooted in miscegenation between a decent representative of his race and an individual of inferior racial stock. To us National Socialists, criminal biology, or the theory of congenital criminality, connotes a link between racial decadence and criminal manifestations. The complete degenerate lacks all racial sensitivity and sees it as his positive duty to harm the community or a member thereof. He is the absolute opposite of the man who recognizes that the fulfilment of his duty as a People's Comrade is his mission in life.'[372]

Frank's stilted verbiage masked a total absence of firm commitment. Not only was it impossible to define his concept of degeneracy in legal terms, but the almost comical invocation of 'criminal biology' afforded little prospect of diagnosing crime, let alone combating it. No, his booming tributes to racial theory called for a quite different interpretation. The racially superior German nation, ran Frank's exegesis of the doctrine, possessed intrinsic value and was therefore 'decent'. Anyone who violated this undefined decency committed a crime against the national community, was subversive and abnormal. As such, he merited ice-cold and merciless (Frank's favourite adjectives) treatment and condemnation. The feeble reference to hypothetical seeds of racial inferiority did not conceal the fact that 'guilt by degeneracy' amounted to no more than the sanctioning by criminal law of a vulgarized Social Darwinist approach.

Frank gave no indication whatever of how national 'decency' should be construed in terms of wholesome popular sentiment. Obviously, current law and general legislative rulings were insufficient to define it. The Reich Legal Director's advice to judges was as follows: it was not their job 'to assist in the implementation of a judicial system which transcends the national community, or to impose universal standards'.

Rather, they must 'maintain the prevailing folkish order of society, wipe out parasites, punish anti-social behaviour and settle disputes between members of the community'.[373] As for wholesome popular sentiment, it was no more than a chimera, even as a legal foundation. 'The basis on which to interpret all legal sources,' preached Frank, 'is National Socialist ideology as expressed, in particular, by the Party programme and the pronouncements of our Führer.'[374]

Nazi ideology was never crystallized by the Party programme, nor could it have been, which left the Führer's pronouncements the supreme fount of legal guidance. After all, what finer embodiment of wholesome popular sentiment could there be than the charismatic saviour and national hero who regarded himself, above all else, as a man of the people?

Hitler's abhorrence of the legal profession rivalled his hatred of the Jews. To him, all lawyers were 'traitors', 'idiots' and 'absolute cretins'. He would not rest, he informed the Reichstag on 26 April 1942, 'until every German realizes that it is a disgrace to be a lawyer'.[375] Yet this was the very same occasion on which he got the Reichstag to confirm him in the office to which he had laid permanent claim ever since the murder of Röhm: 'supreme judicial authority of the German people.' He had long acted as such. Frank made it plain in 1936 that judges had no right of review over the Führer's decisions. Judgements which displeased Hitler were annulled with the aid of his puppets in the Ministry of Justice, and resumed proceedings usually ended in the desired verdict. In 1942 the Reichstag rubber-stamped his request for full powers, 'unsubject to existing legal provisions and by every means that may seem appropriate to him, where necessary to constrain every German to perform his duties, and, in the event of their dereliction, to impose such penalty as he deems fit'.[376]

What so enraged Hitler about the legal system was, quite simply, that there should be an authority whose decisions transcended his own. This authority he abolished, first de facto and then, in the usual 'legal' manner, by Reichstag acclamation. The thing that particularly riled him and sparked off so many outbursts of fury was the reluctance of the courts to become instruments of personal despotism. He threatened in private to do away with the whole pettifogging system and cut the judiciary by 90 per cent, leaving a hard core of 'people's judges' who would swiftly and ruthlessly produce the quota of death sentences which he considered necessary. 'Our judicial system isn't supple enough yet. . . . After ten years' penal servitude, a man is lost to the national community anyway. Who's going to give him a job then? Either you stick such fellows in a concentration camp, or you kill them. The latter course carries more weight at a time like this, because of the deterrent effect. To set an example, it ought to apply to all accomplices as well.'[377] That was in 1942, but many people thought it a healthy approach in peace-time too.

It is a short step from the theory of deterrence to the death penalty. Under a totalitarian system, that transition becomes the key to legalized murder and the perversion of justice.

Rule by wholesome popular sentiment

The idea that moral purity can be enforced by drastic measures and draconian sentences is one of the essential ingredients of wholesome popular sentiment, so-called. Its prevalence is as much a symptom of authoritarian social behaviour as the worship of those twin idols, law and order. From the aspect of social psychology, it serves – like chauvinist-racialist anti-Semitism – to distract attention from one's own shortcomings and behavioural lapses. If 'the others' are defined as bad – even, by this simple mechanism, juridically so defined – one feels a better person. The same notion reinforces a sense of togetherness among all those who are entitled by this crude black-and-white criterion to regard themselves as 'normal'. Hence, too, the autocratic legislator's tactical recourse to 'wholesome popular sentiment'. This secondary effect – the sense of belonging to a wholesome national community – stands high on the list of totalitarian desiderata. It not only consolidates political subservience by according due authority to those who give a community the self-assurance it hankers for, but diverts aggression to those who are clearly distinguishable as inferior or subhuman.

It was, however, in the field of sexual offences or deviations from the norm that this *lex talionis*, alias theory of deterrence, proved particularly ineffectual. The theory assumes that potential offenders can be dissuaded from their intended course of action by fear of harsh penalties. Quite apart from the fact that it has yet to score any statistical successes – experience shows that increased threats of punishment impress neither the genuine criminal nor the casual offender – it credits law-breakers with ascertainable motives and rational, ultimately material, interests. It is sadly and shockingly apparent, however, that the average sexual offender acts on impulse.

Factors of a controllable and rational nature played an equally minor role in the other crimes and offences against decency listed by the Third Reich's penal code and supplementary ordinances. Homosexual acts spring not from evil intent but from a proclivity which the Christian and Western world regards as unfortunate. Abortions are a concomitant of bourgeois morality, and are as much a result of neglected sex education as a product of social pressure. National Socialism wrought no change in this situation, neither by glorifying the illegitimate child nor by imposing stiffer sentences. Sexual intercourse with prisoners of war, which became punishable by special decree, was a natural consequence of the acute shortage of men at home. Its increase is a striking demonstration of how ineffective the régime's racially inspired attempts at control became as soon as they impinged on existential and instinctive factors in the private life of the individual, where 'the other' was oneself. Finally, deterrence failed to impress yet another section of the community: the younger generation. And here the limitations of the totalitarian system became apparent, for the phenomenon referred to as juvenile delinquency was largely a symptom of adolescent protest.

Facts versus figures

It is, therefore, with an eye to the truly tragic inhumanity and ineffectiveness of the penalties imposed that one should read *The Development of Criminality in the German Reich from the Outbreak of War until 1943*, compiled in 1944 by the Reich Bureau of Statistics.[378] Taken at their face value, a few of the figures suggest that the crime rate dropped. In reality, the reverse was true.

Dangerous sex offenders could be sentenced to castration. Individual case histories show that ordinary courts of law, which were the only ones to be covered by the report, did not impose this penalty except in grave instances where the offender had assaulted children repeatedly and was pronounced incurable. Starting with 189 castrations in 1937, the statistical record continued: 238 (1939), 198 (1940), 153 (1941) and 152 (1942). No less than 60 castration orders were issued in the first quarter of 1943. These figures hardly imply a decline in grave sexual offences when one takes into account the conscription of all able-bodied men – and the list does not include what happened at the front.

The same distortion should be borne in mind when one considers offences against Paragraph 175, the law on homosexuality. 8,271 cases

were recorded in 1937 and 7,614 in 1939. The following annual figures
suggest success – 3,773 (1940), 3,735 (1941), 2,678 (1942; Greater
German Reich), 996 (1943, first quarter only) – but the majority of men
were on active service, and male segregation in war-time is an induce-
ment to homosexuality which brings latent tendencies to the surface.

Abortion figures are notoriously unreliable at any stage, and to
estimate unrecorded abortions at 90 per cent of the official total, as this
report does, is to set the figure far too low. In view of the fact that the
birth-rate always drops in war-time, a remarkable constancy emerges.
5,737 abortions came to the notice of the authorities in 1937 and 4,943
in 1939, then 1,962 (1940), 2,715 (1941), 3,116 (1942) and 1,340 (1943,
first quarter only). One might say that the rate had found its own level.
If the fervent birth-rate propaganda had been successful, these figures
would obviously have declined.

The total figure for criminal and moral offences, including homosexuality and abortion, reinforces this impression. After a distinct drop
during the early war-years – a decrease which may be explained by
conscription, an unwillingness to have children in time of crisis and a
mood of moral rearmament stimulated by the outbreak of war – the
annual figure swung back to its old level.

The new regulations were patently incapable of discouraging sexual
intercourse with prisoners of war. It had been easy enough to persuade
the German housewife that the elderly Jew living opposite was racially
inferior and beneath her notice – he didn't appeal to her anyway, she
knew him of old, and, besides, she had her husband. What was quite
impossible was to convince the hard-working war-time grass-widow
that the Frenchman or Pole who toiled alongside her at her place of
work and shared her loneliness – possibly fair-haired, relatively un-
exotic and frequently attractive – was an inferior specimen. 1,909 cases
were brought under Paragraph 4 of the 'Ordinance for the Safeguarding
of German National Military Potential' in 1940, 4,345 in 1941, and
9,108 – yet another jump of 100 per cent – in 1942.

Much imprecision attaches to these official returns from the Reich
Bureau of Statistics. The figures are fundamentally unreliable because
they fail to allow for one vital factor: the countless victims of denunciation who, merely on suspicion of having committed crimes of indecency
and without ever being brought to trial, were carted off to concentration camps in accordance with Heinrich Himmler's prophylactic
methods of racial purification.

Two more figures may help to amplify this review of the Third

Reich's balance sheet *in re* moral rejuvenation. Female crime, in which
the Bureau included offences against the foregoing ordinance, rose
from 15.4 per cent in 1937 to 27.8 per cent in 1941 and 39.9 per cent in
the first half of 1943. The annual figures for juvenile delinquency in the
same period were 5.5 per cent, 11.8 per cent and 17.6 per cent.

So threats of draconian punishment bore little fruit. The certified
number of sexual offences declined, it is true, but official figures are
misleading. They take no account of the numerous sexual offences
committed by Germans in theatres of war and occupied territories.
They gloss over war-time conditions, in themselves an outlet for every
form of brutality and perversion. They also make no mention of
instances in which the enraged populace practised 'spontaneous' lynch
law under expert leadership, principally and not infrequently against
foreign workers who had committed 'racial desecration' by consorting
with German girls and women. Finally, the statistics fail to include,
quite apart from offenders who were 'neutralized' by consignment to
concentration camps, those who indulged their sadistic and perverted
urges as concentration camp guards or as members of the notorious SS
units which operated in the occupied territories. The inclusion of these
latter would produce an appalling increase, not only in the number of
sexual offences committed but also in their degree of severity.

If there nonetheless arose in the Third Reich an impression that the
régime's much-vaunted and vigorous endeavours in the field of
morality and good order were successful, and that misdemeanours and
crimes of indecency were on the decline, this was attributable to a
strict security black-out. Only rumours of what went on in the concentration camps reached the public. However, reports of offences in
everyday life were also suppressed on the totalitarian principle that
what may not be, cannot be, and that the wholesome image of law and
order in a well-conducted national community must be preserved at
all costs.

Burnt alive or quartered?

National Socialist police methods were no more effective against sexual
offenders than those of the Weimar period which was so derided for its
decadence. They were less so, if anything, because the obscure pseudo-
biological and racist tenets of good blood and normal conduct only too
often prevented policemen who toed the Party line under supreme SS
command from grasping or gaining an insight into the motives and

mentality of the sexual offender. The Berlin mass-murderer Bruno Luedke, who was only apprehended by chance, is a case in point. Late in January 1943, some children playing in the municipal park at Köpenick discovered the body of an elderly woman who had been strangled and then raped. The police went in search of a foreign worker who could be held responsible for the crime. In the course of their inquiries they came across a tramp who had been roaming the district. Bruno Luedke passed for a harmless, goodnatured imbecile whose petty thefts were attributable to diminished responsibility. His clothes were stained with blood – chicken's blood, admittedly, but chicken's feathers had also been discovered near the scene of the crime. More as a matter of form than anything else, Luedke was brought in for questioning.

' – I pinched the chicken, right enough. The old girl was sitting on a tree, so I went over to her.

– What did you say to her?

– Well, I asked her if she wanted to, but she said no.

– And what did you do then?

– I grabbed her by the throat.'[379]

The authorities would have been satisfied with this confession, which had dropped into their lap without undue suspicion or effort on their part. However, an alert detective ascertained that Luedke's sporadic fits of wanderlust coincided with a series of unsolved sex killings in other places as widely separated as Munich and Hamburg. Luedke further volunteered under interrogation that he had felt sick during the gallows scene in *Jew Süss* and rushed out of the cinema. Thanks to these and other statements, the police at last plumbed the mystery of the multiple killings. Luedke readily confessed and was convicted of fifty-four sex murders spanning the years 1928–1943. He himself claimed to have committed eighty-four, or two-thirds of all the unsolved sex killings for that period.

The police gratefully issued Luedke with a legal aid certificate. They only stumbled on the perpetrator of this long series of atrocities by chance and with his active co-operation, though any experienced member of an efficient CID team would at once have put the mentally retarded tramp on his list of suspects. Quite apart from the temporal coincidence of Luedke's peregrinations with a number of unsolved cases, there was a striking similarity of method. The mass-murderer first strangled his victims and then abused them. Eighty-four sex crimes committed by the same man, most of them under the National

Socialist régime . . . This gruesome tally illustrates how absurd it was to contend that crimes of such gravity were impossible in the Third Reich. It also shows up the incompetence of an allegedly perfect police system which was increasingly harnessed to Party interests and considerations of government policy. Finally, it demonstrates the futility of deterrent measures. To a typical killer on impulse like Bruno Luedke, they meant nothing at all.

As Gauleiter of Berlin, Goebbels itched to set an example. In a letter to the Chief of the German Police, Heinrich Himmler, he demanded 'that the bestial mass-murderer and butcherer of women should not die a normal death on the gallows. I suggest you have him burnt alive or quartered.'[380] Himmler considered the proposal but rejected it on the grounds that it might cause an unwelcome stir. Luedke was handed over to an institute of forensic medicine in Vienna, where he died in the course of experiments which were doubtless aimed at investigating this very exceptional specimen of subhumanity for the advancement of 'criminal biology'.

Although nothing prejudicial was known about his ancestry, Nazi anthropologists of the Frank school strove to accommodate the primitive and mentally unbalanced Bruno Luedke in their doctrinal edifice dedicated to the racially degenerate criminal. However, the real causes and impulses that lead to sex crimes were destined to elude these doctrinarians. There was no room in their stereotyped vision of wholesome humankind for complex personality structures and complicated instinctive factors.

In summer 1940, the regional court at Darmstadt sentenced a nineteen-year-old labourer from the Odenwald village of Ober-Ramstadt to five years' imprisonment under Paragraph 175. The prosecution had indicted him on 127 counts alleging acts of indecency with other men, 51 of which were proved. The sentence was a mild one by current standards because the court's medical adviser explained away the youth's misdemeanours as adolescent aberrations.[381] Press reports of the case betrayed a note of bewilderment. The whole affair was irreconcilable with the tenets of National Socialist ideology. An abominable slough of homosexuality might be conceivable among the corrupt youth of the big cities, spoiled sons of the middle class or intellectually contaminated secondary-school boys. But that such a plethora of homosexual relationships should have existed among honest labourers and craftsmen in the wholesome, healthy countryside, with the youngsters of an entire village involved in and corrupted by unnatural practices – this did not fit into the approved scheme of things and was greeted with utter perplexity. Under the Nazi creed, homosexuality was a symptom of depravity peculiar to degenerate individuals and those tainted with Jewish blood. To quote the gospel according to Heinrich Himmler: 'The village is unacquainted with such problems.'[382]

Drowned in a bog

Reich Legal Director Hans Frank commented with exemplary vehemence on the degenerate's liability under the penal code. 'Particular attention', he said, 'should be addressed to homosexuality, which is clearly expressive of a disposition opposed to the normal national community. Homosexual activity means the negation of the community as it must be constituted if the race is not to perish. That is why homosexual behaviour, in particular, merits no mercy.'[383] The highflown language concealed a simple piece of arithmetic. In terms of population policy, homosexuals were zeros. They negated the community by failing in their duty of racial preservation, in other words, by producing no children – and that, in a Third Reich hungry for population and obsessed with the birth-rate, was an unpardonable crime. As Das Schwarze Korps succinctly and aptly put it, homosexuality was a political, not a medical problem.

The homosexually inclined male was stylized into the prototype of sexual abnormality. It is significant that the homosexually inclined female seldom figured in pronouncements by National Socialist guardians of morality. What mattered to them was man, the warrior and begetter of children. In the blinkered view of these reactionary sexual theorists, woman, being subordinate to man, could not decline her role as a preserver of the species. Being equipped for motherhood by nature, even a Lesbian could and must bear children at the behest of her spouse. Lesbianism presented no practical reproductive problems of any consequence, and these alone were what counted.

The fanatical denigration of male homosexuals worked all the better because it was used to mobilize ingrained bourgeois hatred, not only of 'the others' but also of one's own kind. Frank was far too intelligent and perceptive to push this aspect. Himmler was not. He dished up all the old clichés and added some more of his own devising. Homosexuals were mentally diseased, effeminate and cowardly. They lied and believed their own lies – a peculiarly interesting statement coming from Himmler, because he defined the product of this characteristic as mental irresponsibility. Homosexuals were also blabbermouths who betrayed everything and were incapable of loyalty, or so he lectured his SS generals at Bad Tölz in 1937.[384] Considering the SS principle of allegiance and his own blindly credulous mentality, he could not have delivered a more withering indictment. Nevertheless, these self-righteous and malicious tirades harboured a trace of envy and respect. Himmler's bourgeois conception of moral sickness went hand in hand with a secret sense of inferiority at the thought that these degenerate 'effeminates' possessed special antennae and abilities denied to the normal man. He was well-read enough to be acquainted with the frequent occurrence of homosexual leanings among historical personages of genius from Plato to Frederick the Great, and he was enough of a hero-worshipper to find this 'somehow' uncanny and suppress it in his own way – the SS way.

A similar assessment of homosexuality's quasi-élite qualities can be read into Hitler's pronouncements on the subject. 'He lectured me on the role of homosexuality in history and politics. It had destroyed ancient Greece, he said. Once rife, it extended its contagious effects like an ineluctable law of nature to the best and most manly of characters, solely eliminating from the reproductive process those very men on whose offspring a nation depended. The immediate result of the vice was, however, that unnatural passion swiftly became dominant in public affairs if it was allowed to prevail.'[385]

Hitler is reputed to have said this in January 1934 to Rudolf Diels, inscrutable founder of the Gestapo and ambitious protégé of the Prussian Minister President, Hermann Göring. There is much to suggest that the quotation is authentic. The Führer long tolerated the homosexual proclivities of his SA chief of staff, Röhm, and cloaked them in his own authority because the man's talents and connections were worth more to him than any moral doctrines. One can even detect a note of sympathy and regret that the outstanding qualities of certain homosexuals should be lost to posterity for want of descendants. One can also detect a faint note of menace which enhances the credibility of Diels's account. Adolf Hitler was a pragmatist: as soon as it seemed opportune for quite different reasons – those of power politics – he dropped his friend Röhm and posed as the great exponent of moral purity.

He made the most of this role, too, for his own ends, and simultaneously mapped out the course of future development. On the day he arrested Röhm at Wiessee, and even before the latter's murder, he issued Viktor Lutze, the new chief of staff, with an order of the day containing twelve demands addressed to the SA:

'I expect all SA leaders to help to preserve and strengthen the SA in its capacity as a pure and cleanly institution. In particular, I should like every mother to be able to allow her son to join the SA, Party and Hitler Youth without fear that he may become morally corrupted in their ranks. I therefore require all SA commanders to take the utmost pains to ensure that offences under Paragraph 175 are met by immediate expulsion of the culprit from the SA and Party. I want to see men as SA commanders, not ludicrous monkeys.'[386] With that, homosexuals were finally declared fair game.

Hitler's misgivings about homosexuality stemmed primarily from self-interest. His objection to it as a vice or symptom of effeminacy was only secondary. The main danger, as he saw it, was that it would infiltrate the political leadership and constitute itself a secret Order of the Third Sex. He was also concerned at the thought that population growth might be curbed by the heterosexual abstinence of those affected. It is noteworthy and indicative of his wholly amoral outlook that Hitler by no means regarded the homosexual proclivity as 'genetically bad' by definition.

Arguments based on personnel and population policy can be found far more crudely and vehemently expressed in the recorded remarks of Hitler's most assiduous imitator, the Reichsführer-SS. The body politic would be undermined and laid low, he preached to his SS princelings in recapitulation of his master's theories, if the ruling élite became eroded by homosexual standards – and woe to the normal man when that happened! Hitler spiced his prophecies of doom with an example drawn from the dog-eat-dog rivalries of the past. 'In Silesia, SS-Obergruppenführer von Woyrsch was then (1933–34) caught in the cross-fire from the homosexual SS-Gruppenführer Heines and the homosexual Gauleiter and Oberpräsident Brückner. He was hounded for disrupting this wonderfully harmonious relationship, not because they said "he isn't one of us" but always on moral, political, ideological – National Socialist – grounds.'[387] The Grand Master of the Black Order had no need to tell his satraps how such men should be dealt with in the interests of national security and good blood. They had played an active part in the assassinations of 30 June 1934, of which they were the real beneficiaries. Röhm's crony Edmund Heines had been one of the first to bite the dust. 'But when a man in the Security Service, in the SS or in the government has homosexual tendencies,' Himmler told Kersten in 1940 'then he abandons the normal order of things for the perverted world of the homosexual. Such a man always drags ten others after him, otherwise he can't survive. We can't permit such a danger to the country; the homosexuals must be entirely eliminated.'[388]

In the same way, Himmler dramatized the effects of homosexuality on population growth until they assumed the proportions of a threat to national survival. In 1928, the sociologist Robert Michels estimated the number of homosexually inclined men in Germany at 1.2 million. Himmler and *Das Schwarze Korps* generously rounded this figure off – or, rather, up. On their submission, no less than 2 million men – or 10 per cent of male Germans at the height of their physical powers – were contaminated by this 'frightful legacy from the liberalistic period'.[389] Somewhat illogically, Himmler informed the Advisory Board for Population and Racial Policy that these figures were to blame for the enormous surplus of women in the German Reich.[390] Meanwhile, the SS weekly used banner headlines to brand homosexuals as enemies of the State. A nation which needed to raise its annual birth-rate by 1.5 million could not dispense with the reproductive services of hundreds of thousands of men.

This clarified the current requirement or 'national-political task': merciless re-education 'without regard to the pros and cons of the pundits'.[391] Most of these creatures, lacking in all poise, all personal determination and strength of character, appeared to be merely sick. But: 'Compel them to work methodically – something which few of them have ever done in their lives – segregate them from "normal" people under strict surveillance, prevent them from self-indulgently playing the invalid to an audience, force them to see a reflection of their own impossibility in others of their kind, and a change sets in with remarkable speed. The "invalid" recovers. The "abnormal" man turns out to be quite normal. He merely passes through a phase of development which he has failed to undergo in his youth.'[392] To each his own. Homosexual prisoners in concentration camps, identifiable by a pink triangle, were to be reared into healthy German males by hard labour. Besides, one could always separate 'the chaff from the still usable wheat'.[393] The Reichsführer, whose intimate knowledge of SS camps afforded him a better grasp of their potential, greeted the *Das Schwarze Korps* suggestion with scepticism. One might be able to lock up 20,000 male prostitutes and attempt to re-educate them, but millions of homosexuals were another matter. Himmler contemplated more extreme measures. Homosexuals, he told Kersten, must be eliminated root and branch. Addressing his SS generals, he extolled the sagacity of the ancient Germans, whose custom it was to drown their homosexuals in bogs. 'That was no punishment, merely the extinction of an abnormal life. It had to be removed just as we pull up stinging nettles, toss them on to a heap and burn them.'[394]

An ardent admirer of German antiquities, Himmler was able to enlist scholarly research and commendation for this view. SS-Untersturmführer Karl August Eckhardt recounted in *Das Schwarze Korps*[395] how the noble Germans of old used to regard homosexual behaviour as racial treason and punish effeminates by drowning them in bog and fen. The medieval Church had committed the deplorable error of exterminating homosexuals merely as heretics whom they burnt alive to the greater glory of God – 'although burning at the stake was in many instances replaced by the more lenient penalty of decapitation'. The great debasement of Germanic outlook and Nordic sentiment had come about with the incursion of Western susceptibilities during the enlightenment. Newly interpreted, the homosexual represented more of a sub-species than a degenerate form of human being and homosexuality was punished only as a moral offence, 'which completely upset the criterion of assessment'.

The author of these statements was not just anyone. Professor Eckhardt, legal historian and authority on German law, had held a chair at Berlin University since 1928 and was regarded as one of the luminaries of historical scholarship. His contribution to the nation's moral renascence culminated in the following pronouncement: 'Just as we have readopted the old Germanic approach to the question of marriage between alien races, so we must also, in assessing the racially pernicious symptom of degeneracy known as homosexuality, revert to the Nordic principle that degenerates should be exterminated.'[396]

Although attracted by the Germanic custom of summarily drowning homosexuals in bogs, Himmler regretfully told the Bad Tölz meeting of SS generals in 1937: 'In our case, I must reluctantly concede, it is no longer possible.'[397] His humorous proviso applied only to the bog method of execution. To the head of the Black Order, nothing was impossible. He accordingly did his best to punish homosexual traitors to the race with due regard for ancient Germanic usage and eradicate them, if not from the entire nation, at least from his élite corps.

Summary castration

The new masters made it clear from the outset that homosexuality was prohibited in their realm of wholesome popular sentiment. A decree of 23 February 1933 banned pornographic literature of every description, likewise all public activity by the League of Human Rights. This registered association, whose motto was 'For Truth and Justice', had constituted itself the spokesman of the homosexual minority and publicly advocated the repeal of Paragraph 175. In autumn 1934 the Gestapo took steps to regulate matters by requesting local departments to submit lists of all persons known to have engaged in homosexual activities – detailed lists, as the report from the Hagen department showed: 14 persons previously convicted under Paragraph 175, 16 in course of prosecution and 11 suspected of homosexual tendencies.[398] Methods such as these, which took account of mere suspicion, paved the way for denunciation and arbitrary arrest. The harsher indecency provisions in the new penal code of 1935 afforded still further opportunities to deploy the full rigour of the law, even in the case of minor offences, by invoking wholesome popular sentiment. The smear campaigns against the Catholic Church showed how conveniently these infamous methods could be manipulated. Heavily publicized by a controlled press, trials involving priests charged with moral lapses not only caused a sensation among unbelievers but aroused misgivings among the faithful. What substantially contributed to this was the propagandist skill with which such accusations were hawked around. A fanatic like Himmler could privately declare, in all seriousness, that the ecclesiastical hierarchy was largely a club for homosexuals.

Himmler's suspicions applied, if at all, to his élite SS with its denaturized virility myth. Röhm's SA had demonstrated plainly enough how great this threat could become in a tough fighting organization dedicated to naïve self-idolatry, but it was this very fact which drove Himmler to such pathological extremes in his petty bourgeois abhorrence of homosexual proclivities. His ideal Order had to be pure and wholesome, free from all temptations of mind and body. The measures taken against homosexual members of the SS provided a better guide to future intentions than legal proceedings which were still, of necessity, semi-public.

At the very time when the Reichsführer-SS was stigmatizing lapses in the SA leadership, when Röhm and his young paladins were slaughtered and the Führer issued his virtuous appeal to the SA, the SS Central Office was headed by Gruppenführer Kurt Wittje. Wittje was not relieved of his duties, officially 'because of illness',[399] until May 1935. In reality, he was dismissed from the SS with deprivation of rank on account of homosexual abuses which had long been common knowledge. The veteran Nazi's superior officer sought to excuse him by claiming that he had committed them under the influence of alcohol, but not even such a close associate of the Reichsführer could escape condign punishment. Wittje was lucky, as it turned out, because Himmler now adopted a more drastic procedure.

Cases of homosexuality naturally occurred in the ranks of the SS – one case a month, as Himmler himself admitted in 1937. He went on to define the penalty: culprits were to be stripped of their rank, expelled, and brought before a court. However, senior SS commanders attending the Bad Tölz conference were additionally apprised of a small penal refinement which Himmler requested them to introduce without undue publicity: 'After serving the sentence imposed by the court they will, on my instructions, be taken to a concentration camp and there shot while attempting to escape.'[400]

Eighteen months later the Reichsführer-SS ventured to air his ideas in public. The following kite was flown during a speech to the régime's Foreign Organization at Stuttgart on 2 September 1938: 'I can, for instance, envisage that it may be only a few years before a homosexual in the SS becomes liable to the death penalty.'[401] At this juncture, Heydrich's Security Police Headquarters already contained a political section designated 'IIS – Control of Homosexuality and Abortion'. The sails were set for the period after final victory, when attention could at last be devoted to general aims of national policy which had so far been neglected.

Himmler was particularly distressed by homosexual lapses on the part of his senior officers, and dealt with them himself. His attempts at therapy – he rejected psychiatric treatment – were astonishingly naïve. In the case of one veteran commander whom he had sorrowfully been compelled to downgrade, he accepted the man's word of honour that he would renounce his unnatural proclivities. The offender was sent to prove himself at the front, was again promoted – and promptly suffered a relapse. Himmler's masseur, Kersten, saved the sinner from imminent execution by getting him posted to Norway. Impressed by Kersten's knowledge and understanding of the problem, Himmler invited him to become his official adviser on matters homosexual.

Kersten declined with horror. 'You know yourself,' he told the Reichsführer, 'that, ever since it was known how severely you were dealing with homosexuals, it has become a source of the most malicious denunciations.'[402] Only a little while before, Himmler had confided to his disinterested medical adviser how he proposed to deal with the threat of inherited bisexuality: 'I have long been considering whether it might not be expedient to castrate every homosexual at once.'[403]

Where the Black Corps was concerned, this problem was solved on 15 November 1941 by the 'Führer's Decree Relating to the Maintenance of Purity in the SS and Police'. Having secured Hitler's blessing on his endeavours, Himmler sent a triumphant confidential circular to the SS and police:

'1. In order to keep the SS and police free from homosexually inclined weaklings, the Führer has ruled that any member of the SS or police who engages in indecent behaviour with another man or permits himself to be abused by him for indecent purposes will, regardless of age, be condemned to death and executed. In less grave cases, a term of not less than six years' penal servitude or imprisonment may be imposed.

2. The Führer's decree will not be published because it might give rise to misinterpretation.'[404]

This top-secret ukase invested the SS with yet another special privilege which nullified the competence of the ordinary courts. Although there was little room for misunderstanding, senior SS commanders were lavish in their stringent interpretations of the decree. SS Central Office chief Gottlob Berger laid it down that indecency did not apply to quasi-copulatory behaviour alone. An objective infraction of decency or the subjective lascivious intention to arouse sexual desire would be enough to fulfil the terms of the order. 'This includes touching the body of the other person, even when clothed, also the act of kissing.'[405]

The Führer's secret ordinance was welcomed, and not only by the more racially obsessed members of the SS. Even Goebbels, who was not renowned for prudishness, noted in his diary: 'An extremely beneficial decree, and one which will preserve the élite organization from this cancerous disease.'[406] Goebbels's diary, be it added, was written with a view to future publication.

Nor was it only in SS circles that the supreme penalty was deemed a fitting punishment for sexual degeneracy. Early in February 1942, when the notorious decree was already circulating the special SS courts, a meeting of the Reich Ministry of Justice took place. The chief function of this ministry's various departments was to give instruction in contemporary judicial practice. Its ruling on homosexuality: 'In serious cases, castration will not, except in rare borderline instances and where prospects of success are fully assured, warrant the non-application of Paragraph 1 of the Amendment Law.'[407] Paragraph 1 of the Amendment Law prescribed the death penalty.

Off to the brothel

As seen by Himmler in 1937, the problem of prostitution was innocuous compared with that of homosexuality. The former was susceptible of inclusion by means of specific measures in an 'organization acceptable to civilized people'. If only to prevent frustrated men from straying into homosexuality, it was essential to be 'extremely broadminded'[408] in this respect.

This was a surprising tack to take. Until now, prostitution had figured in National Socialist thinking only as a focus of venereal disease. Literature on sex education moralized in the time-honoured way about the perils and beastliness of intercourse with women of easy virtue: 'They all suffer from chronic gonorrhoea, and in many cases from syphilis as well.'[409] Then there were the more up-to-date arguments according to which prostitutes, being subhuman, were incapable 'save temporarily at most, of voluntarily performing worthwhile productive work by reason of their mental inferiority or innate feeble-mindedness'.[410] These were precisely the characteristics adduced to justify the consignment of all prostitutes to concentration camps, over whose gates loomed the re-educative slogan 'Freedom through Work'. But although pimps, who genuinely did no worthwhile productive work, found their way into concentration camps as antisocial parasites, their protégées, who at least toiled for their money, did not. For all the rhetorical attacks on it, the continued existence of their trade remained unchallenged – and not simply because the world's oldest profession was ineradicable. There were ideological excuses for this ideological failure, and they dictated that prostitution should be 'organized'. In short, it was profitably incorporated in the system.

The Third Reich's most notorious establishment dedicated to the sale of love – the Salon Kitty in Berlin's Giesebrechtstrasse – owed its existence to purely pragmatic considerations. Heydrich's brain-child was ideological only to the extent that his brothel for bigwigs presented the totalitarian system with an added means of surveillance and supervision. In this case, surveillance applied principally to government guests from abroad but also to prominent Party members who failed to grasp the special purpose of this Security Service establishment. The Salon Kitty was staffed by hand-picked hetaerae who were adept in titillating the jaded male palate. Additionally stimulated by alcoholic beverages of comparable quality, guests let slip much that was of interest to the Security Service: minor hints or major State secrets, informative intimacies or items of inside information. SD technicians had ensured that none of these precious disclosures went unheard. Cunningly installed in the pleasure-chambers of the Salon Kitty were sensitive microphones whose verbal harvest was carefully garnered by a monitoring and recording centre in the basement. The elaborate arrangement was essentially a whim of Heydrich's: as the genuinely important embassy staff did not frequent the place anyway, the results in terms of successful espionage were minimal.

The initial campaign against prostitution was eventually succeeded, after passing through phases of tacit disapproval and toleration, by the type of systematic organization which Himmler had already outlined. War supplied the final impetus, for the needs of sex-starved soldiers could not be satisfied by the sight of nude sculptures alone.

Two directives issued by the Reich Ministry of the Interior on 9 September 1939 and 16 March 1940 authorized the establishment of medically supervised brothels throughout Reich territory. At the same time, a highly moral-sounding form of bureaucratism came into play. Official authorization of brothels was simultaneously to assist in the registration of all prostitutes. Any who still dared to work free-lance were to be placed in preventive detention or a concentration camp for 'anti-social behaviour'. For military brothels, premises were to be selected in suitable urban districts where no children or juveniles could be morally corrupted by their proximity. Finally – so stringent were the rules governing State-controlled lechery – no landlord was to profit from such an institution.

Difficulties arose nonetheless – in Würzburg, for example. Having ascertained that there was a need for one, the authorities decided to establish a brothel at No. 5 Karthause. Local residents lodged a protest with the National Socialist Association of Those Bereaved by War, invoking the memory of the sons whom they had sacrificed for

Führer and Fatherland. Their complaint was submitted to Himmler in his capacity as Chief of the German Police. Himmler, in his turn, requested Würzburg's police commissioner for a statement of opinion. This was to the effect that the honest citizens' objections were attributable to their religious outlook, which amounted to proof of nullity. Himmler duly sanctioned the establishment of a brothel at No. 5 Karthause.[411]

If the Nazi guardians of morality considered that arch-conservative Würzburg required a brothel in the interests of public health and military welfare, this was doubly true of larger cities. Goebbels lamented in 1942 that over 15 per cent of the women detained during a recent police raid were venereally diseased, most of them being syphilitic. The new line presented a welcome opportunity, on grounds of sexual hygiene, first to adopt an understanding attitude towards prostitution, whose inevitability had long been accepted, and secondly to extend State discipline to this indisciplined and clandestine sector of national life. The Gauleiter of Berlin and Minister of Public Enlightenment breathed a sigh of the purest relief. 'In the long term,' he declared, 'we shall doubtless be unable to avoid establishing a red light district in the Reich capital, just as there is in Hamburg, Nuremberg and other large cities. A city of four million inhabitants cannot be organized and administered from the aspect of bourgeois morality.'[412]

Once approved, the brothel system had to make its greatest possible contribution to the public weal. This process assumed bizarre forms which suggest that Himmler's hand was at work. One peculiarly esoteric research centre experimented with human semen in an attempt to find a substitute for plasma in blood transfusions. Brothels were enlisted as semen-suppliers. According to one reliable source,[413] prostitutes employed at the Klosterstrasse brothel in Stuttgart were instructed to preserve semen-filled sheaths after each bout of copulation and place them in a special container which was collected at regular intervals by an authorized representative from the research centre. It is hardly surprising that no details of this obscure scientific project leaked out. All those involved had to sign a pledge of secrecy.

The custodians of racial purity were particularly exercised by the sexual needs of millions of foreign workers in all parts of the Reich, which needs represented a 'threat to the body politic'. Soon after the outbreak of war, 'racially desecrative relations' between German women and Poles, who rated as inferior, began to figure with increasing frequency in Security Service memoranda. On 28 February 1940 the

SD reported general hopes for a dispensation which would keep Polish workers supplied with a sufficiency of Polish women, 'If necessary, where the former are accommodated in large assembly camps, in special Polish brothels.'[414] Two years later Goebbels, too, expressed concern: 'The only way of mastering the situation once and for all, I imagine, will be to establish brothels. But that is rather a delicate matter which needs careful handling.'[415]

The Minister of Propaganda showed himself ill-informed. Early in 1941, one of Bormann's circulars made it clear that a good start had already been made on the establishment of brothels for 'workers of alien race' in the Upper Danube region. The Party Chancellery had gone on to suggest that other regions might profit by the experience gained there.

By the end of 1943, 60 brothels for foreign workers had opened on Reich territory 'for the protection of German blood' and another 50 were in preparation. These 'operational centres' were staffed by some 600 prostitutes recruited in Paris, Poland and the Reich Protectorate of Bohemia and Moravia, all of whom were free to return home at any time. The brothels operated under strict medical, sanitary and – needless to say – police supervision. The ladies were obliged to pay a fixed daily fee to cover board, heating, lighting and linen. Their takings were substantial. Some top-class performers served up to fifty clients daily, and one virtuosa employed at Bitterfeld claimed that she often earned as much as 200 marks a day. 'She said she already owned two tenements in Paris and had a friend there who was going to buy her two more. When her contract expired she intended to return to Paris and retire on the strength of her ownership of four houses.'[416]

The SD report undoubtedly erred on the bright side and glossed over the cruel fate of many brothel inmates. Not all of them can have enlisted as willingly and been as happy in their work. The reference to fifty clients a day is in itself an indication of the strains to which they were exposed. On the other hand, there is no doubt that a shrewd professional could earn enough to retire on. As a report from Frankfurt stated: 'Although the Poles do not earn much, the Frenchwomen are in a position to send RM1,000 home to France every month (with the approval of the exchange control office). Generally speaking, the charge per visit ranges from RM3 to RM5. Fees of RM50 and even RM100 have been paid in isolated instances.'[417] As untaxed income – for the exchequer did not benefit from State-supervised fornication –

this represented a sizeable reward for services rendered, though few foreign workers can have afforded to pay such prices.

The public's response to an institution ostensibly devised for its own protection was, to say the least, ungrateful. As more and more Germans were rendered homeless by the intensified aerial bombardment of the Reich, so people found it even harder to understand why the government should spend an average of RM100,000 apiece on setting up brothels for foreigners. On this point, suggested the Security Service, the Party must deliberately direct its propaganda towards enlightening the public on the vital need to maintain German racial purity.

Shave them or hang them?

Meanwhile, many hundreds of thousands of foreign workers conscripted from all over Europe – mainly Poles, Russians and Frenchmen – were involuntarily helping to keep the industry and agriculture of the Greater German Reich in operation. There were also prisoners of war, among them numerous Englishmen and Americans who had long been a familiar sight. People were accustomed to them, not least because even foreigners had adjusted themselves to prevailing conditions with varying degrees of willingness. And these were the creatures whom Party propagandists condemned wholesale as alien blood and inferior stock – human beings like oneself, men on whose help one depended, workmates with whom one lived and toiled side by side.

This was where the rulers of Nazi Germany became enmeshed in a trap which they themselves, in their insatiable lust for power, had set. The home front was suffering from a manpower shortage occasioned by a war of conquest. Vacancies had to be filled by foreign workers, and these foreigners proved conclusively by their skill and efficiency how absurd were the ideological doctrines which preached the inefficiency and inferiority of all non-Germans, all foreigners. How could the women of Germany be persuaded that these men, who had replaced their husbands in field and factory, were, if not subhuman, of inferior stock and unworthy of them? Only one method occurred to the tyrants of the Third Reich – the only method open to them: coercion and threats of draconian punishment.

Soon after the invasion of Poland, which initiated the large-scale shipment of prisoners of war to the Reich and their incorporation in its economy, the penal code was amended to suit war-time requirements. The totalitarian administration of justice was stiffened with new crimes and horrendous penalties. 25 November 1939 saw the publication of the decree for the safeguarding of German military potential. In addition to sabotage, disruption of major industrial concerns, membership of subversive organizations and sabotage against the armed forces of allied countries, Paragraph 4 of this ordinance made unauthorized association with prisoners of war – and, in particular, sexual intercourse – an offence punishable by heavy terms of penal servitude. The SD's morale reports claimed prompt acceptance of this measure by the general public, who had, after all, been prepared for it by the racial protection laws. The same reports also indicated, however, that sexual intercourse between Germans and Poles was far from infrequent. Undeterred, the Security Service declared that the public regarded harsh sentences as altogether justified and expected the authorities to proceed with rigour: 'In many instances, villagers have resorted to self-defence.'[418]

What was termed self-defence on the part of outraged citizens tended to be the local Party officials' way of compensating for the ordinary courts' reluctance to convict in such cases. The senior government representative at Osnabrück reported in August 1940 that an eighteen-year-old girl employed as a kitchen-maid in the PoW hospital at Lingen had confessed to having sexual intercourse with Poles. 'On the instructions of the Kreisleiter, SA men cut off the kitchen-maid's hair in the Adolf-Hitler-Platz at Lingen, in the presence of a sizeable crowd.'[419] The girl was then handed over to the Gestapo.

Not long afterwards, a fifteen-year-old German girl and a Czech girl of nineteen were confined in the pillory at Komotau and then, with their heads shorn, led through the town mounted on a pair of donkeys. Their crime: sexual intercourse with Polish prisoners of war. 'Suspended from their necks were large placards bearing the following inscription: "We two sows had relations with prisoners of war".'[420] Controlled public fury meted out the same treatment to all women who had failed in their duty, but the courts drew a distinction between nationals and aliens: the German girl was sentenced to nine months' hard labour, the Czech to fifteen.

Recommendations on how to punish guilty prisoners of war were issued by the SS Race and Resettlement Bureau. Those who had besmirched German blood, ran a proposal dated July 1940, should be handed over to SS racial assessors. Anyone whom they adjudged inferior would undergo special treatment. 'This special treatment will be effected by hanging.'[421] The assessors were never called in. Bormann eliminated any possible misunderstandings by decreeing the same justice for all prisoners of war. The French and British were to be treated exactly like the Poles: 'Hand over the prisoners in question to the Gestapo for shooting!'[422]

Complaints about the number of German women and girls involved in intimate relationships with foreign males became so frequent that they alerted the Minister of Public Enlightenment. In September 1940, Goebbels instructed all regional Party headquarters and propaganda bureaux to step up their verbal bombardment. It had to be impressed on the public that the association of German girls 'not only with Jews but with all other men of alien blood must be rejected'.[423] That year, barely two thousand cases came before the courts.

The following year there were over twice as many, nearly four-and-a-half thousand. Indignantly, the Racial Policy Bureau in Munich furnished Goebbels with a graphic account of ten cases in which women and girls had been intimate with French prisoners of war employed on their farms. In three instances, the great enlightener of the public could claim that his propaganda had borne fruit.[424]

One seventeen-year-old milkmaid had repeatedly allowed a foreign worker to kiss her. The couple were then caught copulating in a barn. The girl was handed over to the juvenile welfare department, but not before some outraged locals had cut her hair off.

At Bad Aibling, two young women helped a pair of Frenchmen to escape from PoW camp and hid them in the elder's home. When the police turned up, they lied. Their intention had been to smuggle the fugitives into Switzerland by car. The younger woman, aged twenty, had even planned to abscond with them. She was alleged to have had intercourse with one of the Frenchmen, first in a wood and then at her aunt's flat. Both women were sent to hard labour for three years and six months. Their heads were shorn by the indignant populace.

A twenty-seven-year-old maidservant and a twenty-three-year-old farmer's daughter from a village near Dachau were accused of having had intimate and long-standing relations with French prisoners of war, even though they were engaged to German soldiers. Both were pregnant, allegedly by their fiancés. An infuriated mob punished them for their infamous conduct by cutting off their hair.

The pillory was a favourite method of demonstrating wholesome popular sentiment. The public's role was usually confined to that of a half-malicious, half-shamefaced spectator. As for the courts, they tolerated such outbursts of organized popular fury and seldom ventured to criticize those who, with official encouragement, took the law into their own hands.

In the Franconian village of Diespeck, a baker's widow became pregnant by a Pole and was duly arrested. The local Party leader removed her from gaol a few days later and had her led down the village street with partly shorn hair. The pregnant woman was forced to wear placards on her chest and back bearing the words 'Polish whore and Polish sow'. Schoolchildren accompanied the procession. The Kreisleiter treated the local inhabitants to a speech on the purpose and significance of the exhibition in terms of racial policy. Shortly afterwards the woman gave birth and died. The superior court at Nuremberg, which submitted a report on these happenings, cautiously averred that 'The Kreisleiter's actions did not meet with universal approbation'.[425]

In a hamlet in the Bayerisches Wald, the peasant girl Adeline G. became involved with a Polish prisoner of war who had voluntarily stayed on as an agricultural labourer in the Roding district after his release in October 1940. In February 1941 Adeline G. gave birth to a child and was two months later sentenced to ten months' imprisonment by a juvenile court. The Gestapo hanged her Polish lover, Julian Majlca, in a wood near Michelsneukirchen and forced his Polish workmates to file past the body. He was never brought to trial.

Similar treatment was accorded to another Pole, Paul Hwiszd, in the neighbouring district of Nittenau. Berta, the sixteen-year-old daughter of his employer, became pregnant by him during the winter of 1940-41. The presiding judge refused an indictment against the girl and merely instructed the welfare authorities to attend to her after her confinement. Another Polish agricultural labourer charged with a similar offence was removed from court custody and strung up by the Gestapo. Yet another Pole, Jarek, who worked in a Bavarian village and had been involved with two peasant girls, was hanged by the Gestapo from a tree a quarter of a mile south of the village. 119 Poles were compelled to file past the corpse on orders from Himmler himself. The parade was organized by the chief administrative official at Straubing, who supervised it in person.

The provincial court at Nuremberg reported more such incidents during the autumn months of 1941. The list was far from complete because it covered only those cases which had come to the notice of the judicial authorities. Most cases never reached court, and even Nuremberg's official guardians of justice failed to do more than level feeble criticism at the high-handed behaviour of Party bosses and criminal policemen in their reports to the Ministry of Justice. The public did not agree with such measures, they said, carefully covering themselves, because it was felt that executions should be preceded by a judicial sentence.[426]

Members of the public were equally reluctant to intervene. It remains a moot point whether murders perpetrated on alien Poles in these rural districts really accorded with wholesome popular sentiment, or whether citizens were genuinely intimidated by deterrent executions.

By and large, even these acts of terrorism failed in their purpose. Although they did not provoke resistance, they were an utterly ineffective weapon against sexual deprivation and the growing ties between lonely German women and foreign males who had been thrown together at work. In 1942, the number of regular proceedings brought under Paragraph 4 of the military potential ordinance doubled yet again to over 9,000. No less than 122 cases were heard during this period in the Landshut jurisdictional area alone. 'Authoritative circles' conservatively estimated the number of illegitimate children born as a result of these liaisons at 20,000 – more than enough for the racial protectionists to fabricate a doom-laden myth about 'racial infiltration' and call for a universal ban on sexual intercourse by foreigners.[427]

According to court statistics, it was mainly in rural areas that the ice tended to melt between German girls and foreign workers. Not unnaturally, this development was less marked in towns, where employers and foreign labour seldom belonged to the same household. The contrast was certainly not attributable to a more racially conscious National Socialist outlook among townspeople. On the contrary, the absurdity of Nazi doctrines became even more transparent under urban conditions.

The Reich Department of Youth Leadership complained about unworthy behaviour in the ranks of the female youth organizations. It seemed that girl students were in a quandary because even Japanese or Siamese had been officially declared racially valuable and of quasi-Aryan status. Some of their number had so far forgotten their racial instincts as to abandon their allegedly 'normal' inhibitions towards foreigners and consort with orientals – Persians, Indians, and the like! Racially conscious student leaders, who had preserved their proper instincts, deliberately barged into these foreign visitors when they encountered them with German girls, and the police advised them not to be seen with female fellow-students.[428]

Security Service investigators did their best to trace the causes of this rampant racial impurity.[429] They were struck by the fact that young people showed a particular interest in associating with foreigners. Religious outlook also played a not inconsiderable role. People in Catholic areas often adopted a markedly friendly attitude towards their Polish co-religionists, and German citizens refused to testify in cases where they should have denounced their neighbours for being on intimate terms with Poles. By way of excuse, the SD postulated that many were unaware of the extent to which relations with foreigners rated as improper. One could not, for instance, shout from the house-tops what Bormann secretly confided to Party authorities, namely, that association with civilian workers from allied Italy was also undesirable.[430] Maintenance of racial purity was rendered still more difficult by the fact that voluntary workers from abroad were privately accommodated. Even in Berlin, single women showed a distinct readiness to take foreign lodgers. Lastly, there was the question of close contact at work, above all in the country. It was a particular thorn in the side of Party Secretary Bormann that this contact persisted during leisure hours, for instance in the morally parlous environment of the public swimming-pool. It being undesirable to exclude foreigners *en bloc* and reintroduce segregated bathing sessions, Bormann solemnly proposed that racial pollution should be combated by increased supervision and sex education.[431] He further opined that the provocative behaviour of many foreigners – a fact to which the SD had drawn attention – doubtless heightened the dangers of the situation.

In practice, the opposite also occurred. SD reports referred to the 'very pronounced sexuality'[432] of certain 'less estimable' women. One frustrated private soldier, who could hardly have been rated any more estimable by the same standards but was an extremely welcome witness, denounced an unnatural female of this type. She was an eighteen-year-old domestic whom he and a crony had accosted. 'We walked up and down outside the pub until 10 p.m. Did it have to be Frenchmen who had sexual intercourse with her, we asked. We could do the job just as well as her PoW. Well, said the girl, she couldn't promise anything for today. She was expecting the Frenchman to give her a thorough poking in all the right places, and she expected full satisfaction. She also said she planned to try unnatural intercourse as well.'[433]

Experienced judges reduced this abundance of causes to two motives so natural that they conduced to the leniency abhorred by advocates of exemplary punishment. In the first place, many women were suffering from sexual frustration; in the second, farmers' wives were particularly dependent on male labour – two factors which interacted on many levels. The guardians of German racial purity would have no truck with such subtleties. The only excuse for which they could raise any sympathy at all was the one they understood best: coercion. The following statement by a Silesian farmer's wife and member of the National Socialist Women's Association illustrates this. She had two children aged four and seven by her husband, who was away on active service in Russia. In May 1943 she gave birth to a child sired by an East European worker, since fled. 'B. was employed by me. Early in June 1943 he came to me and insisted that I have sexual intercourse with him or he would run off and leave me just at the busiest time of year. He went on and on at me, and since I'm all alone with my sister-in-law on a 30-acre farm, and B. was a good worker, I allowed him to seduce me.'[434]

It was a shrewd story, if not entirely credible. Lenient as the ordinary courts often were, merciless rigour prevailed in the special courts which exemplified the blatant contradictions and brutality of the period.

The SD can hardly have rejoiced to report that many a husband pleaded on his erring wife's behalf, sympathizing with her lapse during his own long absence and assuring the court that, having lived happily together in the past, they would do so again in future.

As for the guilty foreigner, he had little hope of escape once enmeshed in the machinery of 'justice'. On 10 February 1944 Ernst Kaltenbrunner, head of the Reich Central Security Bureau, issued a secret directive. This laid down a special procedure designed to plug any remaining gaps in the judicial preservation of racial purity. 'Foremost among the offences to which gravity must be attached are acts of sabotage, crimes of violence and indecency, and sexual intercourse with German women and girls. These cases must not, as a matter of principle, be passed to the judicial authorities. The only cases transferable to them are those in which a judicial sentence seems desirable in the interests of public opinion and in which it has been ascertained by advance consultation that the court will impose the death penalty.'[435]

It was typical of the unbroken tradition of bourgeois double standards in racial guise that men could safely indulge in conduct which exposed women to grave charges. Sexual relations between German males and women workers from abroad drew verbal condemnation at most. In other respects, the Party refrained from interfering unless it feared a threat to public health. At Bormann's instigation, the Supreme Command of the Armed Forces decreed on 2 January 1943 that relations between German soldiers and female foreign workers in the home front area were unworthy and destructive of military potential owing to widespread venereal disease.[436]

The imposition of a similar ban on sex in front-line areas would have been absurd. The Führer was nonetheless anxious that German males should not squander their seed on the improvement of inferior ethnic groups. In November 1942, Reichsleiter Bormann acquainted Reich Director of Health Conti with his master's wishes in this respect. Pressure on the rubber market was too great for the authorities to have stuffed vast quantities of condoms into the pack of every soldier on the Eastern front, but the conscientious and resourceful Conti hit upon another means of contraception. Going to Himmler, he recommended the mass production of chemical substances for distribution among the female inhabitants of the occupied territories. Raw materials being in short supply, these preparations could not, unfortunately, be of the highest quality. They would irritate the vaginal lining and have other adverse effects, but Conti urged that the ban on such contraceptives be specially lifted in the Eastern territories.[437] Although the Reichs-führer-SS must have been attracted by this potential aid to his final solution, Conti's bold project came to nothing. All else apart, Himmler's model SS was the only military formation whose members were categorically forbidden to have intercourse with women of alien blood. Under a directive dated 9 December 1941, any such offences had to be reported to the Reichsführer personally.[438]

Hitler looked with equal disfavour on soldiers' requests for permission to marry foreigners. Judging by the photographs he had seen, he said, most of these women were crook-backed, bent, ugly, and ill-equipped for genuine German matrimony. He would sooner allow his men to indulge in discreet peccadilloes. Bormann, the brown eminence, reacted promptly once more. He circulated a memorandum approving an order by Colonel-General Eduard Dietl to the effect that members of the armed forces were required to contract marriages with fellow-nationals only. Ethnically related Germanic peoples were included in the ban. Even Norwegian women were relatively inharmonious, most of them being inferior, stunted creatures 'with an Alpine infusion'. Furthermore: 'At home, hundreds of thousands of vivacious German girls – and numerous war-widows too, unfortunately – are waiting for our returning soldiers.'[439]

They alone were to be the recipients of pure German genes. The purpose of sexual intercourse was procreation. In their attitude to contraception among healthy Germans, the Nazi custodians of race were at least as Catholic as the Vatican.

They were even more Papal in the matter of terminated pregnancies. The annual number of abortions in the German Reich was estimated at 6–700,000 at the end of the 1920s. This was a major reason why champions of wholesome public morality tried so hard to upgrade the status of illegitimate children and their mothers. Addressing the consultative committee on population policy in 1937, Himmler quoted a revised annual estimate – 400,000 – which implied that the new policy was proving successful. The Chief of the German Police knew better than that, because he angrily admitted to his SS generals at the same period that the real figure lay somewhere between 600,000 and 800,000. This estimate he supplemented with a few highly arbitrary statistics suggestive of a disastrous drain on the folkish birth-rate. 30,000 of these abortions had ended fatally, he claimed, and 300,000 had left the women permanently sterile. Although these figures were a complete fabrication – he referred on another occasion to 50,000 cases of sterility – they served as a pseudo-humanitarian pretext for dealing relentlessly with all cases of attempted and successful termination. Women could be – and were meant to be – sentenced to hard labour, abortionists to death. Here as elsewhere, the courts' interpretation of the law seemed unduly lenient to those in power. Judges were severely taken to task at a meeting of the Reich Ministry of Justice in February 1942. In the case of self-abortion and abortion by another party, 'the sentences imposed are still too light. It is no longer tolerable in any part of the Reich that a sentence should be determined by factors strongly reminiscent of the idea of social abortion.'[440] Abortion was permissible solely on racial grounds. Where one parent was of impure blood, abortion should be undertaken in the public interest. The 'vital energy of the people' was the supreme law which dictated the degree of punishment to be meted out to the doctor, midwife or quack who terminated a pregnancy. This was especially true in wartime, when the nation's life-force was being tapped by casualties sustained in battle. 'Particular heed should be paid to the position in respect of capital abortion by another party.' The supreme judicial authority recommended capital punishment for second offenders.[441] That was in February 1942. The number of terminations known to the courts had risen sharply since 1940, and the trend persisted.

Visible cracks appeared in the laboriously cultivated image of public

morality and propriety. Neither barbarous sentences by special courts
nor arbitrary police methods proved capable of curbing the moral
effects of war. Although the system's supervisory powers were extended
by every totalitarian method known to an SS machine which grew
more autonomous with each passing day, control of general moral
conduct increasingly slipped from its grasp. The organization of power
structures was outpaced by the spread of disorganized conditions.

In many cases, families were disrupted and sexual problems created
by the evacuation of women and children from cities under threat of
aerial bombardment. Separation had an adverse effect on married
women as well as on the husbands who stayed behind in reserved
occupations. Charges of sexual misconduct by women evacuees were
as frequent as complaints about poor morale, lack of enthusiasm for
work and lax behaviour among their grass-widower husbands.

Soldiers' wives had been familiar with these symptoms of marital
dissolution for an even longer period. As the war dragged on, it
became more and more difficult to rediscover mutual understanding
and sexual harmony during brief spells of leave. Increasingly dependent
upon their own resources, many women asserted their independence
in matters of sex as well. The strict rules governing intersexual relations
began to crumble, yielding to freer and often uninhibited modes of
conduct.

This became particularly apparent when people had an excuse to
let their hair down and celebrate. The following description is taken
from a young soldier's account of his Christmas leave, 1943–44: 'New
Year's Eve was frightful. The streets swarmed with females chasing
field-grey uniforms. Many of them carried bottles containing their
extra schnapps allocation and broke the ice by asking to borrow a
corkscrew. If the soldier didn't have one, they produced one from
their handbag. They weren't just young women, either. There were
forty- and fifty-year-olds among them.'[442]

Scenes like this may not have typified feminine behaviour in war-
time Germany, but they were symptomatic of an emotional state.
Women had been too long exposed to strains which invalidated the
traditional rules of propriety and transformed them into an intolerable
burden. One Security Service report spoke of the noticeable 'sexualiza-
tion of community life' and referred quite explicitly to the sexual
frustration of soldiers' wives. Far from laying the entire onus on them,
it blamed the pernicious influence of those in positions of leadership. The frequency of divorce among locally influential figures and

their blatant affairs with actresses or secretaries set a bad example.[443]

However well founded this criticism may have been, the general effects of promiscuity in high places were inconsiderable. Official appeals for an exemplary standard of moral austerity were equally incapable of stemming the relaxation in bourgeois social conventions. These could be maintained only in normal times, so-called. The pressure of wartime conditions rendered them inoperative, and attempts to prop them up by resorting to intensified coercion only accelerated this process. A threshold had been reached beyond which intimidation became ineffective and resistance began.

The forbidden ideal of democratic freedom

The conduct of the young illustrates how such a seemingly adamantine code of behaviour could disintegrate. Officially recorded cases of juvenile delinquency were more than twice as numerous in 1941 as they were in the peace-time year of 1937. It should, at the same time, be noted that these were less criminal offences than statutory violations attributable to neglect, e.g. loafing, sexual intercourse with adults, indecency between minors, and gang activities. It was not that youthful acts of violence or offences committed for profit – mugging, theft, burglary – showed any dramatic increase. The offences were over-whelmingly of a moral nature, and latent in these eruptions of adolescent instinct was a tendency to protest, not only against rules in general, but against the specific constraints of a system of total human coverage and totalitarian control.

This was particularly manifest in the aforementioned relations between German girls and foreign students. Reports on the subject came in from many university towns. Informants in Darmstadt told of a group of girl students who obviously thought it chic to have foreign boy-friends, whatever their race. They had consorted with Chinese boys in the university stadium, and three girls aged sixteen or seventeen had been sighted walking in the woods with foreigners. Misgivings voiced by BdM leaders had no effect. The Gestapo announced from Dresden that German girls had actually engaged in sexual intercourse with Turkish students from the polytechnic and college of mining. In Berlin, German girls were espied in bars and at the Wannsee lido accompanied by Arabs. That was in summer 1940, and the SD reported: 'All sections of the public are urgently demanding that a move at last be made to deal with this unworthy behaviour. It is felt that, however necessary they may sometimes have been in the past, considerations of foreign policy are out of place today, and that stringent measures could at least be taken against the German girls involved.'[444] In other words, if years of racial indoctrination had borne no fruit, the deficiency must be remedied by law.

It was a vain hope. The courts were already swamped by a rising tide of juvenile immorality. Alarming reports flooded in from all over the country in such numbers as to suggest that the National Socialist educational system was itself at risk. In the East Prussian district of Holland at the end of 1939, a school medical inspection established that many of the girls examined must have had intercourse a short time before. In the rural district of Marburg, a similar state of affairs was discovered among under-fourteens. In Frankfurt, the chief public prosecutor expressed consternation at the increase in crimes of indecency among adolescents. The municipal juvenile welfare department supplied examples. In one case, five Hitler Youth boys aged between fourteen and sixteen had lured some fourteen-year-old girls into an attic. Three of them held them down while the other two raped them. In two other cases, schoolgirls had taken the initiative by visiting soldiers' billets in quest of sexual experience. Not once but several times, and not with one man but several. Their ages: thirteen and fourteen.[445]

The shocked guardians of morality responded with a police ordinance for the protection of juveniles (March 1940) which prohibited loitering in the open after nightfall and forbade visits to bars and places of entertainment on pain of detention.

A report submitted in April 1942 by the provincial court at Munich stated that laxity of outlook and conduct was becoming particularly marked among girls. From the age of fourteen onwards, many of them unhesitatingly engaged in sexual intercourse with members of the armed forces and Labour Service. After Hitler Youth parades, young people roamed the darkened streets, went to forbidden films and allowed themselves to be led astray by corrupt adults. A few cases taken from the records of one juvenile court[446]:

Three boys and three girls, all aged thirteen, met to engage in group sex. Two other boys, aged thirteen and sixteen, procured three nine-year-old girls for the same purpose. A sixteen-year-old boy hired himself out as a male prostitute. A girl at primary school lectured her classmates on sexual technique and the use of contraceptives. Some fifteen- and sixteen-year-old girls mutually agreed that French prisoners of war could 'do it far better than Germans' and verified this by engaging in acts which included 'unnatural sexual intercourse'. Two fifteen-year-old girls moved in with some anti-aircraft gunners and spent several nights practising positions. Other schoolgirls made a business out of sex but were ignorant enough of their racial merits to accept payment in small change. One fifteen-year-old girl was re-proached by her mother for persistently associating with SS men and soldiers. The girl was unmoved. Her retort: 'If she got herself pregnant she'd be just what the Führer was always asking for – a German mother.'[447]

These phenomena were not confined to the towns, where there was a growing incidence of pregnancies, births and venereal diseases among girls in the 14–18 age-group. To quote from the files of the Reich Ministry of Justice: 'It seems that an extremely grim situation prevails in the small provincial town of Giebelstadt (in the jurisdictional area of Würzburg). Grave rebukes were perforce administered to some forty minors and juveniles of both sexes who had committed indecencies together over a considerable period, notably in recent months. Most of the cases involved minors aged between ten and fourteen. This un-pleasant state of affairs is said to derive from the proximity of Giebelstadt airfield and the allegedly licentious conduct of the soldiers quartered there, who have unscrupulously made advances to girls of school age.'[448]

In search of reasons for this drastic decline in moral standards among the young, the Munich court pin-pointed six causes: (a) inadequate parental control in war-time; (b) evening Hitler Youth parades; (c) sub-standard Hitler Youth leaders; (d) youth camps and the employ-ment of juvenile labour; (e) a flood of trashy and obscene literature; and (f) the reduction of police patrols for the supervision of juveniles.[449]

This amounted to a charge that the government and parents had neglected their supervisory duties. To those who, like the Munich judges, viewed the entire complex of juvenile offences in the light of discipline and propriety, this was the obvious explanation. But there was more involved than that. Young people, who were supposed according to the official doctrine to satisfy their associative needs by joining the national youth organization, the Hitler Youth, and its numerous affiliates, were forming groups of their own. It was not enough to dismiss this trend as hooliganism, as immoral or plain criminal. Young people had a quite patent urge to associate indepen-dently, not only outside the organizations prescribed and controlled by the system but in opposition to them.

Some of these gangs evolved their own rules, elected leaders and treasurers, adopted badges and code-names. The *Buschwölfe* ('Bush Wolves') of Munich wore a seven-pointed star and their local rivals the *Charlieblase* ('Charlie Gang') pullovers embroidered with the letters CHARLIE. The Munich judges confined themselves to reporting that the first gang organized communal thefts and the second consorted in air-raid shelters with girls above and below the age of fourteen. But was that all? Far from being modelled on the world of crime, the names, monograms and badges smacked of American films with their sheriff's stars and campus conventions. Juvenile gangs of this type existed throughout the Reich. They came to the notice of the guardians of the law primarily because they roamed around after nightfall, held meetings, attacked Hitler Youth patrols and occasionally molested passers-by. Kassel had its *Bärenbände* ('Bear Gangs'), Düsseldorf the *Klub der Goldenen Horde* ('Golden Horde Club') and *Shambeko-Bande* ('Shambeko Mob'), Ahlfeld the *Schlangenklub* ('Snake Club'). In Wismar they called themselves *Blauer Dunst* ('Blue Mist', an idiomatic phrase which might be rendered 'The Deceivers') and the *Ringbande* ('Ring Gang'), in Braunschweig the *Schreckensteiner* and in Hamburg *Goldene Vierzehn* ('The Golden Fourteen'), in Chemnitz the *Stadtbadbrühe* (literally: 'Municipal Baths Broth').

In 1940, Frankfurt's *OK-Gang* and *Haarlem-Klub* were cleaned up.[450] The club, which had existed since early 1939, comprised eighty-eight girls aged between thirteen and eighteen and seventy-two boys whose ages ranged from fourteen to twenty. They all attended secondary schools and came from better-class homes. Most of them belonged to the Hitler Youth or German Girls' League. Their main interests were hit tunes, dancing, and lounging in coffee-houses. They dressed ostentatiously and seemed uninterested in politics. Inquiries disclosed a picture of active and indiscriminate promiscuity – outdoors, in cafés, at private dances and at a ski-hut near Oberreifenberg in the Taunus. One party invitation read: 'Gentlemen will attend in bathing trunks, ladies with nothing up top, nothing down below, and fresh air in the middle.'[451] Hard liquor flowed freely at these parties, and there were private rooms to which couples could withdraw. Club members derived sexual gratification and new ideas from pornographic literature. Partner-swapping was the rule, and emotional ties were unfashionable. The youngsters slept together 'because there was nobody else'. One sixteen-year-old girl was involved with five boys simultaneously. Another made a point of preserving her virginity but was amenable to any other form of sexual technique. Another had intercourse with her escort in a booth at the *Café Hippodrom*. A seventeen-year-old girl went tarting after a Faith and Beauty meeting but couldn't raise the energy: 'I was so drunk I was bushed – that's why intercourse didn't take place.'[452]

The spectacle of such impropriety – 'cynicism, boundless effrontery' – left police investigators flabbergasted. '12-year-olds exhibited the precocity of 16-year-olds and many 16-year-olds had the sexual maturity of 21-year-olds.'[453] Nor was the phenomenon unique. Frankfurt later spawned the *Ohio-Klub* and the *Cotton-Klub*, where the 'Swing-Jugend' used to congregate. While stating that the 'Swing Youngsters' were Anglophile, the police ascribed their conduct primarily to sexual licence stimulated by dancing to highly syncopated music. However, it had meanwhile become dangerous to be associated, even by hearsay, with the word 'swing', and not merely because of its sexual connotations.

In August 1941 the Minister of Propaganda received an alarming SD report from Hamburg.[454] This claimed that 'hot and swing demonstrations' by youthful Anglophiles had recently assumed 'unpatriotic and reactionarily demoralizing forms'. Records of banned swing music were in wide circulation. Young people were dancing to Anglo-American music and using English conventions and nicknames. Amateur swing bands were springing up like mushrooms. Three hundred youngsters had held a wild jam session at the Alsterpavillon, those involved being 'degenerate and criminally inclined juveniles, some of mixed blood, who terrorized the healthy-minded public by their mode of behaviour and undignified musical excesses'.[455] The report concluded by urging that steps be taken to root out those authors of the epidemic who were known to the Gestapo.

Goebbels read the report and exploded. How could things have gone so far? Why hadn't the police 'simply carted off' everyone present at the jamboree? State Secretary Gutterer issued security chief Heydrich with the following directive: all 'swing youngsters' were to be conscripted into the Labour Service forthwith, then handed over to the Todt Organization for re-education by hard labour.

Seizing upon these instructions with alacrity, the Gestapo interpreted them in its own way. Juvenile courts and Labour Service leaders were spared the chore of dealing with recalcitrant music-lovers because few of them ever came to light. One exception was Hasso Schützendorf, who slipped through the net in October 1942 and took his case to the Hanseatic juvenile court. The Gestapo had stuck him in a concentration camp on suspicion of being a 'Swingjunge'. Here he had his hair shorn, was thrashed with an iron bar and forced to push earth-laden trolleys uphill for a fortnight. The court's medical adviser certified that Schützendorf was suffering from general debility and exhaustion.[456]

The more intelligent wielders of authority, such as Goebbels, Heydrich and Ohlendorf, were well aware of that which remained hidden from the general public and was seldom perceived by the honest guardians of law and order. These symptoms of 'juvenile demoralization' could not be equated with simple phenomena such as hooliganism, unlawful assembly, theft, promiscuity, homosexuality or racial desecration. Quite apart from the fact that these things too, and the scale on which they occurred, were already jeopardizing the whole National Socialist educational system, 'unruliness' in its specific forms could not be simply accounted for by war-time conditions and the inadequate supervision of young people.

Even the outward, individualistic image of the so-called 'swing circles' carried an inherent rejection of the system's regimentation and uniformity. The girls used make-up, affected an air of sophistication, loved garish clothes and nonchalantly displayed their physical charms. This conflicted diametrically with what was expected of decorous BdM girls and had been drummed into them throughout their childhood. The same defiance was latent in the predilection for outlawed Negro music, and protest found its clearest expression in the private associations – gangs and clubs – which grew up extraneously and in opposition to the authorized national youth organizations.

Although poorly articulated and incapable of organized resistance, this protest, so far from being unconscious, was a symptom of definite opposition.

An SD analysis of juvenile demoralization, so-called, appeared on Bormann's desk. From its abundant detail it can be deduced that these 'Anglophile' youngsters harboured an aversion for the Hitler Youth, BdM and Labour Service because organized activities encroached on their spare time. They had no taste for military service. They opposed the war and doubted the veracity of glowing military communiqués. They mumbled 'Morning' instead of greeting each other with a crisp 'Heil Hitler'. The SS Security Service report concluded: 'Their ideal is democratic freedom and American laxity.'[457]

The behaviour of these young people was symptomatic of the problems and changing standards engendered by a transition from the stable social structures of pre-industrial agrarian society to the dynamic social patterns of an industrial society based on the division of labour. National Socialism sought to disavow the reality of this development by means of its pseudo-ideological superstructure – something which not even a totalitarian system can continue to do indefinitely. The Third Reich was nonetheless able, in its mania for purity, to enlist the support of moral concepts which German society had preserved in the face of all social and political vicissitudes: the petty bourgeois moral code and middle-class notions of propriety which had reigned in the late nineteenth century. It was the ethic of the underling, the outlook of the authoritarian personality: anything alien to me and forbidden by my superiors is abnormal.

This was indeed something to build on. Themselves typical of this mentality, the National Socialist rulers used it as a foundation for their edifice of tyranny by wholesome popular sentiment.

The chapter is not necessarily closed. In Theodor Adorno's words, 'German sexual taboos fall within the same ideological and psychological syndrome of prejudice which helped to create popular support for National Socialism and still persists in a form which is, in terms of manifest content, depoliticized. At the right moment, it could also assume definite political shape.'[458]

Glossary

Adolf Hitler German Industry Fund:
Adolf-Hitler-Spende der deutschen Industrie
Adolf Hitler SS Guards:
SS Leibstandarte Adolf Hitler
Advisory Board for Population and Racial Policy:
Sachverständiger Beirat für Bevölkerungs- und Rassenpolitik
Ancestral Heritage (Organization):
Ahnenerbe

Beauty of Labour:
Schönheit der Arbeit

Centres of National Socialist Human Guidance (=day-nurseries):
Stätten der nationalsozialistischen Menschenführung
Compulsory Domestic Service Year:
Haushaltliches Pflichtjahr

Day of National Mourning:
Volkstrauertag
Day of Remembrance for the Movement's Dead:
Gedenktag für die Gefallenen der Bewegung
Domestic Service Year:
Hauswirtschaftliches Jahr

Faith and Beauty:
Glaube und Schönheit
folkish:
Völkisch. Originally a Germanization of 'nationalist', it acquired racialist
and almost mystical overtones which the English word fails to convey.
Hence the attempt to convey them by 'folkish', a neologism when used
in this context.
Fount of Life (Association):
Lebensborn

246

German Central Institute of Education and Instruction:
Deutsche Zentralinstitut für Erziehung und Unterricht
German Children's Troop:
Deutsche Kinderschar
German Farmers' Day:
Ehrentag des deutschen Bauerntums
German Girls' League:
Bund deutscher Mädchen (BdM)
German Labour Front:
Deutsche Arbeitsfront (DAF)
German Labour Party:
Deutsche Arbeiterpartei (DAP)
German National People's Party:
Deutschnationale Volkspartei
German Popular Education Service:
Deutsches Volksbildungswerk
German State Railways:
Deutsche Reichsbahn
German Women's Labour Service:
Deutscher Frauenarbeitsdienst
German Women's Service:
Deutsches Frauenwerk
German Young Folk:
Deutsches Jungvolk (DJ)

Health Service Troop:
Gesundheitsdienstschar
Heroes' Remembrance Day:
Heldengedenktag
Hitler Youth:
Hitlerjugend (HJ)

Investigation and Arbitration Committee:
Untersuchungs- und Schlichtungs-Ausschuss (USCHLA)

Labour Service, see Reich Labour Service
League of Struggle for German Culture:
Kampfbund für deutsche Kultur
Leisure Bureau:
Amt Feierabend

Men's Association for the Control of Immorality:
Männerbund zur Bekämpfung der Unsittlichkeit

National Art Day:
   Tag der Kunst
National Labour Day:
   Tag der nationalen Arbeit
National-Political Institutes of Education:
   Nationalpolitische Erziehungsanstalten (Napola)
National Socialist Association of Those Bereaved by War:
   Nationalsozialistischer Kriegsopferverband
National Socialist Flying Corps:
   Nationalsozialistisches Fliegerkorps (NSFK)
National Socialist German Labour Party:
   Nationalsozialistische Deutsche Arbeiterpartei (NSDAP)
National Socialist German Secondary School:
   Nationalsozialistische Deutsche Oberschule
National Socialist Judicial Association:
   Nationalsozialistischer Rechtswahrerbund
National Socialist Medical Association:
   Nationalsozialistischer Ärztebund
National Socialist Public Welfare Organization:
   Nationalsozialistische Volkswohlfahrt (NSV)
National Socialist Students' Association:
   Nationalsozialistische Studentenschaft
National Socialist Teachers' Association:
   Nationalsozialistischer Lehrerbund (NSLB)
National Socialist Women's Association:
   Nationalsozialistische Frauenschaft
Neighbourhood Assistance (Service):
   Nachbarschaftshilfe

Order of German Women:
   Deutscher Frauenorden

Patriotic Front:
   Vaterländische Front
Plenipotentiary-General for the Utilization of Labour:
   Bevollmächtigter für den Arbeitseinsatz

Race and Resettlement Bureau:
   Rasse- und Siedlungshauptamt (RuSHA)
Racial Policy Bureau:
   Rassepolitisches Amt
Reich Bureau of Employment and Unemployment Insurance:
   Reichsanstalt für Arbeitsvermittlung und Arbeitslosenversicherung

Reich Bureau of Statistics:
Statistisches Reichsamt
Reich Central Security Bureau:
Reichssicherheitshauptamt (RSHA)
Reich Chamber of Fine Arts:
Reichskammer der bildenden Künste
Reich Commissionership for the Strengthening of German Nationhood:
Reichskommissariat für die Festigung des deutschen Volkstums (RKF)
Reich Committee on Tourism:
Reichsausschuss für Fremdenverkehr
Reich Day of Youth:
Reichsjugendtag
Reich Department of Student Leadership:
Reichsstudentenführung
Reich Department of Youth Leadership:
Reichsjugendführung (RJF)
Reich Director of Health:
Reichsgesundheits führer
Reich Director of Sport:
Reichssportführer
Reich Director of Youth Education in the NSDAP:
Reichsleiter für die Jugenderziehung in der NSDAP
Reich Farmers' Leader:
Reichsbauernführer
Reich German Family Association:
Reichsbund Deutsche Familie
Reich Labour Leader:
Reichsarbeitsführer
Reich Labour Service:
Reichsarbeitsdienst (RAD)
Reich Labour Service for Young Women:
Reichsarbeitsdienst für die weibliche Jugend (RADwJ)
Reich Legal Director:
Reichsrechtsführer
Reich Medical Officer-in-Chief:
Reichsarzt
Reich Ministry of Education:
Reichserziehungsministerium
Reich Ministry of Justice:
Reichsjustizministerium
Reich Ministry of Labour:
Reichsarbeitsministerium

Reich Ministry of Public Enlightenment and Propaganda:
  Reichsministerium für Volksaufklärung und Propaganda
Reich Press Office:
  Reichpressestelle
Reich Tourist Association:
  Reichsfremdenverkehrverband
Reich Women's Leader:
  Reichsfrauenführerin
Reich Youth Leader:
  Reichsjugendführer

Secret State Police:
  Geheime Staatspolizei (Gestapo)
Security Service:
  Sicherheitsdient (SD)
Senior SS and Police Commanders:
  Höhere SS- und Polizeiführer (HSSPF)
Sports Bureau:
  Sportamt
State Day of Youth:
  Staatsjugendtag
Strength through Joy:
  Kraft durch Freude (KdF)

Teaching and Research Centre for Runology and Emblematology:
  Lehr- und Forschungsstätte für Runen- und Sinnbildkunde
Travel and Tourism Bureau:
  Amt Reisen und Wandern

Universal German Women's Association:
  Allgemeiner Deutscher Frauenverein

West German Morality League:
  Westdeutscher Sittlichkeitsverein
Women's Association, see National Socialist Women's Association
Women's Auxiliary Service:
  Frauenhilfswerk
Women's Voluntary Aid Service:
  Freiwilliger Frauenhilfsdienst

Notes

Bibliographical abbreviations: BA = Bundesarchiv, Koblenz; IfZ = Institut für Zeitgeschichte, Munich.

(NB. Page numbers refer to passages quoted from translated and untranslated editions alike, but many of the former have been freshly translated from the original German.)

Introduction: The end of 'good breeding'

1   Rauschning, Hermann: *Hitler Speaks*, Thornton Butterworth, London 1939, p. 99.
2   Speer, Albert: *Inside the Third Reich* (tr. by Richard and Clara Winston), Weidenfeld and Nicolson, London 1970, p. 143.
3   Rauschning, op. cit., p. 101 et seq.
4   Sellmann, Adolf: *50 Jahre Kampf für die Volkssittlichkeit und Volkskraft*, Schwelm 1935, p. 107.
5   Ibid., p. 114.
6   Kessler, Count Harry: *Diaries of a Cosmopolitan: Count Harry Kessler, 1918–1937* (tr. by Charles Kessler), Weidenfeld and Nicolson 1971, p. 397.
7   Oven, Wilfried von: *Mit Goebbels bis zum Ende*, Buenos Aires 1949–50; Vol. II, p. 299.
8   Domarus, Max: *Hitler*, Munich 1965, p. 762.
9   Frank, Hans: *Nationalsozialistischer Ehrenschutz*, Vienna 1938, p. 14.

Chapter 1: Rich Man, Poor Man, Beggar-Man

10   *Berliner Illustrirte Zeitung*, 25.12.1898.
11   Gruber, Max von: *Hygiene des Geschlechtslebens*, Stuttgart 1927, p. 116.
12   Ibid., p. 67.
13   Ibid., p. 147.
14   Ibid., p. 146.
15   Ibid., p. 50.
16   Ibid., p. 38.
17   Mayer, August: *Gedanken zur modernen Sexualmoral*, Stuttgart 1930, p. 66 et seq.
18   Franz-Willing, Georg: *Die Hitlerbewegung*, Hamburg/Berlin 1962, p. 104.
19   Hitler, Adolf: *Mein Kampf* (tr. by Ralph Manheim), Hutchinson, London 1969, p. 189.
20   Ibid., p. 203.
21   Ibid., p. 191.
22   Ibid., p. 225.

23 Ibid.
24 Ibid., p. 226.
25 Domarus, op. cit., p. 892.
26 Hitler, op. cit., p. 229.
27 Ibid.
28 Ibid., p. 232.
29 Ibid.
30 Ibid., pp. 230–1.
31 Ibid., p. 231.
32 Ibid., p. 232.
33 Hofer, Walther (ed.): *Der Nationalsozialismus. Dokumente 1933–1945*, Fischer Bücherei 172, p. 30.
34 Strasser, Gregor: *Kampf um Deutschland*, Munich 1932, p. 339.
35 Lauer, Amalie: *Die Frau in der Auffassung des Nationalsozialismus*, Cologne 1932, p. 17.
36 *NS-Briefe*, Yr. 5, No. 18.
37 Hitler, op. cit., p. 401.
38 Lipset, Seymor, in: Goothard Jasper (ed.): *Von Weimar zu Hitler 1930 bis 1933*, Cologne 1968, p. 114.
39 Hitler, op. cit., pp. 39–40.
40 Rauschning, op. cit., p. 89.

Adolf Hitler

41 Heiden, Konrad: *Adolf Hitler*, Zurich 1936–37, Vol. I, p. 340.
42 Richter, Alfred: *Unser Führer im Lichte der Rassenfrage und Charakterologie*, Leipzig 1933, p. 17 et seq.
43 Jetzinger, Franz: *Hitler's Youth* (tr. by Lawrence Wilson), Hutchinson 1958, p. 107.
44 Kubizek, August: *Adolf Hitler*, Graz/Göttingen 1963, p. 79.
45 Ibid.
46 Hitler, op. cit., p. 277.
47 Ibid., p. 295.
48 Strasser, Otto: *Hitler and I* (tr. by Gwenda David and Erich Mosbacher), Cape, London 1940, p. 82.
49 Ibid.
50 Rauschning, op. cit., p. 259.
51 Strasser, Otto, op. cit., p. 78.
52 Diehl, Guida: *Die deutsche Frau und der Nationalsozialismus*, Eisenach 1933, p. 42.
53 Hoffmann, Heinrich: *Hitler was my Friend* (tr. by Lt-Col. R. H. Stevens), Burke, London 1955, p. 141.
54 Boberach, Heinz: *Meldungen aus dem Reich*, Munich 1968, p. 141. (Similar jokes had been in circulation for years. Kurt Hirche [*Der 'braune' und der 'rote' Witz*, Düsseldorf/Vienna 1964] dates its immediate precursor in 1937:

He who rules like a barbarian
and imitates Napoleon,

> was born in Austria,
> trims his whiskers English-fashion,
> salutes like an Italian,
> makes German girls have children
> but can't produce any himself –
> there's a German for you!

Or again: Hitler and Mussolini bathing, one in bathing-trunks and the other naked: Adolf wants to conceal the last unemployed member of the German national community, Benito to look down at the last Italian rebel.)

55 Speer, op. cit., p. 92.
56 Ibid.
57 Picker, Henry: *Hitler's Table Talk* (tr. by Norman Cameron and R. H. Stevens), Weidenfeld and Nicolson, London 1953, p. 353.
58 Ibid., p. 474.
59 Zoller, Albert: *Hitler privat*, Düsseldorf 1949, p. 196.
60 Picker, Henry: *Hitler's Tischgespräche*, Stuttgart 1965, p. 321.
61 Ibid., p. 164.
62 Speer, op. cit., p. 92.
63 Bullock, Alan: *Hitler: A Study in Tyranny*, Odhams, London 1964, p. 726.

Chapter 2: The Handmaid of the Lord

64 Domarus, op. cit., p. 450.
65 Ibid.
66 Reber-Gruber, Auguste: *Weibliche Erziehung im NSLB*, Leipzig/Berlin 1934, p. 9.
67 Gottschewsky, Lydia: *Männerbund und Frauenfrage*, Munich 1934, p. 9.
68 *Reden an die deutsche Frau*, Berlin (n.d.), p. 15.
69 Domarus, op. cit., p. 451.
70 *Offizieller Bericht über den Verlauf des Reichsparteitages*, Munich 1938, p. 235.
71 Tremel-Eggert, Kuni: *Barb*, Munich 1934, p. 76.
72 Siber, Paula: *Die Frauenfrage und ihre Lösung durch den Nationalsozialismus*, Wölfenbüttel 1933, p. 16.
73 Darré, Richard Walther: *80 Merksätze und Leitsprüche über Zucht und Sitte aus Schriften und Reden*, Goslar 1940, no p.
74 Diehl, op. cit., p. 70.
75 *Das Schwarze Korps*, 24.4.1935.
76 Ibid.
77 Domarus, op. cit., p. 451.
78 Ibid.
79 Ibid., p. 450.
80 Diehl, op. cit., p. 74.
81 Domarus, op. cit., p. 531.
82 Ibid.
83 Ibid.
84 Diehl, op. cit., p. 76.

85 Domarus, op. cit., p. 531.
86 Reichenau, Irmgard (ed.): *Deutsche Frauen an Adolf Hitler*, Leipzig 1933, p. 9.
87 Ibid., p. 15.
88 Ibid., p. 30.
89 Ibid., p. 9.
90 BA 149 – 70/14.
91 Reichenau, op. cit., p. 21.
92 Domarus, op. cit., p. 565.
93 Ibid., p. 567.
94 *Tagewerk und Feierabend der schaffenden deutschen Frau*, Leipzig/Berlin 1936.
95 Ibid., p. 7.
96 Schunke, Johannes: *Das Recht im Leben der Frau*, Halle (n.d.).
97 *Tagewerk* etc., p. 10.
98 Ibid., p. 35.
99 Ibid., p. 39.
100 Ibid., p. 23.
101 Sopp, Frieda: *Der Arbeitsdienst der deutschen Mädchen*, Berlin 1940.
102 *Völkischer Beobachter*, 22.1.1939.
103 Domarus, op. cit., p. 1708.
104 Lauer, op. cit., p. 14.

Joseph Goebbels

105 Heiber, Helmut (ed.): *The Early Goebbels Diaries* (tr. by Oliver Watson), Weidenfeld and Nicolson, London 1962, p. 97.
106 Heiber, Helmut: *Joseph Goebbels*, Berlin 1962, p. 38.
107 Ibid., p. 29.
108 Heiber, *Diaries*, p. 27.
109 Ibid.
110 Ibid., p. 28.
111 Ibid., p. 42.
112 Ibid., pp. 45–6.
113 Ibid., p. 56.
114 Ibid., p. 57.
115 Ibid., p. 82.
116 Ibid., p. 83.
117 Ibid., p. 84.
118 Heiber, *Goebbels*, p. 273.
119 Ibid., p. 260.
120 Gamm, Hans Jochen: *Der Flüsterwitz im Dritten Reich*, Munich 1963, p. 274.
121 Ibid.
122 *Stern*, 11/1970, p. 106.
123 Ibid.
124 Speer, op. cit., p. 150.

Chapter 3: Mundane Pleasures

125 Goebbels, Joseph: *Der Angriff*, 2 vols, Munich 1935–39, p. 282.
126 Ibid., p. 385.
127 Rosten, Curt: *Das ABC des Nationalsozialismus*, Berlin 1933, p. 199.
128 Kotze, Hildegard von/Krausnick, Helmut (eds): '*Es spricht der Führer*', Gütersloh 1966, p. 164.
129 Picker, *Tischgespräche*, p. 321.
130 Oven, op. cit., Vol. II, p. 41.
131 Heyen, Franz Josef: *Nationalsozialismus im Alltag*, Boppard 1967, p. 300.
132 Kirkpatrick, Clifford: *Women in Nazi Germany*, Jarrolds, London 1939, p. 105.
133 Wulf, Joseph: *Die Bildenden Künste im Dritten Reich*, Gütersloh 1963, p. 254.
134 Tremel-Eggert, op. cit., p. 337.
135 Domarus, op. cit., p. 298.
136 *Das Schwarze Korps*, 20.7.1939: 'Das geht unsere Frauen an.'
137 Wulf, op. cit., p. 255.
138 *Frankfurter Zeitung*, 10.9.1938.
139 Heiber, *Goebbels*, p. 317.
140 Ibid.
141 Heiber, *Diaries*, p. 59.
142 Picker, *Tischgespräche*, p. 214.
143 Ritter, Reinhard Gerhard: *Die geschlechtliche Frage in der deutschen Volkserziehung*, Berlin/Cologne 1936, p. 62 et sqq.
144 Ley, Robert: *Wir alle helfen dem Führer*, Munich 1937, p. 132.
145 Ley, Robert: *Deutschland ist schöner geworden*, Berlin 1936, p. 91.
146 Starcke, Gerhard: *Die Deutsche Arbeitsfront*, Berlin 1940, p. 10.
147 Ley, Robert: *Soldaten der Arbeit*, Munich 1938, p. 71.
148 François-Poncet, André: *The Fateful Years* (tr. by Jacques Le Clercq), Gollancz, London 1949, p. 209.
149 Ibid.
150 *Völkischer Beobachter*, 1.8.1938; 'Münchner Beobachter' Supplement.

Ernst Röhm

151 Bracher, K. D./Sauer, Wolfgang/Schulz, G.: *Die nationalsozialistische Machtergreifung*, Cologne/Opladen 1960, p. 884.
152 *Münchner Post*, 30.6.1931.
153 Klotz, Helmut: *Der Fall Röhm*, Berlin 1932, IfZ MA 610/20.
154 Ibid.
155 Ibid.
156 Bennecke, Heinrich: *Hitler und die SA*, Munich/Vienna 1962, p. 253.
157 Letter of 5.10.1932; IfZ, Fa 36.
158 Klotz, loc. cit.
159 Letter of 15.9.1932; IfZ MA 127/1.
160 BA, SA 402.
161 Hofer, op. cit., p. 65.

Chapter 4: Warriors and Mothers

162 Domarus, op. cit., p. 533.
163 Rauschning, op. cit., p. 51.
164 Klose, Werner: *Generation im Gleichschritt*, Oldenburg 1964, p. 91.
165 Hansen, Heinrich: *Die Presse der NSLB*, Frankfurt 1937, p. 1.
166 Krieck, Ernst: *Nationalpolitische Erziehung*, Leipzig 1932, p. 89.
167 Eilers, Rolf: *Die nationalsozialistische Schulpolitik*, Cologne/Opladen 1963, p. 17.
168 Jörns, Emil/Schwab, Julius: *Rassenhygienische Fibel*, Berlin 1933.
169 Ibid.
170 Rauschning, loc. cit.
171 Eilers, op. cit., p. 38.
172 Ibid., p. 17.
173 Rauschning, op. cit., p. 247.
174 Krieck, op. cit., p. 83 et seq.
175 Neberhorst, Horst (ed.): *Elite für die Diktatur*, Düsseldorf 1969, p. 222.
176 Ibid., p. 228.
177 Ibid., p. 180.
178 Ibid., p. 277 et seq.
179 Ibid.
180 Ibid.
181 Ibid., p. 415 et seq.
182 Neberhorst, op. cit., p. 143.
183 *Das Reich*, 5.4.1942.
184 Ibid.
185 Ley, *Wir alle* etc., p. 132.
186 *Das Reich*, loc. cit.
187 Müller, Albert: *Die Betreuung der Jugend*, Berlin 1943, p. 45.
188 Maschmann, Melitta: *Fazit*, Stuttgart 1973, p. 151.
189 *Das Schwarze Korps*, 5.3.1936.
190 Kelley, Douglas M.: *Twenty-two Cells in Nuremberg*, Greenberg, New York 1947, p. 91.
191 Ley, op. cit., p. 133 et seq.
192 Kotze/Krausnick, op. cit., p. 165.
193 Picker, *Tischgespräche*, p. 228.
194 Ibid.
195 *Völkischer Beobachter*, 12.6.1934.
196 Matthias, Friederike: 'Grundsätzliches zur Reform der Höheren Mädchenschule' in Reber-Gruber, op. cit., p. 27.
197 Gamm, Hans-Jochen: *Führung und Verführung*, Munich 1964, p. 298 et sqq.
198 Reber-Gruber, op. cit., p. 38.
199 *Nationalsozialistische Mädchenerziehung*, Yr 1934–35, No. 3.
200 *Völkischer Beobachter*, 14.1.1940.
201 *Frankfurter Zeitung*, 10.9.1938.
202 *SS-Kalender 1937*, August, Eher Verlag, Munich.
203 *Nationalsozialistische Frauenschaft*, Berlin 1937, p. 10.

204 *Nationalsozialistische Monatshefte*, 1.4.1930 issue, p. 43.
205 Domarus, op. cit., p. 531 et seq.
206 Ibid., p. 721.
207 Ibid., p. 531.
208 Schirach, Baldur von: *Die Hitler-Jugend*, Berlin 1934, p. 86.
209 *Organisationsbuch der NSDAP*, Munich 1937, p. 267 et seq.
210 Schirach, Baldur von: *Wesen und Aufbau der Hitler-Jugend*; speech of 12.5.1936 quoted by Gamm, *Führung* etc., p. 315 et seq.
211 Schirach, *Die Hitler-Jugend*, loc. cit.
212 Hofer, op. cit., p. 88.
213 Domarus, op. cit., p. 855.
214 Schirach, op. cit., p. 169 et sqq.
215 Schmid, Lisl: 'Lehrerin und weibliche Hitlerjugend' in: Reber-Gruber, op cit., p. 116.
216 Gamm, op. cit., p. 330 et sqq.
217 Ibid., p. 325.
218 Ibid., p. 317.
219 Ibid., p. 318, p. 326.
220 Klose, op. cit., p. 144 et sqq.
221 Ibid., p. 93.
222 Ibid., p. 92.
223 cf. Kaiser, Hugo: *Frau und Familie*, Halle (n.d.).
224 Siber, op. cit., p. 22 et seq.
225 Bürkner, Trude: *Der BDM in der HJ*, Berlin 1937.
226 Maschmann, op. cit., p. 27.
227 Oven, op. cit., p. 41.
228 Klose, op. cit., p. 109 et seq.
229 Gamm, op. cit., p. 344.
230 Ibid.
231 Yeh-Sheng Tsay: *Der Reichsarbeitsdienst*, Würzburg 1940.
232 Diehl, op. cit.
233 *Das Schwarze Korps*, 15.9.1938.
234 Sopp, op. cit., p. 74.
235 Heiber, Helmut (ed.): *Reichsführer!*, Stuttgart 1968, p. 264.
236 IfZ MA 127/1.
237 Hirche, Kurt: *Der 'braune' und der 'rote' Witz*, Düsseldorf/Vienna 1964.
238 Kersten, Felix: *The Kersten Memoirs* (tr. by Constantine Fitzgibbon and James Oliver), Hutchinson & Co., London 1956, p. 75 et seq.
239 Ibid., p. 77.

Hermann Esser

240 BA, SA 402.
241 Seraphim, Hans-Günther (ed.): *Das politische Tagebuch Alfred Rosenbergs*, Taschenbuch 219, p. 74.
242 BA, R43 II/1150b.
243 Ibid.

Chapter 5: Bundles of Joy

244 Hitler, op. cit., p. 377.
245 IfZ, MA 423/Bl. 4723 et sqq.
246 Ibid.
247 *SS-Kalender 1937*, March, Eher Verlag, Munich.
248 Domarus, op. cit., p. 544.
249 Ibid., p. 640.
250 Müller, op. cit.
251 IfZ, MA 452/Bl. 2528 et sqq.
252 Heiber, *Reichsführer!*, p. 91.
253 Ibid.
254 *Das Schwarze Korps*, 25.1.1940.
255 Ibid.
256 SD-Meldungen aus dem Reich: IfZ, MA 441/7-Bl. 8365.
257 Kersten, op. cit., p. 54.
258 Schoenbaum, David: *Hitler's Social Revolution*, Weidenfeld and Nicolson, London 1967, p. 200.
259 IfZ, MA 330/Bl. 4115.
260 Ibid.
261 Ibid.
262 Ibid.
263 Usadel, Georg: *Zucht und Ordnung*, Hamburg 1942, p. 21.
264 Höhne, Heinz: *The Order of the Death's Head* (tr. by Richard Barry), Secker & Warburg, London 1969, p. 433.
265 Heiber, op. cit., p. 251.
266 Ibid., p. 211.
267 Ibid., p. 219.
268 Ibid., p. 269.
269 Ibid., p. 305.
270 IfZ, MA 330/Bl. 4112 et seq.
271 Ibid.
272 Ibid.
273 d'Alquen, Gunther: *Die SS*, Berlin 1939, p. 25.
274 Hirschfeld, Magnus, et al.: *Sittengeschichte des Zweiten Weltkriegs*, Hanau 1968, p. 240.
275 Ibid., p. 243.
276 Ibid., p. 244.
277 IfZ, MA 311/Bl. 1595 et seq.
278 Manvell, Roger, & Fraenkel, Heinrich: *Heinrich Himmler*, Heinemann, London 1965, p. 91.
279 Heiber, op. cit., p. 249.
280 IfZ, MA 256/Bl. 417 et seq.
281 Heiber, op. cit., p. 228.
282 Manvell/Fraenkel, op. cit., p. 92.
283 Ibid., pp. 92-3.

284   IfZ, MA 127/1–Bl. 1797.
285   Glaser, Hermann: *Das Dritte Reich*, Freiburg 1961, p. 139.
286   Hassell, Ulrich von: *Vom andern Deutschland*, Zurich/Freiburg 1950, p. 62.
287   IfZ, MA 136/1–Bl. 946.
288   IfZ, MA 136/1–Bl. 961.
289   BA, NS 6/414.
290   Vaerting, Mathilde Themis: *Die Frau in unserer Zeit*, Darmstadt 1952, p. 55.
291   IfZ, MA 136/1–Bl. 1002.
292   Hirschfeld, op. cit., p. 603 et sqq.
293   Ibid.
294   IfZ, MA 3/5.
295   Ibid.
296   Kersten, op. cit., p. 74.
297   Ibid., pp. 176–7.
298   Ibid., p. 176.
299   Ibid.
300   Maschmann, op. cit., p. 151 et seq.

Martin Bormann

301   Trevor-Roper, Hugh: *The Bormann Letters* (tr. by R. H. Stevens),Weidenfeld
      and Nicolson, London 1954, pp. 39–40.
302   Ibid., p. 40.
303   Ibid., pp. 42–3.
304   Ibid., p. 43.
305   Ibid., p. 45.
306   Ibid., p. 46.
307   Ibid., p. 50.
308   Ibid., p. 49.
309   Ibid., pp. 133–4.

Chapter 6: The New Man

310   Domarus, op. cit., p. 232.
311   *Völkischer Beobachter*, 15.10.1934.
312   Brenner, Hildegard: *Die Kunstpolik desit Nationalsozialismus*, 167/168, p. 109.
313   Domarus, op. cit., p. 706.
314   Ibid., p. 878.
315   Wulf, op. cit., p. 185.
316   Brenner, op. cit., p. 113.
317   *Das Reich*, 18.8.1940.
318   Zoller, op. cit., p. 52.
319   Tremel-Eggert, op. cit., p. 46.
320   Brenner, op. cit., p. 19.
321   Ibid.
322   Ibid., p. 29.
323   Schultze-Naumburg, Paul: *Modische Schönheit*, Berlin 1937, p. 95.

324 Ibid.
325 Ibid.
326 Wulf, op. cit., p. 264.
327 Ibid.
328 Ibid.
329 *Das Schwarze Korps*, 25.11.1937.
330 Boberach, op. cit., p. 70 (28.2.1940).
331 IfZ, MA 311/Bl. 1557.
332 Wulf, op. cit., p. 164.
333 *Das Schwarze Korps*, 25.11.1937.
334 Rosenberg, Alfred: *Der Mythos des 20. Jahrhunderts*, Munich 1930, p. 82.
335 Darré, Richard Walther: *Um Blut und Boden – Reden und Aufsätze*, Munich 1940.
336 Domarus, op. cit., p. 1310.
337 Ritter, op. cit., p. 67.
338 Ibid.
339 Boberach, op. cit., p. 192 et sqq.
340 Hofer, op. cit., p. 284 et seq.
341 IfZ, MA 127/1-Bl. 1751.
342 Gruber, op. cit.
343 Lutze, Viktor: *Wesen und Aufgabe der SA*, Munich 1936, p. 15.
344 Usadel, op. cit., p. 15.
345 IfZ, MA 47. Here, in *Festschrift für das Reichstreffen des Reichsbundes der Kinderreichen*, Frankfurt 5–7.6.1937.
346 Schnabel, Reimund: *Macht ohne Moral*, Frankfurt 1957, p. 28.
347 Himmler, Heinrich: *Die Schutzstaffel als antibolschewistische Kampforganisation*, Munich 1936, p. 29.
348 Meier-Benneckenstein, Paul: *Das Dritte Reich im Aufbau*, 1939; quoted in Schnabel, op. cit., p. 29.
349 Schnabel, op. cit., p. 29 et seq.
350 BA, NS2 8 161.
351 Speech by Himmler 1937, quoted in Schnabel, op. cit., p. 28 et seq.
352 BA, BS2–57.
353 BA, NS2–240.

Heinrich Himmler

354 Hofer, op. cit., p. 113.
355 Manvell/Fraenkel, op. cit., p. 5.
356 Ibid., p. 7.
357 Ibid.
358 Ibid.
359 Höhne, op. cit., p. 32.
360 Ibid.
361 Manvell/Fraenkel, op. cit., p. 9.
362 Ibid., pp. 9–10.
363 Höhne, op. cit., p. 49.
364 Ibid., p. 50.

365 Schirach, Baldur von: *Ich glaubte an Hitler*, Hamburg 1967, p. 213.
366 Höhne, op. cit., p. 164.
367 Ibid.
368 Manvell/Fraenkel, op. cit., p. 205.
369 Hofer, op. cit., p. 113.

Chapter 7: 'Degeneracy'

370 Hofer, op. cit., p. 102.
371 Frank, Hans: *Nationalsozialistische Strafrechtspolitik*, Munich 1938.
372 Ibid., p. 32.
373 Hofer, op. cit., p. 101.
374 Ibid.
375 Domarus, op. cit., p. 1874 et sqq.
376 Ibid., p. 1877.
377 Picker, *Table Talk*, p. 302 et seq.
378 BA, NG 908.
379 Hirschfeld, op. cit., p. 323.
380 Ibid., p. 326.
381 BA, R22/3361.
382 IfZ, MA 311/B1. 1828 et sqq.
383 Frank, op. cit., p. 32.
384 IfZ, MA 311/Bl. 1828 et sqq.
385 Diels, Rudolf: *Luzifer ante portas*, Stuttgart 1950, p. 381.
386 Domarus, op. cit., p. 401.
387 IfZ, MA 311/Bl. 1828 et sqq.
388 Kersten, op. cit., p. 57.
389 *Das Schwarze Korps*, 4.3.1937.
390 BA, NS 2/41.
391 *Das Schwarze Korps*, 4.3.1937.
392 loc. cit.
393 loc. cit.
394 IfZ, MA 311/Bl. 1828 et sqq.
395 *Das Schwarze Korps*, 22.5.1935.
396 loc. cit.
397 IfZ, MA 311/Bl. 1828 et sqq.
398 IfZ, MA 131/Bl. 1322.
399 Höhne, op. cit., p. 143.
400 IfZ, MA 311/Bl. 1828 et sqq.
401 IfZ, MA 312/Bl. 2583 et sqq.
402 Kersten, op. cit., p. 59.
403 Ibid., p. 58.
404 IfZ, MA 333/Bl. 7977.
405 IfZ, MA 392/Bl. 2683.
406 *Goebbels-Tagebücher 1942–1943*, Zurich 1948, p. 101.
407 IfZ, MA 624/Bl. 4217.
408 IfZ, MA 311/Bl. 1828 et sqq.

409   Gruber, op. cit., p. 128.
410   Ibid.
411   IfZ, MA 3/5.
412   *Goebbels* etc., p. 55.
413   cf. Bauer, Willi: *Geschichte und Wesen der Prostitution*, Stuttgart 1956, p. 105 et seq.
414   BA, R58/148–59.
415   *Goebbels* etc., loc. cit.
416   BA, R58/190.
417   Ibid.
418   BA, R58/148–59.
419   BA, NS6/419.
420   BA, R22/3376.
421   Kempner, Robert M. W.: *SS im Kreuzverhör*, Munich 1964, p. 197.
422   IfZ, MA 666.
423   IfZ, MA 666/Bl. 2301 et sqq.
424   IfZ, MA 666/Bl. 2349 et sqq.
425   BA, R22/3381.
426   Ibid.
427   BA, R58/158–253.
428   IfZ, MA 666/Bl. 2326 et sqq.
429   BA, R58/158–253.
430   IfZ, MA 3/Bl. 15.
431   IfZ, MA 136/1–Bl. 1563.
432   BA, R58/158–253.
433   BA, R58/185.
434   Ibid.
435   Kempner, op. cit., p. 198.
436   IfZ, MA 127/1–Bl. 1669.
437   IfZ, MA 3/15.
438   IfZ, MA 325/Bl. 8504.
439   Wulf, op. cit., p. 138.
440   IfZ, MA 624/Bl. 4217 et sqq.
441   Ibid.
442   BA, NS1/544.
443   Ibid.
444   BA, R58/152–103.
445   BA, R22/3364.
446   BA, R22/3379.
447   Ibid.
448   BA, R22/3355.
449   BA, R22/3379.
450   BA, R22/3364.
451   Ibid.
452   Ibid.
453   Ibid.
454   IfZ, MA 667/Bl. 4196 et sqq.

455 Ibid.
456 BA, R22/3366.
457 IfZ, MA 667/Bl. 4196 et sqq.
458 Adorno, Theodor W.: 'Sexualtabus und Recht heute', in: *Sexualität und Verbrechen*, ed. Fritz Bauer *et al.*, Frankfurt 1963, p. 307.

Index

of officials, behaviour, 141–2; 'Exalted Women', 142–4; sexual permissiveness, 234–5, 238; *see also* Feminist Movement *and* Motherhood

Women and the Law, 63

'Women's Academies of Wisdom and Culture', 142–3

Woyrsch, Udo von, 200, 219

WRAD (voluntary labour service for girls), 66

Year of Hygienic Duty, 137

Year of Understanding, 134

Youth, *see* BdM, Educational policy, Hitler Youth, German Young Folk *and* Juvenile Delinquency

Zahler, Ludwig, 202

Zander, Elsbeth, 125

Ziegler, Adolf, 184